Readings in Soil Development

Readings in School-Based Curriculum Development

Malcolm Skilbeck
Editor

P·C·P
Paul Chapman
Publishing Ltd

Copyright © 1984. Section One: Chapter 1 P. Gammage; Chapter 2 R. Letch; Chapter 3 M. Plaskow. Section Two: Chapter 4 A. Craft; Chapter 5 L. Kant; Chapter 6 C. Williams; Chapter 7 H. Connell. Section Three: Chapter 8 C. Bayne-Jardine; Chapter 9 E. Davies; Chapter 10 R. Crone; Chapter 11 C. Saville; Chapter 12 T. Joyes; Chapter 13 J. Cosslett; Chapter 14 C. A. Eastgate; Chapter 15 F. Fay; Chapter 16 A. Hodge; Chapter 17 A. Donald; Chapter 18 A. McMahon; Chapter 19 P. Waterhouse. Section Four: Chapter 20 H. Macintosh; Chapter 21 J. Stephenson. Section Five: Chapter 22 J. Rudduck; Chapter 23 N. Russell; Chapter 24 G. Evans. Section Six: Chapter 25 D. Lawton; Chapter 26 R. Slaughter; Chapter 27 J. Hemming. Introduction to the book and to individual sections © M. Skilbeck
All rights reserved

First published 1984
by Harper and Row Ltd, London

Reprinted 1988
by Paul Chapman Publishing Ltd, 144 Liverpool Road, London N1 1LA

No part of this book may be used or reproduced in any manner whatsoever without written permission except in the case of brief quotations embodied in critical articles and reviews

British Library Cataloguing in Publication Data
Readings in school based curriculum
   development.
   1. Curriculum planning—Great Britain
   I. Skilbeck, Malcolm
   375'001'0941   LB1564.G7

ISBN 1 85396 046 2

Typeset by Inforum Ltd, Portsmouth
Printed in Great Britain by
St Edmundsbury Press Ltd, Bury St Edmunds, Suffolk

A B C D E F G   4 3 2 1 0 9 8

CONTENTS

Introduction *Malcolm Skilbeck* 1

SECTION ONE CHANGING THE CURRICULUM: NEW CHALLENGES, NEW ROLES

Introduction *Malcolm Skilbeck* 7
Chapter 1 The curriculum and its participants: perspectives of interaction *Philip Gammage* 11
Chapter 2 New directions in curriculum policy, local and national: changes at the local level *Ron Letch* 29
Chapter 3 Why change the curriculum: new directions at national level *Maurice Plaskow* 39

SECTION TWO NEW DIMENSIONS FOR THE CURRICULUM

Introduction *Malcolm Skilbeck* 49
Chapter 4 Curriculum for a multicultural society *Alma Craft* 53
Chapter 5 The education of girls and women *Lesley Kant* 62
Chapter 6 Low achievers *Coralyn Williams* 72
Chapter 7 Education for international life – a neglected area *Helen Connell* 81

vi Readings in School-Based Curriculum Development

SECTION THREE SCHOOL APPROACHES TO REVIEW, EVALUATION AND DEVELOPMENT

	Introduction *Malcolm Skilbeck*	93
Chapter 8	Case-study of school-based curriculum review *Colin C. Bayne-Jardine*	101
Chapter 9	The role of the headteacher in the management of change *Elsa Davies*	116
Chapter 10	Problem solving via a schools support service *Robert Crone*	124
Chapter 11	Communication and dialogue in the school setting *Chris Saville*	134
Chapter 12	School self-evaluation *Terence B. Joyes*	139
Chapter 13	Curriculum guidance and the role of pupils in the lower secondary school *Jean Cosslett*	148
Chapter 14	Curriculum guidance at 14+ *Carole Ann Eastgate*	154
Chapter 15	Curriculum change in a Catholic secondary school *Francis Fay*	159
Chapter 16	Sixth-form curriculum change *Allan Hodge*	164
Chapter 17	The role of the teacher as an agent of change in further education *Arthur S. Donald*	171
Chapter 18	Reviewing and developing the curriculum: the GRIDS project *Agnes McMahon*	179
Chapter 19	The design, selection and use of resources in curriculum development *Philip Waterhouse*	190

SECTION FOUR HOW CAN WE IMPROVE STUDENT ASSESSMENT?

	Introduction *Malcolm Skilbeck*	207
Chapter 20	Assessing and examining: policies, practices and alternatives *Henry G. Macintosh*	209
Chapter 21	Public examinations or validated school assessment? *John Stephenson*	217

SECTION FIVE *THE SCHOOL AS A CENTRE FOR CURRICULUM RESEARCH AND PROFESSIONAL DEVELOPMENT*

	Introduction *Malcolm Skilbeck*	227
Chapter 22	Curriculum development and teacher research *Jean Rudduck*	231
Chapter 23	Teachers as curriculum evaluators *Neil Russell*	244
Chapter 24	The school as a centre of professional development *Glen Evans*	256

SECTION SIX *CURRICULUM FUTURES*

	Introduction *Malcolm Skilbeck*	271
Chapter 25	Curriculum and culture *Denis Lawton*	275
Chapter 26	Futures study in the curriculum *Richard A. Slaughter*	290
Chapter 27	Curriculum for what? *James Hemming*	305

THE CONTRIBUTORS

Philip Gammage taught in primary schools while studying psychology and is now Professor of Education at Nottingham University. His main academic interests are social psychology and early childhood education.

Ron Letch began his teaching career in Essex schools. He later became an education and youth officer for a large international organization before returning to teaching as a senior lecturer in a college of education. His present post is as a local authority staff inspector responsible for in-service education.

Maurice Plaskow has been a curriculum officer with the Schools Council since 1970, having worked on the Humanities Curriculum Project for three years under Lawrence Stenhouse. He has been particularly involved with the secondary curriculum and with projects in humanities and the arts.

Alma Craft is a principal professional officer with the School Curriculum Development Committee, and was Coordinator for Multicultural Education at the Schools Council. She has evaluated several curriculum developments and has undertaken research into the education of ethnic minority pupils in Melbourne and London.

Lesley Kant taught in London comprehensives before moving into teacher training. At the Schools Council she worked on examinations and assessment developments such as pupil profiles and examination reform, and coordinated the equal opportunities programme. She is currently working as a senior adviser with Norfolk LEA, and is the co-author of *Jobs for the Girls*, a Schools Council publication on girls' career opportunities.

Coralyn Williams (MEd Studies, Queensland) is a lecturer in curriculum studies at Mount Lawley Campus of Western Australia College of Advanced Education. Having taught at primary, secondary and tertiary levels in Western Australia and Queensland, her research interest is in curriculum innovations as they relate to classroom practices. Her recent study leave was spent in the UK and Australia, investigating curriculum for low achievers.

Helen Connell has travelled widely and worked in several countries, including four years in international education with the Australian Curriculum Development Centre. She is trained as a geographer, and has taught in a university geography department. Recently she completed research studies on innovations in primary and secondary school curricula for the Home Office and the Commonwealth Institute.

Colin Bayne-Jardine has been Headmaster at Henbury School, Bristol, since 1976. He read history at University College Oxford, and studied curriculum theory at Bristol University. He taught in the USA, Canada, Glasgow, Devonshire and Bristol before being appointed Headmaster of Culverhay School, Bath, in 1970.

Elsa Davies is Head Teacher at Whitehall School, Uxbridge, and vice-chairman of The English New Education Fellowship. She is the author of several papers on pupil assessment, parental involvement and school policy making, and is a council member of the British Educational Management and Administration Society and the Advisory Centre for Education.

Robert Crone is Senior Master, Laurelhill High School, Lisburn, co. Antrim, Northern Ireland. He is co-author with John Malone of two books on school-based curriculum development *Continuities in Education* (1979) and *The Human Curriculum* (1983).

Chris Saville is Senior Staff Inspector for Nottinghamshire LEA. He has wide advisory experience, following headship, and gained his PhD in 1981 on research into the role of advisers as change agents, at the Centre for Applied Research in Education, University of East Anglia.

The Contributors xi

Terence Joyes has taught in Essex, Derbyshire and Nottinghamshire secondary schools. He was subsequently Leader at the Brookfield Teachers' Centre, Boreham, and is currently Head of The Gade Valley Education Centre, Hemel Hempstead. His research interests are school and individual self-evaluation – process, procedure and political control.

Jean Cosslett has taught in Essex primary and secondary schools since 1967. She obtained her BEd degree at Lucy Cavendish College, Cambridge in 1971–2 and her MPhil (History of Education) from King's College, London in 1977.

Carole Ann Eastgate has been Deputy Head (Pastoral) at King's School, Gutersloh, Germany since September 1982. Before this she studied for an MA in curriculum studies at the University of London Institute of Education. She was formerly Head of Physical Education and Head of House at Twickenham School, Twickenham.

Francis Fay is a year head at a large comprehensive school on the outskirts of Liverpool, where he has taught history and economics for the past eight years.

Allan Hodge obtained his BSc from Bristol University in 1971, and an MA in curriculum studies from the University of London Institute of Education in 1980. Now doing part-time research into the history and politics of secondary curriculum change at the beginning of the twentieth century, he is Head of Social Studies at Carmel College, Wallingford, Oxfordshire.

Arthur Donald graduated from Garnett College with an Honours degree in education and later completed a Masters degree in curriculum studies at London University. He is currently Head of Section (Keyboard Techniques) at London College of Printing.

Agnes McMahon is a Research Fellow in the University of Bristol School of Education. She is currently working on the GRIDS Project and prior to this she was doing research on teacher induction.

Philip Waterhouse's interests are in the management of resource-based learning. He is coordinator of the Council for Educational Technology project on 'Supported Self-Study', which is promoting a move towards more open systems of learning in secondary schools.

Henry Macintosh is Secretary of the Southern Regional Examinations Board, was formerly Secretary of the Associated Examining Board, and has published and lectured extensively on assessment techniques both in the UK and abroad.

John Stephenson is Head of the School for Independent Study at North-East London Polytechnic. Formerly a lecturer in teacher training, he had eight years' experience as an examiner in GCE and CSE and eight years' teaching in secondary schools. He is currently Secretary of the UK Section of the World Education Fellowship.

Jean Rudduck is Professor of Education at the University of Sheffield. She has been involved in a number of classroom-based teacher research studies, including 'Sex-Stereotyping in the Early Years of Schooling', 'Teachers in Partnership' and 'Children's Thinking'.

Neil Russell is Senior Lecturer in Curriculum Studies at the Canberra College of Advanced Education, and was formerly Director of the national Teachers as Evaluators Project, funded by the Australian Curriculum Development Centre. He is currently coordinating an evaluation of materials project to assist teachers working with gifted and talented children.

Glen Evans, after some years of secondary school teaching, held university appointments in Toronto, Melbourne and Brisbane, where he is now Professor of Teacher Education. He was foundation chairman of the Council of the Curriculum Development Centre in Canberra.

Professor Denis Lawton, recently appointed Director of the University of London Institute of Education, started his teaching career in 1958 at Erith Grammar School. He joined the Institute in 1963 and since then has had wide experience in education. His publications include *Politics of the School Curriculum* (1980) and *Curriculum Studies and Educational Planning* (1983).

Richard Slaughter taught for eight years before pursuing research at Lancaster University leading to a PhD: *Critical Futurism and Curriculum Renewal*. He now works as a freelance writer, researcher and consultant in futures and education.

Dr James Hemming taught English for sixteen years before training as a psychologist. He has since worked in education, industry and counselling. His several books include *The Betrayal of Youth* (1980) a critique of traditional secondary education.

INTRODUCTION

Purpose and scope of the book

'School-based curriculum development, a fine idea but will it work?' That sceptical comment, combining acknowledgement of an educational philosophy with disinclination to see it realized in practice, has become commonplace. This volume, a companion to the editor's *School-Based Curriculum Development*, demonstrates that the school can realistically and successfully play many roles in curriculum development. It brings together a wide array of practical classroom experience, research, development and scholarship to illuminate crucial issues in institutional and local development work. Ways and means are suggested of undertaking the numerous and varied roles neatly encapsulated in the term curriculum development. Problems and barriers commonly encountered by schools are discussed in a practical manner. Finally, broader social perspectives that schools need to take into account are given a curriculum setting.

Almost all the papers gathered together here have been written specifically for this book and are published for the first time. As editor, I have had the pleasure and advantage of reading them in draft and final form and corresponding with the authors about them. Having seen them grow over time, and being in a position to interrelate and discuss them in the introductions to the several sections in which they are grouped, I see the individual chapters as closely knit – different and varied facets of the same central body of ideas and experience. Readers may notice significant differences of approach and viewpoint and, in any case, may wish to use the book selectively. For this purpose, it is hoped that the grouping of chapters, the section headings and the introductions to the individual sections will be of assistance. Each chapter is followed by its author's own list of references and additional readings and these, too, should assist readers who wish to follow particular aspects in more detail than is possible in chapters whose scope and length have of necessity to be confined. A further point about the book as a whole is that, since it comprises chapters written for a particular purpose and has been designed to be used in association with the companion volume, there is a linkage of themes between the two books.

These readings, from a multiplicity of standpoints, thus bring a wide experience to bear on school-based curriculum development as a set of ideas, processes and practical tasks to be accomplished. In many parts of the book, practical suggestions are made both for follow-up work and for initiating and conducting curriculum review, evaluation and development. There are particular technical skills which must be deployed in curriculum development, broadly conceived, including techniques for deciding on priorities and goals, group collaboration, the planning and design of experimental projects, data gathering, analysis and evaluation and, by no means least, communication skills. Some of these may be mastered through individual reading and study, others are best acquired in practical situations, others again may be gained through systematic in-service courses.

Although contributors give specific pointers to action and discuss examples of tasks and processes in curriculum development, the book does not aim to serve as a detailed technical manual. While such a manual would have its uses, there seems more need, at present, for a wider-ranging consideration of issues, ideas and experience. In any case, curriculum development can never be adequately reduced to a set of detailed guidelines for action, but must always be, to a significant degree, specific to situations and persons or groups. Principles and suggestions therefore take precedence over rules and detailed steps. Reflection on classroom experience, consideration of research and theory, the exercise of imagination and judgement, collaborative decision making, concrete thinking about problems and how to solve them: these are better starting points for curriculum action than following a recipe book.

The papers assembled in this book will all assist in such activities, provided they are themselves seen as commentaries and reflections on the authors' own experience and thinking about the curriculum, at whatever level and in whichever subject area, process or aspect of education the author has specialized. Even where, as is frequently the case, a chapter is written from and to a particular dimension of the curriculum – learning needs of low-achieving children, the role of the head in curriculum change, teachers as evaluators, or relating curriculum to defined student characteristics – the discussion is invariably suggestive of wider applications which, it is assumed, readers may wish to make, according to individual circumstances.

This book has been written primarily to bring out the fundamental ideas and activities which schools need to address in curriculum review, evaluation and development. These are presented through topics and themes that are generally cross-curricular in character. We have not approached curriculum as an assemblage of subject matter, organized around the familiar topics, themes and subjects of the timetable of primary and secondary schools. There are indeed plenty of resources of this kind for teachers to draw upon and it is assumed that the book will be used by teachers and others in association with those resources. Our grouping of chapters in this book aims to foster a whole-curriculum approach, encouraging reviews, evaluation and development by groups or teams of teachers and consultants (and, it is to be hoped, students, governors, parents and others).

Our understanding of the school curriculum is changing rapidly. No longer can we rest content with the reductionist view that curriculum comprises all the subjects and topics on the timetable or that curriculum is predetermined by vocational or examination requirements. Schools throughout this country are now under an obligation to review their curricula, following publication in 1981 of *The School Curriculum* by the Department of Education and Science and the follow-up circulars. In this book, we consider what this means, nationally, at the local authority level, and in the school setting. What does it mean to review the curriculum? How broad is the scope of review? What *is* the curriculum? Does review lead on to evaluation and is there any point in evaluating unless for purposes of change and development? These are the kinds of questions to which contributors give their answers deriving from rich and varied experience of the educational system.

Characteristic of the curriculum field now, is the pressure exerted by interest groups to have schools respond to their particular conceptions of need. Government has outlined, for the maintained sector, a rudimentary framework for the curriculum; at secondary level this is filled out in very precise detail by examination syllabuses. Yet, despite these and traditional assumptions about what the curriculum ought to encompass, the demands for new approaches, new learnings, grows apace. We discuss ways and means of meeting pressures of this kind, giving examples of how dimensions such as multiculturalism and internationalism can be incorporated without overcrowding or bias.

Since what we most seriously lack in curriculum studies is substantial reporting and evaluation of school experience of curriculum making, the greater part of the chapters in this book consist of teachers' reports of small-scale curriculum development projects, or of studies which focus on school-level tasks, priorities and roles. What will strike the reader is the extent to which such reporting is moving beyond the anecdotal, idiosyncratic and subjective mode which in the past has divided the research and development community from teachers (just as there has been a much needed improvement in the communicative powers of researchers and developers!). Indeed the style of analysis of curriculum innovation is now one where a common language and conceptual framework is available to researchers, theorists, teacher educators, administrators and classroom teachers. Those chapters reporting or relating to school experience of curriculum review, evaluation and development provide good examples of that common body of knowledge.

It is arguable that the greatest single inhibitor of school-based curriculum development in the English system of education is the hold of public examinations, not only on teachers but also on parents and students. Thus, when questioned about their indifference to or weak efforts in curriculum development, teachers commonly blame the examinations either directly or indirectly. These topics are discussed by writers familiar with the administrative practice of examining and assessing. However, to focus on the examination issue would be to overlook structural, attitudinal and resource questions: do teachers have the time, the capacity, the competence, the disposition to do curriculum development? Is development properly a role for the school at all? These and related questions are discussed in the author's companion volume. In the present book, contributors have been asked, on the whole, to accept that there *is* a powerful case for school-based curriculum development, and to concentrate on *how* the job is to be done, and some of the difficulties that have to be faced and overcome on the way. It is very clear that changes in schools themselves will be needed, to bring out stronger professional roles, for example the school itself as a force in the in-service education of teachers, or as a training ground for evaluation expertise. Moreover, curriculum development conceived merely as a set of clear-cut processes of management, monitoring, review and so forth could quickly become a monotonous, routine affair. One of the most vital changes, therefore, is the enhancement of the school's role as an agency of social and cultural development: the curriculum as itself a kind of map or outline of principal features of the culture on the one hand and, on the other, a resource whereby teachers and students working together can play a part in mapping out possible futures. School-based curriculum development must go well beyond what many of its exponents have in the past seen as its basic task.

But just as we must broaden our appreciation of the scope of curriculum development, so must we determine and clarify specific roles and tasks for schools. The production of sophisticated resources and materials for learning cannot be a normal undertaking of schools, nor can they expect to undertake curriculum review, evaluation and development independently of other groups and agencies in society. The interpretation of the fundamental aims of education, major priorities and the general framework of the curriculum are also matters where it might be expected schools will take guidance. Similarly, in the kinds of themes and issues in contemporary life to which they give curriculum prominence, schools must show a close knowledge and understanding of the wider community of which they are part. A most effective way of schools' showing this understanding is in their accepting a role within systems, national and local, and collaborating with public as well as professional groups which have a growing and mostly constructive and legitimate interest in shaping general curriculum policy.

Finally, the experience of curriculum developers and evaluators everywhere points consistently towards a recognition that the school curriculum is a complex entity. This is perhaps summed up best in the view of a curriculum change as a change in a social system, involving persons, groups, roles, interrelationships, values, established institutional practices and customs, and a shift in the distribution of resources. Central to all this is the disarmingly simple goal of embarking on curriculum development to improve students' learning. The claim of school-based curriculum development is that, of all the agencies or means available to us, and notwithstanding its limitations, the school is best able to undertake curriculum development. It does not follow that there is no significant role for other agencies; nor does it follow that curriculum development can be set up as a task, carried out and then put down. The development of the curriculum is, or ought to be, a normal function of the school. What is involved in carrying out that function is complex, but nevertheless manageable and, as we endeavour to show, can be undertaken in quite practical ways.

SECTION 1

CHANGING THE CURRICULUM: NEW CHALLENGES, NEW ROLES

INTRODUCTION
Malcolm Skilbeck

If analysis of the school curriculum draws us inevitably and quickly towards the learning experiences and needs of students, a good starting point is a sound method for addressing the characteristics of learners. A growing preoccupation of teachers is finding adequate ways of characterizing learning needs, processes and outcomes in the school setting. The curriculum means little to the teacher unless it can be related to learning, and the language of teachers is dominated by concrete talk about particular types and qualities of student performances in specific school or school-related settings. Learning theorists, on the other hand, for decades have attempted to construct general explanations of these learning activities, for example through genetic theories of cognition, accounts of behaviour modification and analyses of the relationships among emotional development and school achievements. There has been, unfortunately, relatively little coincidence of the two kinds of accounts, learning theorists' and teachers'. As a result, for more than twenty years, major curriculum development projects in many countries have proceeded largely independently of our systematic knowledge of the psychology of learning even though many curriculum workers have declared their allegiance to a child or learner-centred approach to the curriculum.

In his chapter, Philip Gammage seeks to reopen lines of communication between teachers, learning theorists and curriculum developers. Curricula ought to be, he argues, learner shaped and school shaped. Teachers have a central role in this, but how are they to make use of the knowledge yielded by research and theory, and how are they to demonstrate, in an era of accountability, that their own experiential and intuitive judgements have the full authority of well-structured professional judgements? Teachers normally and naturally attribute traits and tendencies to students. Are they unduly subjective? Do they succumb to stereotyping? Can teachers be trusted to take greater responsibility for the curriculum? By becoming more reflective about their own processes of attribution, more attentive to relationships among the learners' personal history, self-concept and sociocultural circumstances, more curriculum conscious, teachers can fairly claim a major role in curriculum development.

It is in this light that we may see value in new pressures on schools which, to many teachers, have been a source of disquiet. The teacher who is a competent, well-organized and self-critical professional is well able to share responsibility for the curriculum. Such sharing is, as Ron Letch points out, a requirement for the future. Greatly increased interest in curriculum policy by central and local education authorities has been a feature of the 1970s. In the 1980s this is very likely to continue and indeed to intensify. Whilst the role of the local education authority has been, as Ron Letch says, mainly responsive in relation to a series of central government initiatives, we may expect the local authorities themselves, for example through their own curriculum policy statements, guidelines and reviews, to increase their visibility in curriculum matters. Moreover, and especially in secondary education, agencies other than those traditionally identified as 'educational' will increasingly impinge on the school curriculum. If the school is both to respond to these pressures and to maintain its own central role in curriculum design and development, the local education authority must play its part through information and advice, by providing and organizing much needed opportunities for professional development and by assisting schools in their utilization of scarce resources.

Supporting this account of rapid and substantial changes in the curriculum activities of local and central government, Maurice Plaskow documents two decades of transition in national curriculum initiatives. Since the early 1960s, a succession of reports, circulars, funding arrangements and other initiatives from central government have helped to bring to the fore, first, a broadly based liberal philosophy of education and, in recent years, more utilitarian or at any rate more socially functional views of what the curriculum of the school should comprise. Maurice Plaskow's account outlines some of the most important of these recent changes, setting them against another, broader, older and more liberal concept of schooling, which, in its heyday, the Schools Council promoted. Personal fulfilment, sensitivity in interpersonal relations, the enlargement of the imagination and access to a complex cultural heritage are what, he reminds us, the Schools Council aimed to foster in the large-scale programme of projects and other activities designed to support schools in their curriculum making. With the disbandment of the Council and the creation of new, separate agencies for curriculum and examinations, alongside a vastly increased role for the officials of the Department of Education and Science and Her Majesty's Inspectorate, the national arena changed dramatically in the early 1980s. School curriculum making cannot proceed independently of these events, but few schools have responded adequately to them, partly because of inadequate communications within the education system as a whole, partly because of a long-standing belief that school autonomy incorporates a disregard of or even resistance to central government departments and agencies.

CHAPTER 1

THE CURRICULUM AND ITS PARTICIPANTS: PERSPECTIVES OF INTERACTION

Philip Gammage

The term curriculum is extremely wide and is usually taken to mean not only the formal provision of sequenced, agreed portions of disciplines, but also pedagogical organization, teaching style and evaluation. Any curriculum involves people in planning, selecting, sequencing, 'matching' and evaluating. This chapter seeks to emphasize the social-psychological context of all this; especially to remind readers that 'matching' (a currently fashionable term) is a difficult and chancy thing to achieve, requiring considerable sensitivity from the teacher. No programme of good ideas, however well conceived, however attractively packaged, can ensure it. The curriculum context is full of beliefs, approximations and causal inferences (attributions), the social-psychological reality of teaching.

Introduction

Presumably, for institutionalized education to take place, some crude consensus, or at least the political will and power to attempt either formulation or imposition of its substitute, has to be arrived at. 'Consensus' may be largely illusory and may depend more upon the realities of power than upon agreed aims. But whatever the political processes, formal education will depend upon four main features:

1. some notions of a suitable curriculum and/or groupings of knowledge essential for:
   a) all people
   b) some people
   c) a few people;

2. some notions of a structure of organizations by which curricula may be transmitted;
3. specially designated and trained persons assigned to duties relating to the types of transmission listed at (1);
4. recipients grouped in such ways as to both facilitate and ritualize some reasonably economic form of transmission.

To these may be added certain other features which sometimes appear to take even more prominence in formal education than at first sight appears necessary or desirable, for example selective and control functions. Such functions are usually embedded in the traditional values of the society and some are highly ritualized. Public examinations, certificates, degrees, memberships of professional institutes or of learned societies: these are so often taken as the legitimations proper to the appropriate and effective deployment of time in formal education. For there to be winners of such 'glittering prizes', there have to be losers too; and most children and adults who undertake education are fully aware that not everyone 'wins'; more, the incentive of winning itself may not seem worth while or desirable to as many as educationists might think.

Children and schooling

When one looks specifically at the contributions of the social sciences to education one is struck by two broadly different perspectives:

1. Early childhood education has (until recently) been largely dominated by psychology.
2. Secondary education has been much more a field of sociological investigation.

Such perspectives are crude and in no way discrete. But if one subtracts the largely psychodynamic writings on adolescence from commentary on secondary education, psychologists have much less to say on learning or on curriculum specific to that age group than to younger age groups. Likewise, until the preoccupation (during the 1960s) of sociologists with nursery education as a vehicle for the amelioration of social imbalance, sociologists appear to have had relatively little to contribute to the education of young children. Yet the preoccupations of one group – and the subsequent research – seem incomplete or inadequate without the context provided by the other. How, for instance, might one view psychological perspectives or the developing self-concept and its intertwining with schooling without recognizing the impact of the larger issues of, say, ethnicity, gender, or class? Additionally, the cultural context is itself rather more fluid than we might think. Concepts of children and of childhood alter. As Newson remarks, children are very much cultural products; there can be no such thing as a 'culture-free child' (Newson 1982, p.71). Children and childhood are not necessarily the same from century to century, nor even from decade to decade. It is not merely a case of earlier physical and mental maturity; not merely the effects of the secular trend of decline of age at menarche (Tanner 1978), but the ways we view a *state* of childhood. As adults and caretakers we may assume our definition carries cultural salience and political weight. But children learn through actively interacting with the environment *as it is*. In western technological societies children are generally encouraged to explore the environment, to ask questions, to try things out. In media-conscious societies in particular the child may be more in touch with the here-and-now than his parents. Schools are sometimes forced to recognize this; for example microprocessors in primary schools are probably better understood by the 9 year olds using them than by most of their parents! Parents may also have remarkably short memories, or sometimes be unaware of the rapidity of change about them. For instance, how many parents are aware that in Britain in the 1950s the overwhelmingly normal thing was for the children to be born at home, whereas nowadays almost all children are born in hospital? In one generation a fundamental and far-reaching change has taken place. The state of childhood may, suggests Postman (1983), be disappearing altogether. Such a view may be regarded somewhat sceptically; for certainly, the child's psychological development, like the physical, still needs plenty of time under the eye of concerned caretakers. Equally, there are many qualitative physical and cognitive differences between adults and children which cannot simply be ignored. Nevertheless, there is a good deal in what Postman says, and children are sensitive barometers of cultural change and of its impact on us all. Sheperd and Ragan (1982) say that contemporary society changes with such rapidity that those concerned with the curriculum, 'must constantly re-examine the social scene' (p.462).

Concepts of learning also change over time: not only the validity of content, the demise of a subject area, the development of a new one, not only in terms of the rapidity with which content may expand or alter in certain disciplines, but in terms of what we know of learning as a process. We know that first-hand experience and involvement are major motivators, that learning occurs best when linkage with previous learning is explicit.

We also know, though rarely admit, that much that is formally learned at school is of precious little practical use. We suspect that, at worst, some learning may be no more than ritual 'busy-work', designed to occupy rather than edify. We are also more aware of what schools are for. They are not necessarily about meaningful learning, absorbing inquiry, exciting challenge; they are often about social engineering, about conformity, about orientation to authority, about guardianship. We also know that aspects of schooling, such as those listed above, are not particularly conducive to actual classroom curriculum learning. Indeed, they may actively thwart it by providing irksome duties, conventions and characteristics which cloud the children's minds and obscure disciplined inquiry.

William James once suggested of formal education that, 'In the last analysis it consists in the organisation of resources in the human being, or powers of conduct which shall fit him to his social and physical world' (James 1901, p.29). Sixty-five years later one of the conclusions of a major American report with far-reaching policy effects was that, 'Schools bring little influence to bear on a child's achievement that is independent of his background and general social context' (Coleman et al. 1966, p.325); explicit among the conclusions of that report being the view that schools make very little difference to children and, implicit, that if they wished to do something more akin to James' notions, then schooling would have to be much better fitted to the entering characteristics of children concerned.

Naïve psychology and the classroom

As James also observed, pedagogy and psychology run side by side, and the two should be considered 'congruent features' of good education. Certainly, since the earliest days of teaching, teachers and others have been aware of the importance of trying to assess something of what the learner perceives. More recently, or relatively so, people have been equally concerned with the teacher's perceptions; and nowadays most observers would concede that knowledge of the context of the learner in the home, school and community adds a vital dimension to the planning of learning.

Scientific psychology can sometimes provide us with clear examples of procedures with regard to particular problem solving which may themselves prove helpful to the teachers; and it is aphoristic to say that the curriculum is about 'not only the nature of knowledge, but also the nature of the knower, and the knowledge-getting process' (Bruner 1966, p.72). Indeed, Bruner has repeatedly stressed that some perceptions of the child's system of representation or frame of knowledge are fundamental to the task of the teacher if he or she intends to present information in a form likely to be used by the child's expanding mind. Whilst most teachers recognize this, and its emphasis forms an oft-repeated part of their training, the reality of a busy classroom, or of having to impose externally examined syllabuses, makes it extremely difficult to achieve. Ideally, one would possess appropriate diagnostic material such that one could quickly, yet reasonably accurately assess (rather than assume) the exact psychological characteristics which the child brings to any given task. But the stuff of normal classroom interaction, of normal curriculum transactions, may be frequently much less systematic than that; and we infer, assume, posit and judge in order to fit transaction and learning into some intelligible whole. In short, we as teachers become skilful in our planning and manipulation of the curriculum to the extent that we can employ a sort of naïve psychology of attribution. If we didn't attribute and infer then we wouldn't know; if we were to resort to batteries of diagnostic materials, even supposing they existed, we could be in danger of falling into the trap (which is *sometimes* fallen into by infant teachers anxious to record everything) of allowing testing and recording to overtake teaching. As a friend once succinctly put it, 'weighing the pig all the time, rather than fattening it'.

Attribution and the curriculum are not unlikely bedfellows. One of the modern fields of social psychology, attribution psychology, focuses on the ways people perceive the causes of behaviour. With one or two exceptions (e.g. Hopson and Scally 1981) curriculum theorists appear to have avoided the area; possibly because of its close links with already problematic schema, such as social learning theory and intrinsic motivation. Whatever the reasons, an awareness of attribution does *in the broadest terms* seem relevant to those considering education, since education is about the transmission and exchange of ideas and attribution is about the interpretation and integration of impressions of the self, persons and contexts in which ideas may be exchanged. Is such knowledge helpful to thinking about the curriculum itself?

Attribution theory has its origins in the work of Fritz Heider who believed that people wished to predict something of their environment and to give meaning to it. It differs from scientific psychology precisely because it is concerned with the 'layman's analysis', that is with how we attribute cause to behaviour and situations in everyday life. Though human behaviour is not that amenable to prediction and generalization, we do go through life attributing cause and effect – both to ourselves and to others –

often on the slenderest of evidence. Indeed the 'evidence' may be more to do with states of mind within us, than with external phenomena. Teachers, I suspect, need to be very aware of this, since they attribute much to pupils which they cannot directly ascertain. Pupils likewise attribute to teachers. We *think* we detect some appropriate information or some consistency which gives us a causal model or set of assumptions on which we may then seek to set a whole sequence of transactions. But we are motivated to obtain certain information we deem relevant according to our own previous experience of making (apparently successful) causal attributions, and consistency, though important, is not necessarily as important as is the need to feel that we may reach towards *prediction* and *control*. Of course, causal understanding also depends on the accessibility and availability of information to us, and there are likely to be times when we 'make interpersonal judgements under different inferential sets' (Jones et al. 1972, p.xii). Gahagan (1975 pp.46, 47) says, 'It is important to remember that the attribution process is fraught with possibilities of error . . . [there is] some evidence that we attribute more intentionality to an action the more serious its outcome . . . [and] the degree of relevance that the outcomes of an action have for us personally' has been found to affect our judgement.

Judgement is of course a form of awareness crucial in ensuring 'matching', achieving that 'goodness of fit' of the curriculum to the child. It may come about through negotiation, a currently fashionable term, or it may be the result of highly specific observation and structuring of minute elements of a curriculum; most likely, however, is that it comes semiintuitively, through an awareness by the teacher that the transaction should involve a meeting of minds. Morris (1972) suggested that it was not helpful to talk of child-centred or teacher-centred approaches, that ideally one should think in terms of *transaction-centred* approaches. Others have talked of the affective curriculum (Weinstein and Fantini 1970) in an attempt to deal with the matching of the transaction to the apparent interests, concerns and feelings of the child. Yet most formal education takes place in large-group situations. In such situations it is notoriously difficult to deal with people on a one-to-one basis for any substantial amount of time. Consequently, much curriculum planning relies heavily on that fourth feature listed at the beginning of this paper, on the recipients being grouped so that roughly homogeneous curriculum communications will suit them all. To do this, however, the learners' entering characteristics are usually largely ignored, even if known, and the curriculum is designed from principles other than those much associated with knowledge about the recipients. At best the curriculum is asssumed to fit here, but not there, in need of modification or extension as the teacher goes along. For the lucky child there is a sensitive teacher altering, reshaping and fitting elements of the curriculum to the varying signals and alerts perceived during teaching. Experience leads to the 'elbow in the bathwater' technique, a form of naïve psychology which helps one more accurately to attribute so that the art of teaching modifies the inflexibility of the externally conceived curriculum. Though diagnosis of the learner's condition and stage are essential for anything more than the occasional (and sometimes fortuitous) match between curriculum and pupil, in default of diagnosis sensible awareness and sensitive attribution may prove helpful substitutes.

Popular myth has it that schoolteachers have no time for psychological or educational theory. Yet, when listening to them talk to colleagues, or to parents, one realizes how much they actively employ it. Complex outlines of possible reasons for behaviour, motives, perceptions and needs for control or satisfaction are all causally linked and expressed with conviction often accompanied by details taken from careful observation.

At a very general level research suggests that children usually attribute success in a task to internal factors, such as ability or persistence; and failure is usually ascribed to external, less easily controlled factors, such as lack of help from teachers or parents, bad luck, or inappropriately designed tasks. The child is doing this continually and so is the adult. It is an awareness of both sides of the process and of their *combined* impact upon the curriculum which is so important.

One aspect of causal attribution is the process of self-attribution. It is part of our interpretive feedback on the world. The child comes to school already loaded with a cargo of rich experiences: some of these will have given him opinions about himself, and will have affected the way he sees his control, or lack of it, over events, the extent to which he can attribute responsibility (for success and failure) to himself and to others. This differential attribution of responsibility to the self is a major outcome of our early socialization and appears directly linked to self-esteem and to expectations of others.

Many studies have shown some relationship between self-esteem and school achievement. Somewhat fewer have taken direct account of self-attribution of responsibility in school situations, and those that have have brought to light some curious anomalies and conflicts. For example, studies of low-achieving children have noted that (unlike the general view described earlier) such children often perceive failure as something intrinsic to them. There are also some odd sex differences which suggest that females

Figure 1.1 'the complex interweaving of motivational and cognitive development'

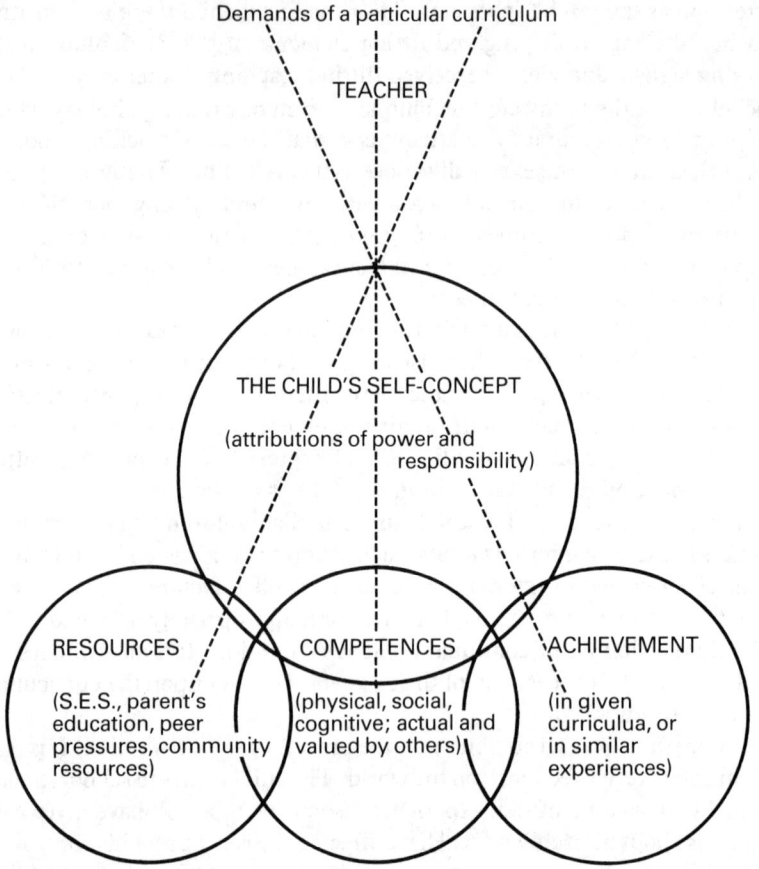

make more external attributions for both failure *and* success. De Charms is somewhat more definite in his North American research and sees the child as, 'immersed in the basic problem of being a personal cause of effects on other people', and later refers to the 'complex interweaving of motivational and cognitive development' (1976, pp.201, 202). Whatever the research perspective, such 'complex interweaving' is a constant feature of classroom reality, and how well the child's psychological resources meet curriculum demands depends upon many variables within that web of interaction. The latter can be diagrammatically represented, though in no way precisely assigned, as shown in Figure 1.1.

Locus of control

Closely associated with such research as that of de Charms have been numerous studies stemming from Rotter (1966) on locus of control. Such studies have tended to demonstrate that 'internally' oriented children feel more in control of their own lives, attribute more responsibility to themselves, possibly show greater persistence and perhaps are more competent socially. Some of this research has linked the child's socialization, especially in terms of SES and value systems, to his perceptions of generalized control and responsibility. A considerable amount of research has also shown reasonably high correlations between measures of internality and school achievement (Stipek and Weisz 1981). Certainly the concept of locus of control has, as Phares (1976) remarked, 'intuitive appeal' and it seems something with which teachers might be more generally concerned, even though there are hardly any appropriate British school tests which could be used for any rapid diagnosis (Gammage 1982). There are, however, many American tests, of which work stemming from Nowicki is probably the most consistently and directly school related (Nowicki and Strickland 1973; Nowicki and Duke 1983). Work by Arlin (1975) suggests that 'externals' need particularly carefully structured curricula and classroom organization, whereas 'internals' prefer, and possibly do better in, open or child-centred situations.

Curriculum context: expectations and values

If one takes some of the attitudes and values implicit in much early childhood curricula, and particularly in curricula focusing on topic or project work, then the following broad aims would probably be quite typical. Certainly, 'open' or child-centred organizations rely upon the early realization of such aims and then try to build on them as continuing and essential vehicles for further development. Psychological and curricular literature demonstrates this quite clearly (Sanders and Wren 1976; Brophy 1978; Downing and Bothwell 1979; Blenkin and Kelly 1981; Kirby 1981).

1. a sense of personal responsibility for the organization of one's work and for the care of things like books and materials;
2. relative autonomy – knowing when and where to make appropriate choices;
3. a sense of independence and self-reliance, but one amenable to and aware of interdependence;

4. the ability to persist until tasks are completed.

But really that is to start from the wrong end. One must be aware, if of nothing else, that certain programmes have optimal effects for certain kinds of children and that curriculum planners should not rely upon, or presume, certain 'desirable' child-characteristics with which such curricula will succeed. If one heeds research by developmental and social psychologists, then one is aware that certain forms of socialization lead to certain quite distinct cognitive perspectives of the world. Ideally, then, the relevant characteristics of children would be assessed before placement in school were attempted. Added to this, one would have to try broadly to assess and categorize curricular programmes, organizations and perhaps schools, so that information could be matched appropriately. No doubt all this smacks too much of the 'brave new world' or of an authoritarian state. But educational environments are very different (Bennett 1976; Galton et al. 1980; Rutter et al. 1979) and already very different classroom experiences are available to children by chance. Current classroom research does seem to be at the point of identifying broad pedagogical-cum-curricular organizations that suit initially high or initially low-achieving children (e.g. Brophy 1978; Solomon and Kendall 1979; Entwistle and Hayduk 1982).

Recent educational and social-psychological research, therefore, would seem to indicate that Coleman et al. (1966) did not get things quite right, and may even have got much of it wrong. Schools and teachers *can* make a difference to children's achievements. They make it in a variety of ways:

a) in the ways in which transaction/teaching style can communicate particular expectations or evaluations of a child which override the immediate impact of an ill-matched or difficult element in the curriculum, which enhance motivation and self-attribution in the child (unfortunately, the converse situation is equally true);
b) in the ways in which differential access to different emphases in or levels of the curriculum can be made available to children within one organizational setting;
c) in the ways in which teachers take serious account of the different motivational and self-attributional patterns of children within a single subject or topic curriculum;
d) in the ways in which the ethos/atmosphere of the school as a whole suits, compensates for or modifies certain child characteristics;
e) in a variety of as yet ill-understood ways associated with (d) and acting through the hidden curriculum.

Although it is unclear how it happens, we can also note that collective teachers' expectations and evaluations have a cumulative effect on children, an effect which may cohere or conflict with the evaluations of peers and parents. The relationships between such variables in pupil performance in a given curriculum are complex and there has been almost no research which has studied such relationships over any length of time (Entwistle and Hayduk 1982). This is particularly true of self-concept reasearch too; few if any have examined those vital but elusive elements of personality in a developmental context. But self-concept, attributional and social-learning studies all clearly emphasize the importance of attributing power and responsibility to the self; and such perspectives stress the highly interactional nature of classroom learning; a learning that involves the child in building up observations about himself and of his performance in given situations. Such observations become internalized and form a part of the ways that child interprets the world. They themselves become crucial to his later success and failure.

The foregoing is already well known, however, and is merely to scratch the surface of person–environment research in respect of schooling. There have been many interactional theories and none has yet developed to the stage where it could provide a detailed 'model' capable of taking into account the everyday life of a child going to school and dealing with his parents, his peers, his teachers and the curriculum. However, three particular features are worth reiterating.

1. The child's reactions to the curriculum are part of his personal history of responses to related experiences; the psychological import (meanings and loadings) will be vital determining factors in his response.
2. The child is an active agent in the process of interaction; and in his construction of the world emotional factors play a vital role; in particular the self-concept may be pro-active and have a 'knock-on' effect.
3. It is possibly in relation to the emotional context of the curriculum that the teacher can most modify, alter or stimulate the reactions at (1).

Taking it into account

In a research project of 'unconventional methodology and unusually long duration in a disadvantaged urban neighbourhood', Pedersen, Faucher and Eaton (1978) examined the influence of classroom teachers on children's later adult status. The investigators happened to notice that IQ change varied by first-grade teacher, and so they altered the original thrust of their investigation from IQ change towards teacher effects. Specifically, they found 'a positive correlation between children's exposure to one first-grade teacher (Miss A) and their success as adults many years later' (Entwisle and Hayduk 1982, p.4).

If, as Carew and Lightfoot (1979) suggest, the interaction between teacher and child is multifaceted and embedded in complex webs of different perceptions and values, then the curriculum has to be child and school *shaped*. Furthermore, the evaluation of curricular success, which is often expressed in terms of those 'glittering prizes', may be crude and inadequate for the vast majority. Evaluation which has salience for the child has to have meaning in terms of the child's and parent's values as well as those of school and society; not merely in terms of how far the child has travelled this or that road in relation to his peers, but what the curriculum gives the child which *he* recognizes as worth while. We sometimes think that if a child comprehends what he is doing, that is sufficient in itself. And perhaps we have advanced further than the time of the apocryphal story of the dominie's interchange with the Scots lad. The lad complained that he didn't understand what he was doing. 'Aye', the dominie replied, 'and ye're not meant to understand, merely to learn it!' But even 'I do and I understand' is to my mind insufficient. The counsel of perfection ought to be 'I do, I understand, and I hold valuable'. Some suggest that relevance is the key to children's valuing the curriculum, especially during secondary education, but adolescents' notions of relevance are often transitory and sometimes odd. They can be notoriously short-term, affected by whim and fashion. To seek relevance alone would be to court disaster, for the curriculum to be valued only according to criteria of immediacy, instrumentality or popularity.

All this is merely to illustrate that knowledge about the values, expectations and concerns of pupils is slowly developing, and that awareness of shifts and changes can alert and sensitize teachers accordingly. This knowledge is not of course restricted only to those areas of social-psychology on which this chapter touches. Cognitive psychologists, especially those associated with school learning, have repeatedly stressed the importance of careful curriculum evaluation in effective teaching. In the past they have tended to be fairly firmly wedded to 'objectives' approaches to the curriculum. But some recent developments in cognitive psychology have been more concerned with continual monitoring of learning outcomes *and* processes, and of adjusting the levels of exposition and task to the changing levels of pupil awareness (Biggs and Collis 1982). This is closer to the formative evaluation taken seriously by some writers on curriculum theory (e.g. Scriven 1967, or Hamilton 1976).

Sociologists might well point out that there are large issues still in need of research and clarification. Some of those which clearly affect the curriculum are processes of role stereotyping and of social values learning as they relate to teacher attitudes, texts and resource materials. These are not just aspects of class or of equality of opportunity as portrayed during the 1960s. The issues of ethnicity and of gender in the curriculum are very much current preoccupations of some sociologists and must be taken seriously. Linguists, too, have hardly stood still during the 1970s. Systematic development work has been going on; some of it demonstrating that differences in attitudes to *literacy* rather than overall differences in oracy seem more likely to predict subsequent educational attainment (Wells 1981), and this has helped clarify work of the 1950s and 60s (by Bernstein, for instance, as well as many others).

But, how might teachers and others take account of the sorts of issues presented in this paper? Is the theory and the research at all translatable in ways which busy teachers might utilize? Figures 1.1 and 1.2 are provided simply as pointers to discussion which may aid teachers in the overall strategies of curriculum design or evaluation. Such diagrams are, at best, merely convenient shorthand checklists to help one establish that vital things are not forgotten. They take one from the global interactions of Figure 1.1 to the in-class guidelines of Figure 1.2.

The class as a group

Much of the foregoing has referred to the importance of individual child-characteristics and of the sorts of ways these bear on the curriculum. But schooling relies on groupings of recipients for its economic functioning. The realities of teaching are of working with groups, estimating general curricular 'fit' before specific individual match is taken into account. Such reality means that the classroom already has a particular interpersonal atmosphere, and effective curriculum organization may depend upon the exploitation of certain group feelings at the expense of others. Thelen says of the schoolroom that the behavioural sciences have helped us see, 'that the classroom group can be viewed as a small society; that the "fit" between its mix of personalities and the personality of the teacher has a lot to do with the effectiveness of the teacher' (1981, p.120). He reminds us that there are three different, though interrelated, types of group which exist within the class.

1. *The psyche-groups*, self-chosen, friendship groups generating much

24 Readings in School-Based Curriculum Development

Figure 1.2 Curriculum planning and awareness check. In-class guidelines

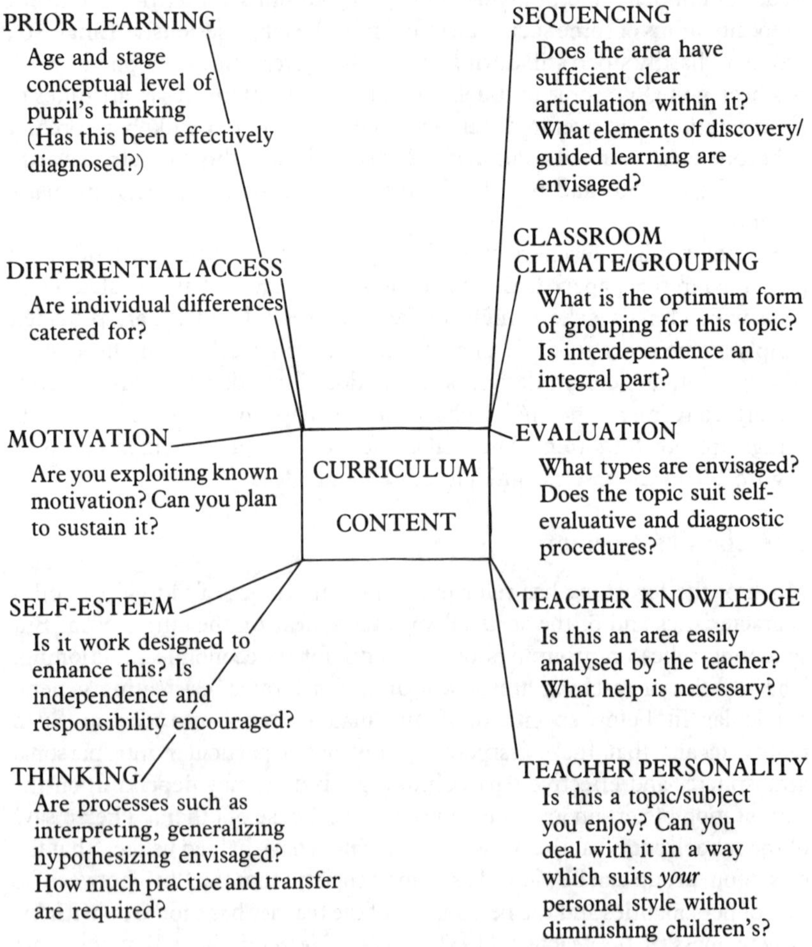

PRIOR LEARNING
Age and stage conceptual level of pupil's thinking (Has this been effectively diagnosed?)

SEQUENCING
Does the area have sufficient clear articulation within it? What elements of discovery/guided learning are envisaged?

DIFFERENTIAL ACCESS
Are individual differences catered for?

CLASSROOM CLIMATE/GROUPING
What is the optimum form of grouping for this topic? Is interdependence an integral part?

MOTIVATION
Are you exploiting known motivation? Can you plan to sustain it?

CURRICULUM CONTENT

EVALUATION
What types are envisaged? Does the topic suit self-evaluative and diagnostic procedures?

SELF-ESTEEM
Is it work designed to enhance this? Is independence and responsibility encouraged?

TEACHER KNOWLEDGE
Is this an area easily analysed by the teacher? What help is necessary?

THINKING
Are processes such as interpreting, generalizing hypothesizing envisaged? How much practice and transfer are required?

TEACHER PERSONALITY
Is this a topic/subject you enjoy? Can you deal with it in a way which suits *your* personal style without diminishing children's?

Source: adapted from Gammage 1982

interpersonal activity and learning. These help individuals to 'discover and maintain their identity'. The problem for the teacher is how to use their strengths and minimize any destructive forces.
2. *The socio-group*, the involuntary nature of the class as a whole. Children have to come to school, are cohort stratified, are assigned this or that teacher.
3. *The task group*, the raison d'être of the children's presence. They are there to work, to learn things chosen by teachers and other adults, to proceed with a curriculum. There are criteria and processes which give legitimation to the teacher's power and control, and recognition to those who are 'productivity-oriented'.

Yet, as Thelen also says, one of the more interesting questions about classrooms is 'Whose culture will dominate?'. It may be that through power and authority the teacher's perceptions (of middle-class culture?) will dominate. But teachers do not necessarily succeed in establishing such a cultural perspective. In certain communities it may be a temporary and outward show. For certain different, disadvantaged or difficult groups, 'the achievement motive is likely to remain unaffected' (ibid. p.134).

Children have to attend school, and most parents and not a few educationists think in terms of 'transmitting' the appropriate curriculum. Certainly, ritual recognitions of engagement with the right curriculum are required. But in the end the child may learn little of what was intended, for he has not valued that on offer. *The real challenge of the curriculum remains embedded in the interaction, in adaptation and engagement.* Conceptions of education as received wisdom, or even as techniques of problem solving, are deficient. Unless we have curricula which have value for the child, which both relate to *and expand* his cultural and group norms, as well as have academic worth, unless we constantly expand our knowledge of the vehicle, humane interaction, in ways which speak to the child's condition and which commit and engage him, our curriculum is likely to be ritual time-filling and we will deserve the dislike of school which so many children express.

> Though the act of learning is something no teacher can achieve on behalf of the learner, nevertheless the learner has to be brought to this act by the skilful persuasion of a professional teacher. This can only be accomplished when relationships are such that there is mutual understanding between learner and teacher . . . (Kirby 1981, pp.90–91)

Throughout this paper I have stressed the fundamental importance of attribution processes in teaching and learning. Causal attribution has become a sophisticated and currently moderately well-researched area of social psychology; and, as research progresses, we can look forward to a possibly finer understanding of the complexities of self-perception, motivation, expectancy and prediction in human behaviour. But at a more basic level as well it has much to offer teachers and curriculum planners, since it focuses on both the continual everyday predictions and diagnoses that the teacher makes in teaching *and* the levels of involvement and responsibility which the child feels for his own success or failure in learning. Even some minimal awareness of attribution is likely to enhance our knowledge of (and belief in) the interactional nature of the curriculum. This in turn should increase our sensitivity as teachers and improve the 'fine-tuning' of our curriculum, our transactions and our evaluation.

References

Antaki, C. and Brewin, C. (eds) (1982) *Attributions and Psychological Change*, London: Academic Press.
Arlin, M. (1975) The interaction of locus of control, classroom structure and pupil satisfaction, *Psychology in the Schools*, vol. 12, pp. 279–286.
Bennett, N. (1976) *Teaching Styles and Pupil Progress*, London: Open Books.
Bernstein, B. (1971) On the classification and framing of educational knowledge, *in* Young, M.F.D. (ed.) *Knowledge and Control*, London: Collier-Macmillan.
Biggs, J.B. and Collis, K.F. (1982) *Evaluating the Quality of Learning*, New York: Academic Press.
Blenkin, G.M. and Kelly, A.V. (1981) *The Primary Curriculum*, London: Harper and Row.
Brophy, J.E. (1978) Interactions between learner characteristics and optimal instruction, *in* Bar-Tal, D. and Saxe, L. *Social Psychology of Education*, Washington DC: Hemisphere.
Bruner, J.S. (1966) *Toward a Theory of Instruction*, Cambridge, Mass: Harvard University Press.
Carew, J. and Lightfoot, S.L. (1979) *Beyond Bias: Perspectives on classrooms*, Cambridge, Mass.: Harvard University Press.
Coleman, J.S., Campbell, E.Q., Hobson, C.J., McPartland, J., Mood, A., Weinfeld, F.D. and York, R.L. (1966) *Equality of Educational Opportunity*, Washington DC: US Government Printing Office.
De Charms, R. (1976) *Enhancing Motivation*, New York: Irgington Publishers.
Downing, L.L. and Bothwell, K.H. (Jr.) (1979) Open-space schools: anticipation of peer interaction and development of co-operative interdependence, *Journal of Educational Psychology*, vol. 71, no. 4, pp. 478–484.
Entwistle, D.R. and Hayduk, L.A. (1982) *Early Schooling: Cognitive and affective outcomes*, Baltimore: Johns Hopkins University Press.
Gahagan, J. (1975) *Interpersonal and Group Behaviour*, London: Methuen.

Galton, M., Simon, B. and Croll, P. (1980) *Inside the Primary Classroom*, London: Routledge and Kegan Paul.
Gammage, P. (1982) *Children and Schooling: Issues in childhood socialisation*, London: Allen and Unwin.
Hamilton, D. (1976) *Curriculum Evaluation*, London: Open Books.
Hopson, B. and Scally, M. (1981) *Lifeskills Teaching*, London: McGraw Hill.
James, W. (1901) *Talks to Teachers on Psychology: and to students on some of life's ideals*, London: Longmans Green and Co.
Jones, E., Kanouse, D.E., Kelley, H.H., Nisbett, R.E., Valins, S. and Weiner, B. (1972) *Attribution: Perceiving the causes of behaviour*, Morristown, NJ: General Learning Press.
Kirby, N. (1981) *Personal Values in Primary Education*, London: Harper and Row.
Morris, B. (1972) *Objectives and Perspectives in Education*, London: Routledge and Kegan Paul.
Newson, E. (1982) Child and parent, school and culture: issues in identification, *in* Braham, M. (ed.) *Aspects of Education*, Chichester: Wiley.
Nowicki, S. and Duke, M.P. (1983) The Nowicki–Strickland life span locus of control scales: construct validation, *in* Lefcourt, H.M. (ed.) *Research with the Locus of Control Constucts*, vol. 2, London: Academic Press.
Nowicki, S. and Strickland, B.A. (1973) A locus of control scale for children, *Journal of Consulting and Clinical Psychology*, vol. 40, no. 1, pp. 148–154.
Pedersen, E., Faucher, T.A. and Eaton, W.W. (1978) A new perspective on the effects of first-grade teachers on children's subsequent adult status, *Harvard Educational Review*, vol. 48, pp. 1–31.
Phares, E.J. (1976) *Locus of Control in Personality*, Morristown, NJ: General Learning Press.
Postman, N. (1983) *The Disappearance of Childhood*, London: W.H. Allen.
Rotter, J.B. (1966) Generalised expectancies for internal versus external control of reinforcement, *Psychological Monographs* (General and Applied), whole no. 609, vol. 80, no. 1.
Rutter, M., Maughan, B., Mortimore, P. and Ouston, J. (1979) *Fifteen Thousand Hours*, London: Open Books.
Sanders, S.G. and Wren, J.P. (1976) The open-space school. How effective? *Elementary School Journal*, vol. 77, pp. 57–62.
Scriven, M. (1967) The methodology of evaluation, *in* Tyler, R., Cague, R. and Scriven, M. (eds.) *Perspectives of Curriculum Evaluation*, Chicago: Rand McNally.
Sheperd, G.D. and Ragan, W.B. (1982) *Modern Elementary Curriculum*, 6th edn, New York; Holt, Rinehart and Winston.
Solomon, D, and Kendall, A.J. (1979) *Children in Classrooms*, New York: Praeger.
Stipek, D.J. and Weisz, J.R. (1981) Perceived personal control and academic achievement, *Review of Educational Research*, vol. 51, no. 1, pp. 101–137.
Tanner, J.M. (1978) *Education and Physical Growth*, 2nd edn, London: Hodder and Stoughton.
Thelen, H.A. (1981) *The Classroom Society*, London: Croom Helm.
Weiner, B. (1979) A theory of motivation for some classroom experiences, *Journal of Educational Psychology*, vol. 71, pp. 3–25.

Weinstein, G. and Fantini, M.D. (eds) (1970) *Towards Humanistic Education*, New York: Praeger.
Wells, G. (1981) Some antecedents of early educational attainment, *British Journal of Sociology of Education*, vol. 2, no. 2, pp. 181–200.

CHAPTER 2

NEW DIRECTIONS IN CURRICULUM POLICY, LOCAL AND NATIONAL: CHANGES AT THE LOCAL LEVEL
Ron Letch

Autonomy has been a keyword in British education for some time. Schools and teachers have held their right to decide both what should be taught and how it should be taught to be one of the indicators of their professionalism. In practice, however, there have been external constraints which have had a strong influence on the curriculum teachers offer in schools. Resources such as money for books and other learning materials are controlled by the employer, in most cases the local education authority. Likewise the number of staff in relation to pupil numbers is determined by the local education authority. External examinations such as the General Certificate of Education and the Certificate of Secondary Education have a strong hold on the secondary school curriculum and in some authorities the selection procedure at 11+ is still significant in the influence it brings to bear on what is taught in primary schools. Agreed syllabuses for religious instruction are the main guides for what should be taught in this area of the curriculum, and although not rigidly followed by all teachers, they act as a limiting factor on what may or may not be taught. Thus, although many teachers may bridle at the suggestion that others outside the profession should influence what is taught in schools, in practice such influence has always existed. The issue has not really been one of whether or not the curriculum should be in the exclusive charge of teachers, but rather how much of their responsibility should be shared by others. It might even be said to have gone further than this. How should such collaboration take place? Will it be a partnership where teachers, elected members, parents, governors and other interested parties work together, each recognizing the particular skills and insights the others bring? Or will it be the more external agencies having to force their way into the jealously guarded professional autonomy of teachers? The most hopeful signs are where partnership is the main mode of operation. Although this may mean that teachers have to be prepared to give ground, the discussion and negotiation which is required when the partners have to find common ground is invaluable in helping the growth of mutual understanding.

Central government and the curriculum

Since local government reorganization in 1974, a number of developments at both a national and local level have caused local authorities to look more closely at their responsibility for school curricula and to reassess their role in influencing or directing what goes on in schools. The so-called Great Debate of the mid-70s drew attention to the many inadequacies of schools, and the Department of Education and Science Circular 14 of 1977 was a document designed to collect information from local authorities about their policies and practices in curricular matters. The impact of this circular at local level was considerable, and for many authorities the exercise of collecting this information revealed how little they knew about their schools. The report on Circular 14/77 was published in 1979 (DES 1979). It revealed a considerable variation in practice across the country and indicated that the Government intended to encourage local authorities to take a much more active part in determining what went on in schools. It said:

> The Government must bring together the partners in the education service and the interests of the community at large: and with them seek an agreed view of the school curriculum which would take account of the range of local needs and allow for local developments . . . (pp. 2–3)

The Government's own response to Circular 14/77 was to issue in January 1980 a discussion document *A Framework for the School Curriculum*. In it the Secretaries of State made it clear that they intended to require each local authority to produce a clear and known policy for the curriculum offered in its schools. However, the document also made reference to two other factors which would significantly influence the way local authorities could respond. These factors, falling schools rolls and the need to limit public expenditure, do not sit well together. In March 1981, the DES issued the amended paper *The School Curriculum*. This was accompanied later in the year by DES Circular 6/81 which stated what each LEA should do about *The School Curriculum*. This was to:

a. review its policy for the School Curriculum in its area, and its arrangements for making the policy known to all concerned;
b. review the extent to which current provision in the schools is consistent with that policy; and
c. plan future developments accordingly, within the resources available. (para. 5, DES Circular 6/81)

Local education authority responses

These government documents plus the Primary Survey (DES 1978) and the Secondary Survey (DES 1979a) both by Her Majesty's Inspectorate, caused considerable debate at local level. Some authorities had begun discussions before the publication of *The School Curriculum* in 1981. However, one point of significance in all the discussions was that it was the local authority taking charge of discussion about the curriculum, *not* the teachers. It is true, of course, that most authorities took considerable care to involve teachers and school governors in discussions, but the LEAs were taking a more positive role in curriculum matters than at any time since the 1944 Education Act.

The two factors mentioned above could not but avoid influencing discussions. The falling birthrate means that schools overall in England and Wales are faced with a reduction of their rolls by a third in the ten-year period between the late 1970s and late 1980s. The implications of this relate to the problems of maintaining a balanced curriculum in small schools. Where local authorities are laying down guidelines for the curriculum to be offered in their schools, they have to give careful thought to the minimum size of school in which such a curriculum can be maintained. As recent governments have sought to reduce local government expenditure, there has been little or no 'cushion' to protect schools with rapidly falling rolls in order to enable them to retain staff who are needed to teach significant areas of the curriculum. For example, if science is to be offered to *all* pupils up to the age of 16, the resource implications, both in terms of laboratory space and teachers, are considerable. The result of falling rolls and limited finance has been that many authorities are engaged in closing small schools and amalgamating others. This is happening in both the primary and secondary sectors, and decisions relating to such closures have often been influenced by the discussions elected members have had about curriculum matters.

One further requirement of Circular 6/81 was that '. . . authorities and governors of schools . . . should assess regularly how far the curriculum – in the schools as a whole and for individual pupils – matches the stated aims' (para. 7). However, by 1981 many authorities had already started the process of setting up guidelines for schools to use in monitoring their progress and achievement, and in 1980 Gordon Elliott was able to report that 69 out of 107 local authorities had initiated or completed discussions on the topic of self-evaluation.

Preparing teachers for change

Thus by the end of 1981 debate on curriculum matters and evaluation were well under way in most parts of the country. However, there is no guarantee that debate will lead to action and most authorities have had to give thought to how they can support and stimulate active discussion and development of curriculum matters in schools. One example of how such development might take place comes from the *Red Book* inquiry of Her Majesty's Inspectorate. The original *Red Book*, published in December 1977, was entitled *Curriculum 11–16 Working Papers by HM Inspectorate – a contribution to current debate* (DES 1977a). It was intended to stimulate debate nationally, but particularly to be the basis of a collaborative effort between five local education authorities, their advisers, schools and groups of teachers, and a number of HMIs. An interim report of the first three years' experience of these groups was published in 1981, entitled *Curriculum 11–16: A review of progress – a joint study by HMI and five LEAs* (DES 1981a). It highlights a number of important points for all local authorities and schools to bear in mind when undertaking curriculum appraisal. First, any such exercise is costly in time and is not something which can be achieved quickly. Second, the activity is probably best carried out collaboratively involving LEA advisers, teachers of all levels of seniority and HMI where possible. Third, the activity of curriculum appraisal has considerable implications for staff development. Working together to solve a common problem is an excellent way for teachers to grow professionally and it also reveals areas where further training may be necessary.

Alongside interest in the whole curriculum were concerns for some of the discrete elements or subjects. The Inspectorate's Primary Survey (DES 1978) had, for example, highlighted the particular problems relating to science and mathematics teaching. Recognition was given to the need for teachers to receive further training in the teaching of science (para. 5.83). Some authorities took up these comments and set up local inquiries into the state of science and maths teaching in their own schools. As a result of the findings, certain LEAs have launched substantial in-service programmes to help teachers acquire the necessary skills and knowledge to enable them to set up imaginative teaching programmes in their own schools. Alongside such in-service programmes authorities have encouraged the development of curriculum guidelines in most areas of the primary curriculum. Working parties of practising teachers, usually led by a local authority adviser, are normally responsible for producing these guidelines. Part of the programme they devise may well include dissemination courses which endeavour to introduce the guidelines to all schools. The courses are also intended to help teachers understand the principles underlying the documents and to plan ways in which they can apply these guidelines in their own schools.

Parental influences and interests

Local authorities have not been the only group to take an increasing interest in the school curriculum. The Taylor Report, *A New Partnership for our Schools* (DES 1977), was an indication of the growing interest of parents in all aspects of the life of schools from their government to the curriculum. *The School Curriculum* (DES 1981) made particular mention of the involvement of parents (para. 10) and the 1980 Education Act enables parents to have greater choice in the selection of schools for their children, requires schools to publish a prospectus which includes information about the curriculum they offer, and requires secondary schools to publish their public examination results. This opening up of schools has not only enabled parents to be better informed about their education service, but has also given schools the challenge of producing curriculum information for parents which is readily understood by them and not presented in professional jargon which can only be understood by teachers. The influence of the 1980 Act has not been entirely helpful however. Parental choice at a time of falling rolls has introduced an element of competition between schools which is not always conducive to curriculum development. There is a tendency for parents to be conservative in their expectations of schools, often basing these on their own past experiences as schoolchildren. Thus headteachers may be reluctant to allow imaginative experiments in the curriculum for fear of their adverse affect on pupil recruitment.

At a time when there is a great need for the curriculum to be dynamic in order to respond to the rapidly changing world which surrounds schools, it is a little ironic that an Act intending to increase parental choice may have the opposite effect. It may encourage a sameness about schools which are reluctant to move away from a limited and overtraditional view of the curriculum. This dilemma is often shared by members of the local advisory service. Encouraging schools to be imaginative in curriculum terms is not easy when schools are faced with parental pressure to retain traditional patterns, when resources may well be restricted because of financial constraints, and maintaining a balance of teacher expertise is difficult in a contracting service.

The role of other government departments

The Department of Industry Scheme to place a microcomputer in every school has been another external influence on schools. The scheme was launched in June 1981 and was quickly taken up by secondary schools and later by primary schools. The initial impact of the scheme in terms of curriculum development has been negligible, as many schools had given little thought to the implications of using microelectronics in any ways other than supplementing mathematics and physics teaching. However, by 1984 the scene has begun to change. Local authorities, universities, institutes of higher education and many other bodies have begun to become involved in offering courses to teachers which go beyond simply understanding the language of microcomputers and being able to operate them. The emphasis of these courses is increasingly the application of computers across the curriculum. Many local authorities have appointed advisers with special responsibility for encouraging and supporting microelectronics education in schools. It is interesting to note that at a time of financial constraints money has been made available for an area of the curriculum which appears to be related to national needs. *The School Curriculum* (DES 1981) devoted a special paragraph (51) to drawing attention to microelectronics and the steps the Government are taking to promote developments in schools. The problem for schools and local authorities, however, is to give these developments enough time and money to take them beyond being merely a cosmetic exercise. To enable teachers of all subjects to use microcomputers to develop and broaden students' opportunities within their own discipline requires a substantial in-service training programme and also the development of suitable software. Developments in both these requirements are slow, and like so many other major curriculum initiatives in the past, there is a danger that microcomputers will become no more than a bolt-on-addition to the curriculum rather than an integral and necessary part of the whole learning experience of pupils.

The Manpower Services Commission and the Youth Training Scheme

The Department of Industry are not the only noneducation government department to exert a strong influence on the curriculum of our schools. The Department of Employment through the Manpower Services Commission have brought considerable pressures to bear on schools and further education. Two major MSC initiatives are currently influencing schools in a way the outcomes of which are difficult to predict. The first of these, the Youth Training Scheme, launched in September 1983, has significance for the shape and size of sixth forms in secondary schools. This scheme, which is a new and permanent training system for young people under 18, offers all trainees a year of experience of work with high-quality training, with a minimum of three months' off-the-job training and education. The scheme offers a real alternative to young people who might otherwise have stayed on at school for a year in the sixth form. The effect of this is two-fold. First, it reduces the potential size of a school's sixth form at a time when falling rolls are already causing problems. Second, schools are beginning to question what effect the YTS should have on the pre-16 curriculum.

Tony Watts, writing in the *Times Educational Supplement* on 13 May, 1983, suggests at least two possible outcomes. Either schools may react by reverting to a more academic curriculum, leaving the vocational element of education to others, or it could lead to their removing some of the examination pressures at 16+, moving towards a more skill-based and experience-based curriculum. This second point relates to the other MSC initiative which is affecting educational provision in some local authorities.

In December 1982, the Prime Minister announced an MSC scheme to stimulate technical and vocational education for 14–18 year olds. The pilot scheme was for ten projects to be set up which would offer four-year courses for up to a thousand students per project. Finance for these projects is provided by the MSC *not* the DES. The intention of the scheme is to offer these young people opportunities to acquire qualifications and skills which will be of direct value to them at work; to better equip them for employment; to give them opportunities to develop initiative, motivation and enterprise; to construct a bridge from education to work; and to improve the collaboration between LEAs, industry and commerce, so that the curriculum has industry's confidence. These ambitious objectives indicate the growing pressure on schools to provide a curriculum for young people which prepares them for the 'real world'. Some indication of the enthusiasm with which this scheme was received by local authorities is that, despite the very limited amount of time given to them to submit proposals, over sixty authorities responded. Much hard work went into the preparation of those submissions at the local level and many of the authorities which were unsuccessful are now using their submissions as a checklist to review the curriculum provision in their secondary schools. The Government may well feel pleased that they have been able to make such a rapid impact on curriculum change at a local level. Usually such changes occur slowly and almost imperceptibly, and one of the features of the 1980s has been that the Government has taken a more interventionist approach to such change.

This new training initiative has not met with universal acclaim however. It is notable that a number of local authorities did not submit schemes for consideration because of fundamental objections to the philosophy they believed to be behind the idea. It was seen by some to be divisive and contrary to the notion of a common and liberal education for all. These critics believe that the creation of these new schools will be recreating a differentiated curriculum; that is, one that seeks to provide a practical, vocationally oriented curriculum for the less able and a traditional, academic curriculum for those pupils of higher ability. Others believe that only a good general education can prepare pupils for the uncertainty of the future and that an overemphasis on vocational preparation may well prepare young people for a type of occupational future which may not exist.

Public examinations

Apart from the MSC initiatives the public examination system has also been used to bring about change in schools. The new 17+ examination, the Certificate of Pre-Vocational Education, is a particular example. When compared with the incredible gestation period of the 16+ examination, which may yet be still-born, the CPVE may almost be cited as a case of instant birth. Whilst the discussions on a single system of examining at 16+ to replace GCE O level and CSE have dragged on for over a decade, the Secretary of State for Education neatly bypassed the examining boards and announced the new CPVE examination in May 1982. In less than a year the Government was able to say that the new examination would be available to students in September 1983. The Joint Board set up to administer the examination is a significant partnership between the Business and Technician Education Council and the City and Guilds of London Institute. Both bodies have been mainly concerned with examining courses for further education in the past, and the traditional schools examining bodies for GCE and CSE have only nominal representation on the new Joint Board. This new group examination with its emphasis on preparation for working life will be the first qualification in recent years whose syllabuses are laid down from the start and controlled by central government. There are already signs that as the new examination gets under way in schools it will have the effect of causing teachers to reexamine the 14–16 curriculum they offer. The downwards effect on the curriculum of YTS and CPVE may be considerable.

Conclusions

The role of the local authority in all these changes is mainly a responsive one. Clearly there is a need for LEAs to support schools in their efforts to react to the pressures and demands of parents, employers and government as they affect the curriculum. The Local Authority Advisory Service has a key role to play in offering such support and can do this in several ways. First, there is the need to keep schools well informed about the many developments which are taking place and the impact these may have upon them. Second, there is the need to provide as many and varied opportunities for teachers to update their professional expertise as resources will allow. The many changes outlined in this chapter make an increasing demand on teachers in areas for which they were not originally trained. Third, there is the need to help schools make the most of the resources they have at their disposal, to help meet changing demands and to boost and maintain teacher morale. Facing such a range of demands in a period of falling rolls and limited finance is trying, even for the most devoted of teachers.

To enable the local education service to survive these changes and to emerge strong and vigorous requires a special sort of partnership between schools and their local authority. It requires a sense of mutual trust, in that schools need to know that the LEA will only make reasonable demands upon them which are designed to benefit the children whom they serve. They need also to know that the LEA will do all it can to provide adequate resources for schools to do the job expected of them. At the same time LEAs have the right to expect schools to be open to the influence and opinions of others and to seek to cooperate in providing an educational experience which will prepare children for the uncertain world of tomorrow.

References

Department of Education and Science (1977) *A New Partnership for our Schools* (Taylor Report), London: HMSO.
Department of Education and Science (1977a) *Curriculum 11–16*, London: HMSO.
Department of Education and Science (1978) *Primary Education in England*, London: HMSO.
Department of Education and Science (1979) *Local Authority Arrangements for the School Curriculum* (Report on Circular 14/77), London: HMSO.
Department of Education and Science (1979a) *Aspects of Secondary Education in England*, London: HMSO.
Department of Education and Science (1980) *A Framework for the School Curriculum* London: HMSO.
Department of Education and Science (1981) *The School Curriculum*, London: HMSO.
Department of Education and Science (1981a) *Curriculum 11–16: A Review of Progress*, London: HMSO.
Elliott, G (1980) *Self Evaluation and the Teacher* Part 2, London: Schools Council.
Watts, A. 'Schools and the YTS': *Times Educational Supplement* 13 May, 1983.

CHAPTER 3

WHY CHANGE THE CURRICULUM: NEW DIRECTIONS AT NATIONAL LEVEL
Maurice Plaskow

When the Schools Council (for England and Wales) was set up as a body separate from the Department of Education in 1964, education reflected the buoyancy of the economy, the promise of the life-enhancing technological revolution and the optimism expressed in Sir Edward Boyle's preface to the Newsom Report (Central Advisory Council 1963) that: ' . . . all children should have an equal opportunity of acquiring intelligence, and of developing their talents and abilities to the full'.

In the same year (1964) the Government accepted the recommendation which had been made by the Crowther Committee (Central Advisory Council 1959) that the school leaving age should be raised to 16 – in 1970–1. Although this was later, in 1968, postponed for two years, and did not happen until 1972–3, it did provide an immediate, major task for the Schools Council to devise a programme to help teachers prepare for a cohort of adolescents, many alienated by the school system as analysed in the Newsom Report, who would be a year older and bigger.

Eight months after the Labour Government took office in 1964, Anthony Crosland, Secretary of State for Education, issued a Circular (10/65: 12 July 1965) inviting local education authorities to submit plans for the reorganization of secondary schools on comprehensive lines in order to eliminate selection into separate and different types of secondary school at 11. The scene was set for a major educational advance in a sense to realize more fully the intentions of the 1944 Education Act and the provision of secondary education for all.

The Schools Council saw itself as a body reflecting and responding to the needs of schools. In particular the work of its projects was to be of direct practical help to teachers (rather than 'pure' research) in order to improve the quality and effectiveness of pupil learning.

In order to help teachers gain familiarity and confidence with new techniques and approaches the Council was also largely instrumental in the establishment and development of teachers' centres as agencies for both information and professional development. The national thrust of the ten years 1964–74 could therefore be described as a collaborative effort to achieve Sir Edward Boyle's aspiration.

Early on in the curriculum development movement it was realized that classroom change affected both the practice and the attitudes of teachers. The model of teacher/instructor transmitting information was expanded and transformed by concepts such as 'enabler' and manager of resources. Classrooms, it was claimed, should be curriculum laboratories, encouraging inquiry, independent learning and responsibility.

Perhaps the most constructive contribution of the curriculum development movement has been the notion of the teacher as researcher, rather than instructor. Students are partners in a cooperative enterprise in which very little can be taken on authority and where information in any case will be mostly mechanized – or it becomes quickly out of date. Students need the reassurance of success, as well as the confidence to overcome temporary failure as a universal element within the human condition. This was a strong strand in the message coming from the national agencies in the 1970s, reinforced by Her Majesty's Inspectorate in their major surveys of both primary and secondary schools. It created, incidentally, considerable tension within a system still dominated by norm-referenced examinations used as selection devices, which gave many pupils experience of failure rather than success. But that's the story of the 1980s . . .

Dissemination of new ideas was linked, therefore, with a recognition of the need for systematic in-service education as well as a reappraisal of the length and content of the initial training of teachers.

In 1972 the Secretary of State for Education, Margaret Thatcher, presented a White Paper to Parliament with the optimistic title *Education: A framework for expansion*. It set out 'a framework for future action . . . the general direction of a ten-year strategy for the education service'. This was to be achieved on a basis of partnership and consultation, with 'room for a good deal of tactical flexibility'.

It accepted the received notion of growth and opportunity, particularly in providing more places in higher education. 'The Government have sympathy with the sincere desire on the part of a growing number of students to be given more help in acquiring – and discovering how to apply – knowledge and skills related more directly to the decisions that will face them in their careers and in the world of personal and social action. This is what is meant by "relevance".' (Secretary of State for Education 1972)

When the remit was given to the Crowther Committee in 1956 plans were being laid to extend initial teacher training courses to three years on the assumption that during the 1960s the number of teachers entering the service would allow a reduction in pupil–teacher ratios at the same time as training better qualified, more professional teachers. The three-year course was then lengthened to four years and degree status. Indeed, the Crowther Committee advocated a twenty-year programme of educational development, envisaging that by 1980 half the boys and girls in the country should be in full-time education to 18.

In fact the 1960s saw a rapid increase in the number of children in schools, and fewer teachers. Throughout the 1960s and 70s the education service, while receiving increased resources, was struggling to cope with more pupils, reorganization both of buildings and structures, and changes within society which posed new challenges to traditional curricula.

The Newsom Report had already suggested that what was on offer was inappropriate for many young people: 'schools will need to present education in terms more acceptable to the pupils and to their parents, by relating school more directly to adult life, and especially by taking a proper account of vocational interests . . .' This was a resonant theme which was to resurface with even greater clamour thirteen years later, after the Prime Minister, James Callaghan, had made a major speech at Ruskin College in 1976, in which he was very critical of the education system.

The buoyant optimism of the 1960s and 70s received a severe setback in the mid-70s when economic recession was suddenly triggered by the massive and unexpected rise in the price of oil, rising inflation and the effects both these factors and the impact of new technologies had on employment. A scapegoat was needed to share the blame for the recession with Arab oil sheikhs, economists, trades unions, inadequate management: education and particularly schools were an easy target. The criticism of schools combined the lack of relevance in the curriculum with an alleged decline in 'basic skills', which had been a repeated refrain in the Black Papers, the first of which appeared in 1969.

The days of laisser-LEA and schools-faire were over. It was clear that any future government would take a more vigorously interventionist stance towards education, and attempt to relate the school curriculum to 'the needs of society' and, in particular, 'wealth-producing industry'. This was underlined in the Green Paper which followed in 1977, issued by the Labour Government:

> It is vital to Britain's economic recovery and standard of living that the performance of manufacturing industry is improved and that the whole range of government policies, including education, contribute as much as possible to improving industrial performance and thereby increasing the national wealth. (DES 1977)

In the same year, 1977, the DES also issued a complex questionnaire to LEAs, asking for information about curriculum arrangements. Circular 14/77 (DES 1977a) reminded LEAs of their duties under the 1944 Education Act for providing both an efficient and a sufficient education related to pupils' age, aptitude and ability.

Authorities were stunned by its boldness. Curriculum committees proliferated; discussion documents and curriculum guidelines began to appear. The formalization of accountability was upon us. The move towards greater community involvement with schools, including what is taught, embodied in the 1980 Education Act in the strengthening of governing bodies on which parents were to be represented as of right, forced schools to begin to articulate and analyse their teaching programme, in order to describe it – and possibly also defend it – to their clients.

After digesting the LEA responses to Circular 14/77 (DES 1979) the succeeding, Conservative, Government produced in 1981 a document on *The School Curriculum*:

> Every school should seek to give every child an adequate grounding in literacy, numeracy and other essential skills needed in our increasingly complex and technological society. The Secretaries of State have an inescapable duty to satisfy themselves that the work of the schools matches such needs. They must work with their partners in the education service so that their combined efforts secure a school curriculum which measures up to the whole range of national needs and also takes account of the range of local needs. (DES 1981)

Secondary schools in particular have therefore found themselves in a dilemma over the last fifteen years. Assaulted by a clamour of strident and changing external pressures, a sudden reversal in financial circumstances and a dramatic decline in student numbers which is forcing school closures and mergers at the same time as major shifts in educational aims and public rhetoric, it is not surprising that writing about the curriculum has become one of the few major growth industries. A headteacher member of the

Bullock Committee on *Language for Life* naughtily suggested that 'the problems conscientious schools have had implementing a "language across the curriculum" policy result from the fact that few schools have a curriculum across which to put it' (Marland 1981).

Nor can it be unexpected that stronger central initiatives should have been taken in an attempt to fill an apparent vacuum; to provide an appearance of authority to replace uncertainty and instability. In the autumn of 1981 the Department of Education and Science issued a new Circular (1981) to Local Education Authorities, asking for an account, within two years, of their curriculum policies. It might have been thought that the Schools Council would be a suitable agency for providing curriculum guidance, and leadership based on collaboration with schools and LEAs built up steadily over the years.

But, in April 1982, the Secretary of State, Sir Keith Joseph, announced that he was not convinced by the report of the independent inquiry into the Schools Council, which had taken place the previous year, which recommended that it should be allowed to continue (DES 1981a). He proposed to disband it, creating in its place two separate bodies: an Examinations Council funded and under the control of the Department of Education and Science, and a more modest Curriculum Development Committee. Both would have members nominated by the Secretary of State, instead of being representatives of organizations as previously. This further underlined the intention of the Government to set the pattern and control the direction of future developments, both in curriculum and examinations.

The arguments became angrily polarized between a search for a 'modern' form of liberal education and a more instrumental view summarized by a member of the Confederation of British Industry Special Programmes Unit in a letter to the *Times Educational Supplement*:

> All aspects of the education system – whatever the stage or level – should and must take account of the economic and industrial realities of the society we live in. Within the harsh context of restricted resources and the absolute need to achieve a cost-effective economy, I see no place for education merely for its own sake . . . Education which casually overlooks the future functional needs of society not only compromises the full potential of pupils but undermines ultimate economic growth . . . I suggest that schools have had adequate time and opportunity to implement a programme along these (vocational/technical) lines but they have failed to deliver because of their built-in context of 'operational' complacency. (Bowmen 1983)

Even the director of the Manpower Services Commission, referring to the new Technical and Vocational Education Initiative (TVEI), could explain it in terms of providing 'a real alternative alongside academic options . . . (it) will be about the *application* of knowledge, rather than the acquisition of knowledge solely' (Holland 1983). See pages 35–36 above.

During 1982 the Manpower Services Commission (MSC) was busily developing its plans for a massive Youth Training Scheme (YTS) for 16–17 year olds, to begin in September 1983. Added to that came the TVEI which announced an intention to create experimental courses in schools for 14 year olds which would build a strand of technical education/training into the secondary curriculum for students willing to follow that direction.

All these actions and declarations blurred the focus of the challenge and dilemma facing a bewildered and somewhat demoralized education service as it tried to adapt itself to rapidly changing technology, social uncertainty and curriculum confusion. Not only had the secure educational goals of the academic tradition been called seriously into question, but a new direction had not been clearly enough determined to enable routes to be charted.

Secondary schools, including those bravely trying to design a comprehensive philosophy and practice, were still essentially constrained by a subject-based tradition. The examination system is subject-bound, validated by the universities who legitimize the content of knowledge. Teachers are trained in subject specialisms, serve on examination boards, and thus have an interest in defending the system against radical change.

Much of the early curriculum development of the 1960s, sponsored by bodies such as the Nuffield Foundation in the UK, was centred on the revision of subject teaching (maths, science, modern languages). Most of the work of the Schools Council in the 180 projects of its first ten years was subject based, too: curriculum reconstruction, not curriculum redevelopment; a refurbishing within existing frameworks and façades, not a new creation redesigned from a rethought concept. Lawrence Stenhouse described the two kinds of curriculum change as curriculum *renewal* and curriculum *innovation*:

> Curriculum renewal is a matter of updating materials, of keeping pace with developments of knowledge and of techniques of teaching. Curriculum innovation involves changes in the premises of teaching – its aims and values – and consequent changes in the teacher's thinking and classroom strategies. (Stenhouse 1973)

There were projects which attempted a redefinition and set new directions, but these were received with suspicion, even hostility; in particular the work which Stenhouse himself directed in the Humanities Curriculum Project (1967–72). Describing the project's intentions in the Schools Council's magazine in 1970, Stenhouse wrote of the conditions necessary to liberate English education from its elementary tradition:

> We need to establish a new climate of relationships with adolescents which takes account of their responsibility and is not authoritarian. Education must be founded on their co-operation, not on co-ercion. We must find a way of expressing our common humanity with our pupils and we must be sensitive to the need to justify the decisions of authority to those affected by them. At the same time we need gradually to develop the capacity for independent study and enquiry with the flexibility of mind which this implies. In short, we need to transform our pupils into students. (Stenhouse 1970)

How is this to be accomplished in a world of conflicting values? In a society which proclaims the values of democratic pluralism, which seeks the goals for its young people of autonomy with responsibility, which increasingly emphasizes the need for generic rather than specific skills which will support adaptability and transfer of learning, the task facing schools is to 'construct meaning from experience' (Eisner 1983), not concentrate on mindless tests of minimum competence.

The drive towards a narrowly functional, instrumental training system is a nineteenth-century relic which was given a more human and civilizing gloss even during the depression of the 1930s. A memorandum issued by the Minister of Labour in 1934 described a scheme for young people to assist:

> the prevention of demoralisation . . . to give boys and girls a real interest in life, to keep their minds and fingers active and alert and their bodies fit, to teach them something which will be of real use to them whether at home or work, and without trying to train them for specific occupations, to give them the type of mental and manual instruction which will help them to become absorbed or reabsorbed into employment as soon as an opportunity may occur.

The Schools Council's *Practical Curriculum* (1981) in its opening chapter set out broad aims which could well be taken as an agenda for a central curriculum agency:

> Schools should help their pupils to know and remember, and to feel, to be capable, to understand and to value . . . Preparation for adult life requires a curriculum which includes moral education as well as political and economic understanding. Human nature and contemporary society requires a curriculum which nurtures aural and visual as well as verbal skills. The challenge is to blend aims and process in an effective, broad and largely common curriculum.

This is the task which confronts schools in the next stage of educational, social and political development. There seems little doubt that external pressures of falling pupil-numbers and reduced finance will hasten a move towards greater agreement on a curriculum framework. The increased participation of parents and community will widen the arena for debate and, one hopes, achieve progress towards a reconciliation between conflicting pressures arising from unhelpful extremes. Schools are in the business of producing neither wholly individual scholars, nor well-indoctrinated, utilitarian citizens. The aims remain those elegantly expressed in one of the earliest Schools Council Working Papers (1965):

> The main issues are, not so much what ground to cover in the sense of what subjects to teach, but what information, ideas and experiences to grapple with, through what media, and by what means. The problem is to give every man some access to a complex cultural inheritance, some hold on his personal life and on his relationships with the various communities to which he belongs, some extension of his understanding of, and sensitivity towards, other human beings. The aim is to forward understanding, discrimination and judgment in the human field – it will involve reliable factual knowledge, where this is appropriate, direct experience, imaginative experience, some appreciation of the dilemmas of the human condition, of the rough hewn nature of many of our institutions, and some rational thought about them.

References

Bowmen, Bill (1983) The price of complacency, *Times Educational Supplement*, 11 March.
Central Advisory Council (1959) *15 to 18* (Crowther Report), London: HMSO.
Central Advisory Council (1963) *Half Our Future* (Newsom Report), London: HMSO.
Department of Education and Science (1977) *Education in Schools: A consultative document* (Green paper), London: HMSO.
Department of Education and Science (1977a) *Local Education Authorities: arrangements for the school curriculum* (Circular 14/77), London: HMSO.
Department of Education and Science (1979) Report on Circular 14/77, London: HMSO.
Department of Education and Science (1981) *The School Curriculum*, London: HMSO.
Department of Education and Science (1981a) *Review of the Schools Council* (Trenaman Report), London: HMSO.
Eisner, E.W. (1983) *Cognition and Curriculum*, London: Longman.
Holland, Geoffrey (1983) Interview in *Newscheck*, Careers and Occupational Information Centre, MSC, June.
Marland, M. (1981) Serendipity time, *The Guardian*, 3 March.
Minister of Labour, memorandum from (1934) *in* Rees, Teresa L. and Atkinson, Paul (1982) *Youth Unemployment and State Intervention*, London: Routledge.

Schools Council (1965) *Raising the School Leaving Age* (Working Paper 2), London: HMSO.
Schools Council (1981) *The Practical Curriculum* (Working Paper 70), London: Methuen Educational.
Secretary of State for Education (1972) *Education: A framework for expansion*, London: HMSO.
Stenhouse, L.A. (1970) Pupils into students, *Dialogue* No. 5, London: Schools Council.
Stenhouse, L.A. (1973) Innovation and stress, *Times Educational Supplement*, 19 January.

SECTION 2

NEW DIMENSIONS FOR THE CURRICULUM

INTRODUCTION
Malcolm Skilbeck

The school curriculum is an amalgam of many influences, ideas and resources. Despite the assumption made by many critics that it is stratified by distinct subjects and relatively impervious to demands for change, it has dimensions which cut across and through subject boundaries and has always been in a state of evolution. At times, deliberate attempts have been made to foster dimensional change, as for example when discovery and inquiry-based approaches to teaching were being actively fostered across the curriculum in primary schools or when across-the-curriculum language policies were being advocated. Other examples are the arguments advanced in the Government's curriculum policy paper, *The School Curriculum*, for education for industrial life and a multicultural society, or by individual schools vigorously developing common policies for student assessment or a broadly uniform policy of curriculum review and evaluation.

In this context, what is meant by a dimensional approach is the attempt to build into the whole school curriculum policy and practice, regardless of subject specialization, a general theme or standpoint. Usually, this attempt does not entail a plea for new subjects but relates to all or several parts of the curriculum. As already indicated, the idea of a dimensional approach is not new. What we need to be alert to, however, is changing priorities, the emergence of new dimensions, or the neglect of dimensions which are educationally important yet lack powerful political, social or economic back-up. In this section, we have four papers, each dealing with a single dimension: education for a multicultural society, the education of girls and women, low-achieving students and education for international life. These by no means exhaust the general themes or standpoints of which contemporary school-based curriculum needs to take account. They are, rather, examples of dimensions which have been very widely neglected until quite recently and which still lack adequate support and recognition.

First, education for a multicultural society is an example of a dimension in curriculum making which receives a great deal of attention in some schools and local education authorities and is still largely ignored in others. Perhaps this is because of confusion over what is at stake. Education for a multicultural society goes far beyond special provision for ethnic minority pupils, important as that is. Multiculturalism is an impoverished concept as long as its application is restricted to minority groups. Alma Craft points out the subtle but crucial difference between education *in* a society – where multiculturalism is reflected in diversity of subcultural groups and a growing pluralism of values and institutional arrangements – and *for* a particular kind of society. What she has in mind is the work that schools need to do in order to build up a communitywide sense of the richness and the fulfilment open to all in a society which positively values diversity. Drawing on research which is largely based on the experiences of schools endeavouring to educate for a multicultural society, Alma Craft suggests a number of practical ways of moving ahead. What is needed is, first, a willingness by teachers to see the value of and educational opportunity in a multicultural curriculum, followed by reviews by schools of their own current practice and of the experience of others in across-the-curriculum approaches.

Next in this section is a chapter by Lesley Kant on the education of girls and women. Like multiculturalism, this topic suffers from a belief that it refers only to particular groups. An adequate response, in curriculum terms, requires reconsideration of the education of boys and men as well as girls and women. Despite the passing, in 1975, of the Sex Discrimination Act and the subsequent establishment of the Equal Opportunities Commission, initiatives of some schools and local education authorities and the contributions of national projects through the Schools Council and elsewhere, sex differentiation in education still works to the disadvantage of girls and women. Lesley Kant documents this disadvantage as it operates through major elements in education: promotion procedures, learning materials, school organization, disciplinary processes, pedagogy, and pupil–teacher interactions. Sex bias, sex discrimination and sex stereotyping are, she argues, being reinforced – not, as yet, significantly reduced – by the education system. Affirmative action by schools themselves can be a major factor for change. The review, evaluation and redevelopment by the school of its whole curriculum is a necessary step if educational and other forms of equality are to be attained by girls and women. This is not something that can be achieved by the piecemeal or partial evaluations and in-school development exercises so widely favoured. What might seem to be a practical limitation on the scope of a curriculum review can too easily prove to be an effective means of ensuring the ineffectiveness of the change envisaged or hoped for.

Although most commonly discussed in relation to secondary age pupils, the curriculum challenge presented by low-achieving pupils is no less real in the primary school. It is a feature of dimensions as defined here that they cannot be restricted to any single age or stage. Coralyn Williams reports the findings of a study project undertaken in both England and Australia, and of numerous studies and reports, in England, Scotland and Australia, which document the unsatisfactory education many low achievers receive in our schools. The focus of her inquiry is the secondary school yet, as she points out, the problems begin with the first tests, classifications and teacher assessments young children receive on entry to primary school. Low achievement and low ability are not the same, yet they are often confused in a general tendency by schools to devote the better part of their energy and resources to those students who are likely to succeed in the examination system and in the long drawn out process of selection for further or higher education. There are, fortunately, exceptions to this generalization. Individual teachers and schools, local authorities and national agencies have shown how such changes as those in school organization, subject matter, teacher expertise and attitudes are necessary and can be made. However, the problem discussed by Coralyn Williams lies deep within our schooling structures and processes. Focused attention through whole-school review, evaluation and redevelopment of the curriculum, and commitment to the principle of an adequate and interesting education for *all* students is necessary. So, too, is a comprehensive reform of initial teacher training.

Of the four dimensions discussed in this section, that which is receiving least official notice is education for international life. The curriculum, as numerous studies have shown, seems to be incurably devoted to the nation state or the locality. The idealistic notion which underlies internationalism in all of its forms is the unity of mankind in a commonly shared world. International education is global in its reference and its values. But how can these ideals ever reach children if school curricula very largely ignore them? Helen Connell, in her chapter, points out the connections between these lofty ideals and the realities of everyday social life. Neglect of this dimension is, in a profound sense, neglect of the contemporary world. Schools can –

and some do – play several roles to improve matters, which range from the construction of a whole-school policy to the appraisal of problems students are likely to face in their own encounters with ideological and value issues. As Helen Connell indicates, both national projects and programmes, and individual school experiences can be utilized by schools that are willing to accept the challenge to help educate their students for the international life which – whether they realize it or not – they are all coming to share.

CHAPTER 4

CURRICULUM FOR A MULTICULTURAL SOCIETY
Alma Craft

In a democracy, the school curriculum seeks to meet the needs of individual pupils as well as preparing them appropriately for adult life. Curriculum development therefore needs to take account of any major social change, such as the increase in cultural diversity in modern Britain. Education *in* a multicultural society aims to help children of all cultural groups maximize their potential achievement: education *for* a multicultural society aims to give all pupils knowledge and understanding appropriate for a school, locality or adult world where they will meet, live and work with fellow citizens from a variety of cultural backgrounds.

As with other cross-cultural themes, school-based developments in multicultural education have no obvious starting points or growth patterns. The catalyst may be the particular needs of a group of pupils, an individual staff enthusiast, a specific problem in school or classroom, a local authority policy directive, or an in-service activity. This chapter examines the notion of multiculturalism and outlines some of the implications for teaching in a culturally diverse society.

What is multiculturalism?

A cultural group is a collection of people whose common origins or experiences have socialized them into a distinctive pattern of behaviour and beliefs. In this sense, *every* society can be described as 'multicultural', as it is composed of numerous cultural groups, including those based on sex, age, occupation, region, social class, religion, language, or country of origin. Discussions of multiculturalism usually focus particularly on those cultural groups which are loosely referred to as 'ethnic minorities'. This term generally describes groups of individuals who share a religious affiliation, linguistic heritage, or migration history. In some cases such groups also have common external characteristics such as colour of skin, hair-type, facial features, personal mannerisms or style of dress.

Recently, there has been an upsurge of interest, research, writing, debate, policy making and resource provision concerning the needs and opportunities of a multicultural society; there are a variety of possible explanations for this, but three factors seem particularly relevant.

First, during this century, the population of Britain has become more heterogeneous than ever before. Large numbers of Irish, for example, have continued to seek employment and opportunity here. Jews fleeing the pogroms of Russia and the persecution of the Nazis have come to settle in large numbers. Since the Second World War, waves of settlers from the New Commonwealth, and now from the European community, have enlarged our labour force. Secondly, many of these ethnic minority groups can be easily identified by their religion, language, appearance or country of origin. Individual ethnic minority members may find this a great source of strength through a sense of belonging, but it can also make them easy prey for prejudice, hostility and discrimination, including anti-Semitism in the case of Jews and racism where colour differences are involved. Both the possible benefits and potential dangers of ethnicity are now attracting serious social and political attention.

A third and most significant factor has been the change in our response to this heterogeneity. A society can react to the presence of ethnic minority cultures in several ways. In some cases, the different cultures may exist and develop separately alongside each other, with social and sometimes geographical segregation (as in South Africa, or to a degree in Nothern Ireland). Elsewhere, new cultures may be absorbed to a greater or lesser extent into the host culture, with the newcomers being expected to adapt and adjust to the dominant norms. Alternatively, there may be an attempt to develop 'cultural pluralism', or 'multiculturalism' where each culture is valued and respected in its own right, and where the existence of a variety of cultural patterns is seen as a positive asset for society and for the individual. For a long time, the prevailing emphasis in Britain has been on the absorption or assimilation of different cultural groups within a relatively homogeneous society. However, since the late 1960s, there has been a shift towards an acceptance of cultural pluralism; legal, social and educational policies and practices have begun to support cultural diversity and the concept of multiculturalism.

Multiculturalism and education

While the emphasis was on assimilation, schools concentrated on teaching English language and customs to ethnic minority pupils so that they could be quickly absorbed and compete on equal terms with their peers. Schools and teachers strove to provide equality of opportunity for all their pupils, and were disappointed to find many ethnic minority pupils continued to underachieve; there was also concern about intercultural prejudice and hostility in the classroom, the playground and outside school.

Educational policy statements from central government have endorsed the notion of cultural pluralism, but there is some controversy and confusion about what this means in practice in schools. Should multicultural education be concerned mainly with meeting the particular needs of ethnic minority pupils in the interests of greater equality of educational outcomes? Should it concentrate on preparing *all* pupils to accept and appreciate cultural diversity to provide a more fruitful framework for work on particular needs, and to improve intercultural relations through promoting mutual respect? Or should its main aim be to reveal and combat racist attitudes and practices? Each of these is a necessary and essential part of multicultural education, but none is sufficient on its own – they are interlocking and interweaving parts of one whole. Multicultural education programmes need to strike a balance between the continuing concern for equality, the notion of respect for diversity and the need to develop sufficient intercultural understanding to provide for social cohesion.

How does a multicultural perspective affect the curriculum?

A multicultural perspective therefore has implications for the particular curricular needs of ethnic minority pupils, and also for the curriculum appropriate for all pupils growing up in a culturally diverse society. Although the two aspects are closely interlinked, it may be helpful to consider them separately.

The particular needs of ethnic minority pupils are immediately apparent where classes are culturally and linguistically diverse. Curriculum strategies are likely to include:

Supporting the English language development of pupils whose first language or dialect is not English
An increasing proportion of ethnic minority pupils are now born here, and so the earlier language 'immersion' programmes and withdrawal

classes for special tuition in English as a second language are giving way to work which builds on the child's interaction with teacher and peers in the mainstream classroom, and which helps develop the functional language needed for classroom learning in all areas of the curriculum.[1] This has become part of schools' focus on the importance of language across the curriculum for all pupils.

Supporting pupils' mother tongue

Some schools and localities have large numbers of pupils with a shared mother tongue, and a growing number are providing mother tongue teaching in mainstream primary schools, in order to facilitate the transition from home to school, to maintain and develop bilingualism as a valuable resource for the individual and for society, and to enhance pupils' attitudes and performance through the development of a sense of identity and self-esteem. There is also increasing interest in the teaching of community languages in secondary schools as a curricular subject, equivalent to the more traditional modern languages such as French or German.[2] In addition, monolingual teachers with multilingual classes are developing strategies for supporting children's home languages, which also aim to raise all children's awareness of the language diversity around them.[3]

Welcoming cultural diversity in the classroom

Innovative teachers throughout the country have responded to diversity in their classrooms by preparing resources about cultural groups, and materials with draw upon the varied cultural experience of their pupils. As with mother tongue teaching, such support for home cultures can be very helpful for ethnic minority pupils, and also signals to the whole class that different cultures are valued by the school.

Inevitably, there has been some wasteful overlap in resource development: an embryonic computerized information service at Bulmershe College of Higher Education is attempting to systematize information about locally produced materials[4] and a comprehensive guide to existing resources and sources is now available.[5]

School–community links

The importance for teacher and pupil of good relationships with ethnic minority parents can hardly be overstated. The range of possible strategies and the issues involved are extending and exemplifying the post-Plowden emphasis on home–school liaison in general.[6]

Pedagogy

Researchers are beginning to investigate teaching styles in multicultural classrooms, and to suggest that collaborative, inquiry-based learning may be both appropriate and effective.[7] On the other hand, it has been suggested that some ethnic minority pupils might benefit from more formal teaching methods.

Many schools and local education authorities have already made substantial contributions towards meeting the needs of ethnic minority pupils, with the appointment of advisers and specialist teachers, and the establishment of resource centres. The second – interlinked – requirement in multicultural education is for an appropriate curriculum for *all* pupils, and this aspect of the work is now receiving increasing attention. It is argued that this is an essential part of all teachers' professional responsibility. Whether they teach in an inner city school or in a rural village, all their pupils are growing up into a world of diverse religions, languages and ethnic groups, and it is necessary and appropriate for the formal and informal curriculum of all schools to have a multicultural and anti-racist dimension. Teachers are beginning to see that taking account of cultural diversity is an opportunity to enrich the curriculum; they are also realizing that education for intercultural understanding and tolerance must be part of the core curriculum. In this sense, many people argue that multicultural education is simply good education, and will involve the following elements:

A critical appraisal of all school curricula, materials and examinations
The initial efforts of some LEAs and schools have tended to concentrate only on the more obvious aspects of cultural diversity – the celebration of different festivals, clothing, foods etc. – and these are often criticized as representing other cultures as strange, exotic and static. Other attempts to introduce multicultural studies as a curriculum subject are concerned with culture maintenance for ethnic minority pupils alone (e.g. Black Studies) and are now seen as potentially divisive. However, with experience, these initiatives can develop and deepen. In many schools, they are leading to an examination of the whole curriculum to ensure it is culturally fair and is permeated with a multicultural perspective. Teachers of all curriculum subjects are beginning to review their teaching to include examples from a wide range of cultures, and to avoid a solely Eurocentric approach which may offer a condescending and stereotyped view of the rest of the world. Such a multicultural curriculum is appropriate for *all* pupils, not just those from ethnic minority backgrounds.

Initially, social studies and religious studies were two curriculum areas which tried to introduce their pupils to other cultures and faiths. More recently, historians have been encouraging their pupils to consider major historical events with greater objectivity so that, for example, the voyages of discovery or the spread of colonialism are also studied from the viewpoint of the countries 'discovered' or colonized. Geographers, similarly, are calling attention to the interdependence of world trading nations, and to the danger that purely descriptive accounts of economically poorer nonindustrial regions may imply inferiority and/or lack of initiative by the local population. Humanities teachers have always drawn examples from European cultures and are beginning to extend the range further afield; they are also becoming more sensitive to the stereotyped views of other cultures which are portrayed in some literature and art, and the part these can play in generating prejudiced views and attitudes. Science and mathematics teachers are beginning to call attention to the multicultural origins of these subjects; home economics teachers are realizing their extensive opportunities to build on the international differences (and similarities) in cookery, dress, home making and child rearing.

Anti-racist teaching

There are also many opportunities within the curriculum for teaching which deliberately sets out to challenge stereotyping and the discriminatory treatment of other cultures – this is now often referred to as anti-racist teaching. For example, literature and drama provide a rich source for discussion of prejudice; biology can investigate the role of inheritance and environment in 'racial' characteristics; geography can help explore the reasons for internal and international migration and all its implications for the individual as well as for society; social science and social education courses can discuss the causes and effects of intercultural tension and can develop young people's critical evaluation of the 'facts' of racism and ethnocentrism; religious studies can consider the moral basis of race relations legislation.

The aim is to give pupils from the majority culture a realistic perception of the minority experience, and to encourage pupils from minority groups to retain or regain their trust in the majority. Such direct teaching about cultural relations is extremely difficult, and if mishandled can be explosive and counterproductive. It is most likely to be effective as a central feature of an eclectic multicultural education programme which affirms cultural, linguistic and religious diversity. Teachers' organizations such as NAME (National Association for Multiracial Education) and ALTARF (All London Teachers Against Racism and Fascism) are very active in publicizing ideas and debate about anti-racist teaching through conferences and publications.[9]

Some teachers also argue that there are structural inequalities in our society which constrain some ethnic minorities as a weak and powerless 'underclass'; they maintain that Britain is a profoundly racist society, and that the curriculum therefore needs to include strategies for community and political action to effect radical changes in the social structure.[10]

Sensitivity to diversity

There is a good deal of teacher and pupil material available (of varying quality) which provides *information* about other cultures. But teachers and pupils first need help to recognize the limitations of their own understanding of the diversity within as well as between cultural groups, and to realize that their views of other cultures may often be stereotyped or even racist. There is considerable interest in race awareness sessions which use psychological techniques to probe underlying feelings, particularly 'white' attitudes towards 'black' and 'brown' people, but many teachers dislike this style of approach.[11] One alternative is the Nottingham University 'Lifestyles' pack which aims to develop teacher sensitivity in a nonthreatening atmosphere, and leads participants to explore the complex and dynamic character of all cultures.[12]

School policy

In an increasing number of primary and secondary schools, staff are collaborating to draw up guidelines to ensure that the whole-school ethos and organization reflect a positive attitude to cultural diversity, and are alert to the dangers of unintentional discrimination. The process of preparing such guidelines can stimulate further school-based developments in multicultural education; once the institutional guidelines exist, they provide support for individual staff members who are already engaged in multicultural activities, and they can influence classroom and library resources, corridor visuals, classroom playground and staffroom behaviour, staffing policy and relations with the community, as well as curriculum content and assessment strategies.

Multicultural curriculum development, anti-racist teaching, increased sensitivity to diversity and whole-school policies are all vital aspects of education for a multicultural society. These are being given strength and formal backing by the publication of a number of firm statements on dealing with racist activities or organizations, or the attitudes of individuals in schools.[13]

Conclusion

As indicated here, multicultural education covers a wide variety of policy and practice; there is an equally wide range of interest and expertise among schools, teachers and teacher educators. Recent initiatives in multicultural education can be seen as both stimulus and response: there are guidelines for selecting learning experiences and for choosing fiction or textbooks;[14] examining boards are beginning to appraise syllabuses, forms of assessment and papers to ensure they reflect and meet the needs of our multicultural society;[15] a number of publications are beginning to explore in detail the specific implications for particular subject areas;[16] and the Swann Report on the education of ethnic minority pupils is bound to be an important milestone.[17]

Heated debate about definitions, aims and methods is likely to continue; evaluation of new developments is rare; dissemination slow and patchy. However, none of this is unique to multicultural education, and amidst the problems and polemics there is a growing number of teachers willing to try out new ideas and activities in their schools and classrooms and enthusiastically committed to the ideal of multiculturalism.

Notes and references

1. See, for example, videotapes of ILEA's SLIP (Second Language in Primary Classroom) Project, and the new ILEA SLIM (Second Language in the Mainstream Classroom) Project, ILEA Learning Materials Service.
2. a) Reid, E. (ed.) (1983) *Minority Community Languages in School*, (Papers from 3rd Assembly of National Congress on Languages in Education), London: Centre for Language Teaching (CILT).
   b) Broadbent, J., Hashmi, M., Sharma, B. and Wright, M. (1984) *Assessment in a Multicultural Society: Community languages at 16+*, York: Longman Group.
3. Houlton, E. and Willey, R. (1983) *Why Support Bilingualism?* York: Longman Group;
   (1984) *Teaching in the Multilingual Classroom*, London: Edward Arnold.
4. Access to Information on Multicultural Education (AIMER), Bulmershe College of Higher Education, Reading RG6 IHY.
5. Klein, G. (1984) *Resources for Multicultural Education: an introduction*, Revised edn, York: Longman Group.
6. Tomlinson, S. (1984) *Home and School in Multicultural Britain*, London: Batsford.
7. Adelman, C. et al. (1983) *A Fair Hearing for All: relationships between teaching and racial equality*, Reading: Bulmershe College of HE.
8. Stone, M. (1981) *The Education of the Black Child in Britain*, London: Fontana.

9 See *Multiracial Education*, NAME journal, published three times a year, and ALTARF newsletter and occasional publications, available from Lambeth Teachers' Centre, Santley Street, London SW4.
10 See, for example, Mullard, C. (1983) The problem of World Studies in a multicultural society, *World Studies Journal*, vol. 4, no. 1.
11 See, for example, All Faiths for One Race (AFFOR) (1983) *Race Relations Teaching Pack*, Birmingham.
12 The 'Lifestyles' Pack, Nottingham University School of Education, 1983.
13 See, for example, National Union of Teachers (1982) *Combatting Racialism in Schools*.
14 Schools Council (1982) Information Leaflet on *Multicultural Education*, London.
15 Schools Council (1983 and 1984) *Assessment in a Multicultural Society* – a series of eight subject-specific booklets, published for the Schools Council by Longman Group, York.
16 a) Lynch, J., (ed.) (1981) *Teaching in the Multicultural School*, London: Ward Lock Educational.
   b) Craft, A. and Bardell, G., (eds) (1984) *Curriculum Opportunities in a Multicultural Society*, London: Harper and Row.
17 The Report of the Swann (formerly Rampton) Committee of Inquiry into the Education of Children from Ethnic Minority Groups, due to be published during 1984.

CHAPTER 5

THE EDUCATION OF GIRLS AND WOMEN
Lesley Kant

The history of female education bears eloquent testimony to those who campaigned for girls' educational rights in the nineteenth and twentieth centuries.[1] In 1975 the Sex Discrimination Act finally outlawed most of the last remaining barriers to equality, by establishing equal access to educational facilities and equality of treatment for girls. On paper, a girl is legally entitled to the same educational opportunities as her male peers. What then is a matter of concern?

It is relatively recently that schools have been criticized for their role in perpetuating sexual inequity. Concern tends to focus on the concept of sex differentiation rather than the overt sex discrimination outlawed by legislation. It is argued that even when girls have equal access to the educational opportunities of their male peers the more subtle processes of sex-bias and sex-stereotyping continue to undermine the principle of equality. This differentiation is described more fully below.

Curriculum

Sex differences in curricular areas have been comprehensively catalogued by Her Majesty's Inspectorate.[2] These reveal that particularly at the secondary level of education the subjects studied by girls and boys differ. Few schools now offer *boys'* or *girls'* crafts or science subjects as alternatives in the first three years of secondary schooling, although legally none should. Many coeducational secondary schools however operate a system in which girls and boys are free to select the subject of their choice. This freedom tends to result in sex-stereotyped choices: few girls opt into craft design and technology; few boys choose home economics or needlecraft.

In physical education sexual division is strongly observed. Not only are there clear distinctions between girls' and boys' games but even those sports favoured by both sexes tend to be separately played and PE departments in coeducational schools usually sport teachers in charge of boys' and girls' PE respectively.

Examinations

Sex differences in subjects taken for public examinations are even more strongly observed. Department of Education statistics for 1980[3] show that at 16+ there are still slightly more entries from boys although the number of girls entering for examinations has increased considerably since the present system of examinations was introduced in 1951.[4] Girls however are more likely than boys to gain a classified result. At 18+ the gap between the sexes has widened and at GCE A level for every four subject entries from boys, there are only three from girls. Boys are more likely to stay on at school till 18 and are likely to be entered for more subjects.

Subject preferences are also strongly sex-typed. Twice as many boys enter for chemistry and four times as many enter for physics; the science girls are most likely to take is biology. Girls dominate in the languages, humanities and arts. Few schools erect sex barriers to examination entry and the option system which occurs at about the third year of secondary education offers supposedly free choices. Yet the choice occurs at a particularly critical stage when most young people are unable to anticipate fully the consequences of their decision. A matter of general educational concern must be the imbalance of the educational experience of both sexes but qualifications in physical science and mathematics are a passport to a wide range of industrial, scientific and technological employment opportunities. Girls then are most disadvantaged by these apparently free choices.

Unlike other disadvantaged groups, the problems for girls in terms of examination performance tends to be underrepresentation rather than low achievement; where girls make unconventional choices they succeed.[5] Current research suggests that the messages transmitted to girls through that which is explicitly taught and that learned through the social and cultural values of the school system influence their choice of subjects and their expectations of further and higher education and employment opportunities.[6] These messages are subtle but persuasive and require more detailed consideration.

Staffing structures and teacher roles

Although school teaching is a profession in which the sexes are almost equally represented and in which there has been a long tradition of female service, men tend to occupy the better-paid and most senior positions. Men account for roughly a quarter of primary teachers, yet they occupy almost two-thirds of the headships and just under a half of the deputy head posts.[7] The resulting message is that responsibility and power are male prerogatives and that the role of women is subordinate to that of men.[8] The trend towards coeducation which was viewed unquestioningly as a concomitant of the move towards comprehensive schooling in the 1950s and 60s has also been effective in reducing the numbers of women in senior positions: girls-only schools were one of the last professional bastions of female promotion.

Various reasons for this imbalance have been suggested; the truth is that few women apply for senior positions, fed on a diet of limited expectations, low self-image and the myth that they are less dedicated than men. There is also considerable evidence that sexual discrimination still operates when women do apply; they are subjected to questions on domestic responsibilities unlike their male colleagues, and their work experience is evaluated differently.[9]

School resources and materials

School textbooks, classroom readers, children's fiction, examination texts, resource packs convey messages to girls and boys about their place in society and the sorts of roles they are likely to play on leaving school. Numerous analyses have been made on the content of curriculum materials. Walford[10] and Harding[11] have surveyed science materials and found illustrations and diagrams heavily biased towards males. Pictures of men performing dynamic tasks are common; when girls appear they tend to undertake a passive or trivial role such as blowing bubbles or floating on the Dead Sea. Eddowes[12] finds mathematics textbooks provide similar stereotypes: women and girls are seen performing domestic tasks round the home while their male counterparts are involved in dynamic leisure activities such as boat building, car riding and playing games. Two American researchers underline the force of the messages: Torrance[13] on girls' performance in science and Fennema[14] who considers the effects of girls' achievement in mathematics. Stones[15] has comprehensively analysed children's fiction and draws similar conclusions about the sexist images which are presented by writers: they represent a world far more stereotyped than the real world inhabited by the pupil readers.

Even in English where girls' performance has tended to be superior to that of boys there is still a considerable bias towards male authors in the texts set for English literature examinations. Female authors are rarely included in set texts yet novel writing is a discipline in which they have traditionally excelled.

School organization

School organization frequently segregates pupils by sex through lists, registrations, meetings and interviews. In one school a notice-board, helpfully positioned so that boys and girls could consult job options, offered *Girls' jobs* and *Boys' jobs*. Most pastoral systems tend to reinforce sex differences, both by their recording systems and by their disciplinary arrangements. Buswell[16] suggests that one of the most important messages which the pupils perceive from the day they enter school is 'they are a boy or girl first and foremost'.

Discipline

Few would deny that in its most extreme forms punishment is sexually differentiated, for it is rare for girls to be caned and regrettably still fairly common for boys to receive corporal punishment. The few occasions on which girls have received the cane have attracted widespread media publicity. Nevertheless there is also considerable evidence to suggest that differing forms of disciplining are developed for boys or for girls.[17]

Additionally, although boys are likely to be punished more than girls they are also likely to receive more praise. Dweck's interesting conclusion is that girls' diffidence is increased partly because teacher criticism, though unusual, is centred on their intellectual limitations.[18]

Another form of discipline employed by teachers is when girls' behaviour is checked by a process Delamont refers to as 'showing up'.[19] Here a girl's femininity and sexuality is called into question. Fairly typical examples are 'No man in his right mind would want to marry you' and 'That wasn't very lady-like, was it?'. When a girl behaves in an unconventional way her behaviour is considered abnormal and a matter of concern. This also applies to boys. Therefore a boy who is reluctant to participate in robust games is considered a problem and treated as such; a girl who prefers more aggressive activities is admonished to be more feminine.[20]

Teacher behaviour

There is considerable evidence to suggest that both male and female teachers adopt differing approaches to their girl and boy pupils.[21] It has been suggested that both male and female teachers are likely to defer more to boy pupils and devote time and attention to subjects that interest and involve boys, as an insurance against behaviour problems. Topic work frequently tends to reflect boys' traditional interests. Sexual categorization is also used within lessons. Buswell[22] describes how all the girls in the class are embraced collectively in admonishment when only one or two misbehave: 'If the ladies would put away their combs we'll begin.' The expectations of teachers in terms of subjects pupils will study and performance within those subjects also has profound influences on girls' and boys' performance. Teachers who suggest that girls can't do science or that boys who enjoy drama are sissies, are helping to compound existing stereotypes.

Pupil aspirations

At an early stage girls tend to limit their educational and employment horizons. Millman[23] discovered limited expectations in terms of employment after school; this appeared to be as constant for those with good academic qualifications as for those who had achieved badly. Sharpe[24] noted that while the boys tended to have extravagant aspirations, girls' hopes centred on more mundane work.

Peer group pressures

The way in which boys and girls relate to each other in the classroom can also influence the learning outcome and process. Girls tend to undervalue their achievements and to overvalue those of their male peers. Boys express pejorative views of their female counterparts.[25] Boys learn to succeed and girls learn at an early stage that the route to male approval lies in subordinating their ability.

All these factors contribute to a sexually differentiated educational experience for boys and girls and these gender roles learned within and without school have profound effects on later life. There are now many schools and education authorities which have attempted to redress the imbalance in the educational system through positive programmes committed to the promotion of equal opportunities.

Affirmative action

Some schools, such as Haverstock, Clissold Park and Quinton Kynaston Comprehensives in London, Beauchamp College in Leicester, Northcliffe Comprehensive in Doncaster and Laurelhill High School in Northern Ireland, have adopted whole-school policies. Working parties have examined the pupils' learning experiences in some detail, articulated policy commitments and introduced a comprehensive programme of intervention. In at least three of these schools a member of staff has been given specific responsibility for initiating work in this area. Other schools have monitored their approaches in diverse areas such as the option system, discipline, dress, careers guidance, examination performance, and as a result have produced guidelines to provide a working base for the elimination of stereotyped practices.

In some cases individual subject departments have articulated concern, motivated by significant underachievement by one sex in particular areas: girls' relatively poor representation in physics and chemistry has frequently been the spur here (although craft design and technology, home economics, physical education and English teachers also tend to be concerned). Methods adopted have been various: some departments have intervened at third-year-option stage through specialist counselling to point out to girls the dangers of dropping physical sciences; others have invited women students and technicians into schools to meet girl pupils and thereby encourage them to view science careers more positively. Some have introduced girls-only classes for an interim period in order to bolster girls' confidence. Occasionally, the content of the science curriculum has been reviewed to make it more relevant to girls' interests and experience.[26] Other departments have reviewed textbooks and materials and eliminated sexist language and images. Courses, such as Girls into Engineering and Futura Girls, have been mounted; photographic displays on themes such as women at work and leisure have been displayed and are typical of other strategies employed. As a result more girls are finding success in physical sciences and are thus able to consider careers in science, technology, engineering and related areas.

Other approaches have included broadening the core curriculum, particularly in the craft design and technology and home economics areas, to ensure boys' and girls' curricular experience is extended to nontraditional craft areas. Hackney Downs Boys School in London has introduced a course from Years 1 to 3 which explicitly addresses itself to sexism within and without the school. Unusually, for a boys' school, it includes a significant home economics component, on the premise that boys must be educated for responsibility in parenthood and home management if girls are to achieve equality at work.

Attention has also centred on areas such as the library or the language that is used within the school. Careful scrutiny plus the compilation of checklists have resulted in the introduction of nonstereotyped materials and guidelines for using sexist material and redressing bias. Other schools have reviewed their staffing structures and policies convinced that a major weapon to advance equality is to appoint more women to senior posts, although the current legislation forbids positive discrimination in this area.[27] However, the Equal Opportunities Commission (see below and note 36) suggests that more careful wording of job advertisement particulars and encouragement to female staff within schools might help to redress the present sexual imbalance.

Local education authorities

Although there has been some dynamic activity from individual schools and teachers, few local education authorities have adopted policies in this area although at the time of writing there has been a surge of interest. Somerset and Tameside LEAs have adopted equal opportunities policies as a result of Equal Opportunities Commission interventions, and Tameside employs two science teachers to work alongside teachers in schools in order to encourage the interest of girls. Manchester LEA has set up a working party which has issued guidelines on good practice to secondary schools and has encouraged the designation of individual school coordinators for equal opportunities. Humberside LEA has formed a working party to produce a policy statement and training materials for school governors. Devon LEA has issued primary guidelines and 'Equal Choice for Girls in the Secondary Curriculum'.

Brent LEA was the first to appoint an adviser for equal opportunities, who has set in train numerous initiatives. Brent's equal opportunities and multicultural advisers attend all interviews for headships and advise governors on appointments.[28] The Inner London Education Authority is the most explicitly committed to the pursuit of equal opportunities. It has made formal policy commitments, established a working party to consider the issue in detail, and produced a document which outlines the strategies it intends to adopt and identifies issues of concern.[29] It has also investigated girls' and boys' performance through statistical analyses and administered questionnaires to teachers and schools in the Authority requesting information both on school initiatives and staffing structures. In 1983 it set up a central equal opportunities unit to develop policy and ensure ILEA's staffing, employment structures and schools reflect fully this commitment to eliminate sexism and racism in Inner London.

A range of projects have focused on aspects of sex differentiation. Amongst the best known are the following ventures:

1. Schools Council's Sex Differentiation in Schools project. This project, part of the Programme 3: Developing a Curriculum in a Changing World, provided a national contact network and helped groups of teachers to set up action research and curriculum development in their schools.[30]
2. Girls into Science and Technology project (GIST) based at Manchester Polytechnic. This has worked in the Manchester area with local schools developing intervention strategies to encourage girls to take up science.[31]
3. Girls and Technological Education (GATE) Project, Chelsea College, London, established through a BP fellowship, provides useful strategies for girls in technological education.[32]
4. Equal Opportunities Information Centre based at the Schools Council. Funding from the Equal Opportunities Commission enabled the establishment of a national equal opportunities in education resource centre and contact directory.[33]
5. Girls and Mathematics Association (GAMMA). This mathematics association for girls was founded in 1981.[34]

The examination boards, another powerful influence on the school curriculum, are formulating criteria for the new 16+ examinations[35] which may include a general criterion on the need to eliminate sex bias within examinations. The Equal Opportunities Commission, set up as a result of the 1975 legislation, monitors educational establishments and regularly publishes bulletins and pamphlets which are available free.[36]

However, the most important role schools have to play in the development of young people is to provide them with the opportunity to develop to the full their individual qualities, talents and skills. In order for this to be effected all those who participate in the educational system must recognize that a sexually differentiated learning experience can never allow girls and women to compete on equal terms. This recognition is an essential prerequisite to the achievement of educational equality for girls and women.

Notes and references

1. Amongst the most celebrated are Frances Mary Buss and Dorothea Beale who pioneered academic education for girls: the North London Collegiate School (founded in 1855) and Cheltenham College respectively; Emily Davies who secured girls' entry to public examinations in 1868 and together with Jemina Clough helped to break down the barrier to higher education; Sophia Jex-Blake and Elizabeth Blackwell who fought for medical degrees for women. Women teachers were one of the earliest groups of female workers to protest against the marriage bar, and equal pay for female teachers was secured in the early 1950s. Strachey, R. (1978) *The Cause*, London: Virago.
2. a) Department of Education and Science (1975) *Curricular Differences for Girls and Boys Education Survey 21*, London: HMSO.
b) Department of Education and Science (1979) *Aspects of Secondary Education in England*, A Survey by HM Inspectors of Schools, London: HMSO.
c) Department of Education and Science (1980) *Girls and Science*, HMI Matters for Discussion, London: HMSO.
3. Department of Education and Science (1980) *Statistics 1980*, London: HMSO.
4. The General Certificate of Education at Advanced (A level) + Ordinary (O level) levels is designed for the most able students academically at 18 and 16 years of age respectively. In 1965 the Certificate of Secondary Education was introduced to provide an examination for middle-ability students at 16 years of age. Examination results in both are graded on a norm-referenced basis. However, over 90% of students at 16 now enter for at least one subject at GCE O Level or CSE. The new 16+ Examination will replace GCE (O) and CSE.
5. Kelly, A. (1978) *Girls and Science* IEA, Monograph Studies No. 9, Manchester: Manchester University Press.
6. Spender, D. and Sarah, E. (eds) (1980) *Learning to Lose*, London: The Women's Press.
7. Department of Education and Science (1980) *Statistics 1980*, London: HMSO.
8. a) Byrne, E. (1978) *Women and Education*, London: Tavistock.
b) Dale suggests women teachers are perceived by pupils as less appropriate disciplinarians than male counterparts. He also suggests women are naturally passive and subordinate!
Dale, R.R. (1969, 1971, 1974) *Mixed or Single-Sex Schools*, vol. I, vol. II, vol. III, London: Routledge and Kegan Paul.
9. National Union of Teachers (1980) *Promotion and the Woman Teacher*, London: The Author.
10. Walford, G. (1980) Sex bias in physical text books, *School Science Review*, vol. 62.
11. Harding, J. (1983) *Switched Off. The Science Education of Girls*, London: Longman for the Schools Council.
12. Eddowes, M. (1982) *'Humble Pi'*, London: Schools Council.
13. Torrance, P. (1963) Changing reactions of pre-adolescent girls to science tasks, in *Education and the Creative Potential*, Minnesota University Press.
14. Fennema, E. (1978) Sex related differences in mathematics and achievement related functions – a further study, *Journal of Research in Mathematics Education*.

15 Stones, R. (1983) *Point Out the Cocoa Janet*, London: Longman for the Schools Council.
16 Buswell, C. (1982) Sexism in school routines and classroom practices, *Durham and Newcastle Review*, vol. IX, no. 46.
17 Delamont, S. (1980) *Sex Roles and the School*, London: Methuen.
18 Dweck's research posits that girls acquire a negative self-image through sexually differentiated criticism. Criticism of boys implies ability which is underexploited. Criticism of girls implies they are intellectually incapable.
Dweck, C. (1977) Learned helplessness and negative evaluation, *Educator*, vol. 19, no. 2.
19 Delamont, S. op. cit.
20 Wolpe, A. M. (1977) *Some Processes in Sexist Education*, WRRC.
21 Clarricoates, K. (1978) 'Dinosaurs in the classroom': A re-examination of some aspects of the 'hidden' curriculum in primary schools, *Women's Studies International Quarterly*, vol. 1, no. 4.
22 Buswell, C. op. cit.
23 Millman, V. (1982) *Double Vision: The Post School Experience of 16–19 Year Olds*, Coventry LEA.
24 Sharpe, S. (1978) *Just Like A Girl*. Harmondsworth: Penguin.
25 Spender, D. (1980) *Man Made Language*. London: Routledge and Kegan Paul.
26 Kelly suggests that more girls will be attracted to science if the content emphasizes the human and social implications of scientific theory and practice.
Kelly, A. (ed.) (1981) *The Missing Half: Girls and Science Education*, Manchester: Manchester University Press.
27 Further details of these and many other school-based initiatives are contained in the Schools Council's Sex Role Differentiation Project Newsletters 1–4, plus two ILEA Supplements: Sept. 1981, April 1982, Sept. 1982, March 1983.
28 Further information on these LEA initiative can be supplied by the authorities concerned.
29 ILEA (1982) *Equal Opportunities for Girls and Boys*, Report by the ILEA Inspectorate, ILEA.
30 The report of the project will be contained in *Sex Differentiation in Schools Report*, London: Longman for Schools Council (forthcoming).
31 GIST, Judith Whyte and Barbara Smails, Manchester Polytechnic, 9a Didsbury Park, Manchester, M20 0LH.
32 GATE Project. Martin Grant/Jan Harding, Centre for Science and Mathematics Education, Chelsea College, London, SW6.
33 Equal Opportunities in Education Resource Centre. Schools Council, Newcombe House, Notting Hill Gate. Development Officer – V. Millman.
34 GAMMA, Jane Ayshford, Girls and Mathematics, 58 Gordon Square, London WC1.
35 The proposal to replace CSE and GCE O level examinations (see note 4) with a single system of examinations at 16+ has been approved by the Secretary of State for Education and the examination boards have been formulating guidelines for the proposed examination (criteria) reform since 1981.
36 Equal Opportunities Commission, Publications Department, Overseas House, Quay Street, Manchester.

CHAPTER 6

LOW ACHIEVERS
Coralyn Williams

In both primary and secondary schools there exist major problems of low achievement and underachievement, ranging from the attitude and performance of children of low ability to the apparent inability of many schools to provide for the needs of children with particular gifts. What is meant by low achievement? How can it be ascertained? What kinds of curriculum changes, changes in school organization and in assessment of performance may be needed to meet the problems of low achievers?

Low achievement within the school context refers to low or poor performance as measured or assessed by the school, usually in some form of test devised within or external to the classroom or school. Low achievement or low attainment* occurs within the norm-referenced framework of schools whereby most pupils within a class are assumed to perform at average level (approximately 50%), another group are expected to perform above average levels (perhaps 25%) and the third group, those we are concerned with, are expected to perform below average levels (approximately 25%), and hence are labelled low achievers, low attainers, or even worse, 'low ability' or 'less able'.

Low attainment is readily ascertained in the present school system, as early as the pupil undergoes the first class or individual test, usually of mathematical or literacy skills. This frequently occurs during the first school year, and if the pupil does not attain average or above-average levels, she/he is immediately relegated to 'low attainer' or 'low ability' status.

---

* Achievement and attainment are used synonymously according to the Oxford Dictionary interpretation of 'accomplishment, completion, thing attained'.

However, a distinction between low ability and low attainment is necessary, for 'low ability' infers that the pupil is performing at maximum level for her/his capabilities, whereas the label 'low attainment' acknowledges that the pupil is performing below 'average' level but may not be performing at maximum personal level.

It is not only the teacher who labels the pupil as a low attainer; even the youngest pupil undertakes self-categorization as soon as she/he becomes aware that class peers are performing tasks at higher levels. An illustration of this I observed in a grade 3 classroom in Queensland, where a 7-year-old girl, having completed a tables test, immediately marked every answer wrong before the teacher called out the correct answers. The pupil's self-perception was quite accurate, the answers were all wrong and this was evidently a daily occurrence. The major problem here is that such a pupil, very early in school life, equates low attainment with low ability. As teenagers, such pupils will generally refer to themselves as 'dumb', thus fulfilling the expectations of both themselves and teachers that approximately 25% (or more) of the school population are not only low attainers but 'less able' or have 'less ability'.

What, however, is the basis of such categorization? Most school tasks and tests are comprised basically of the literacy skills of reading and writing and these components become more and more significant the higher up the educational ladder the pupil proceeds. This means, of course, that the more significant tests (and examinations) become, the more obvious the label of low attainer. Unfortunately the label low attainer is generic, for it is assumed that the pupil is as incompetent at all educational activities as she/he is at reading and writing. Such pupils are assumed not to have any special talents, abilities or gifts. It is evident then that the schooling system, by means of its normative grading and assessment procedures, produces low attainers purely on the basis of narrowly defined school criteria.

These pupils suffer major problems within the present school system. Because of poor literacy (and usually numeracy) skills, they are denied access to the wider and higher curriculum. Once relegated to low-attainer status it is almost impossible to become upwardly mobile in normative terms. A compounding problem of the low attainer is the assumption, not always admitted, that low attainers have low 'intelligence', for intelligence is measured, of course, in terms of these same literacy skills of reading and writing, a highly 'intellectual' activity. Within the school system there appears little recognition that intellectual activity, in particular problem solving, can take forms other than reading and writing. Furthermore, problem-solving activities in which such pupils frequently demonstrate 'above-average' aptitude are generally relegated to low-status subjects and, because of their practical focus, are considered 'nonintellectual' activities. This is evidenced in traditionally practical subjects such as art and home economics which, in recent years, have increased their theoretical components (and, of course, reading and writing), presumably to attain status by becoming more academic. Again, such subjects have become less accessible to the low-achieving student, as recently demonstrated in a visit to an Australian secondary school where it was brought to my attention by an art teacher that the accredited art course was not appropriate for low achievers because of its 50% theoretical component and written examination. School for these pupils is thus an expected 'fail' experience because the focus of school studies is upon their nonattainments and rarely, if ever, provides opportunities for development of their individual talents, abilities, gifts or skills.

What is the present state of curriculum in relation to such pupils? It appears that in many junior schools and some middle schools, where 'tests' are not a focal point of educational activity, low attainers are less obvious, perhaps because pupils with poor literacy skills have opportunities to excel in other activities, such as expressive arts. However, the more significant testing becomes at secondary level (and this includes 'grading' assignments), and the more evident the streaming into A level, O level, Certificate of Secondary Education, and other categories,* the more the low attainer is evident and the less the curriculum becomes relevant.

Why is this so? Apart from teacher talk which occupies the major part of the school day for secondary students, students spend most time in reading and writing worksheets, workbooks, assignments and blackboard notes. (This is perhaps a consequence of teachers' attempting to 'cover' the required examination content and also to cater for individual pacing.) The problem of the low achiever in such a classroom is that because of poor literacy skills most of these activities are unintelligible and such a pupil proceeds through school, learning little other than alienation. Despite numerous reports documenting such effects and disadvantages, for example the Newsom Report in England and Wales, and more recently the Pack Report in Scotland, and, in Australia, the Priest Report, *Schooling for*

---

* In Australia, the mode of streaming varies from state to state, for example, in Western Australian students in Years 11 and 12 (The final years of secondary school) are streamed into Tertiary Entrance or Non-tertiary Entrance (BSE) subjects, and in Years 7 to 10 are categorized according to Advanced, Intermediate and Basic levels for the four core subjects.

15 and 16 Year Olds and the McGowan Report, the secondary school evidences little change for low achievers. (Parliament of N.S.W. 1981)

Because of the organizational structure of secondary schools – subject departments, specialist teachers, short time allocations and class movements – low achievers are further disadvantaged. No one teacher is really responsible or accountable for the learning of an individual pupil. As subject classes are short, frequently only 40 minutes, the individual teacher has little time to identify individual attainments and frequently is unaware that the pupil cannot read, comprehend and write required activities. The required mobility of the teacher and class frequently prevents teachers from providing adequate resources for the whole range of pupils in any one classroom. For such pupils (and indeed it could be argued for every secondary pupil) the bewildering number of specialist teachers (perhaps ten), the constant changing of class location, frequent inability to read even a timetable and lack of skills to perform required activities, build up to a 'no-learning' or 'anti-learning' school experience.

However, such information, although readily available from departmental yearly statistics (particularly in the centralized state systems of Australia), is rarely acknowledged as significant in terms of effects upon teaching and learning. Furthermore, as Power (1981) demonstrates, secondary teachers dislike teaching low achievers. Where classes are streamed, and this appears the norm in Australia for mathematics and science, this problem of teacher rejection is compounded. It is interesting to note that schools have attempted to respond to the consequent rejection by secondary students, as demonstrated in the growth of pastoral care programmes. These programmes, however, no matter how well intentioned, more frequently are additives to the present secondary school structure, and therefore appear, in the main, 'band-aid' attempts which fail to address those organizational structures contributing to student alienation.

What, then, should schools do for low achievers? First, it appears that educators and teachers should equate low attainment with 'underachievement' rather than with 'low ability' or 'less able' status. Philosophically teachers must acknowledge that all pupils can learn, have intelligence, and will exhibit individual talents, abilities, gifts and skills given a stimulating educational environment. Testing and examinations should be recognized as reinforcing failure situations but not providing legitimate learning activities. The narrow academic curriculum must be challenged by teachers who need to develop a wider view of intelligence and of curriculum. A far greater emphasis will be needed on practical problem-solving activities and on developing personal qualities such as initiative, responsibility and effective communication.

It is pleasing to note that individual teachers, headteachers and senior staff have taken up this challenge, more frequently at the 16+ years level than in the junior secondary school. They have been supported by LEAs, local tertiary institutions and the Schools Council. Such educators have accorded low achievers status, both in terms of resources, including selected staff and appropriate facilities and materials, and in the development of appropriate curriculum focused upon life skills and community learning. In place of the normative grading system, certification and assessment have proceeded by means of the profiling of students' strengths and competencies and by offering award schemes, which may be totally school based or may utilize schemes such as those available through the City and Guilds of London Institute. These programmes are alternative in nature, that is, the students are streamed out of the mainstream tertiary-dominated courses. In Australia many examples of alternative programmes for low achievers are evident at the junior secondary level. However, my investigation found such courses were highly dependent upon an individual supportive principal or deputy-principal together with an individual concerned, committed and competent class (not subject) teacher (usually from a primary, social studies or English-teaching background) working in isolation from the mainstream secondary teachers. Unfortunately, up to the 15+ years level, most courses are subject to assessment by the normative grading system required by the particular state. As in the UK, it appears that much more freedom for developing appropriate curriculum is available in the senior secondary school where low-achieving students have opted (or been pushed) out of tertiary entrance courses.

It is evident that within the present organizational structure and climate of most secondary schools such suggestions pose major problems of implementation. If schools are to provide learning opportunities for *all* pupils rather than for the academic élite, schools must become more client centred. The 'bottom 30%' must be recognized as having legitimate access to learning and to adequate resources, including staffing and materials. Norm-referenced testing and streaming, and segmented timetable, specialist teachers for every subject, inappropriate learning materials, the low status of practical and nonexaminable subjects, the continual fail experience, and teaching by low-status and inexperienced, even incompetent, teachers must be challenged by the school as a whole, with the headteacher and senior staff firmly committed to providing a 'comprehensive' rather than academic curriculum for all students.

This, of course, involves the secondary school taking a holistic view of pupils and schooling. Departments will need to surrender their power and control through a cooperative venture of more generalist teachers and courses (particularly lower secondary). The contribution of practical pursuits to intellectual activity must be recognized, less testing will free more 'learning' time, provision of adequate learning materials for all children for all activities must be made, and students must be given more practical options in order to develop special abilities. Schooling should be extended from pencil/paper activities to educational activities and experiences which will facilitate pupil initiative, responsibility, cooperation and communication.

Despite these problems, in both the UK and Australia, renewed interest and action is evident at the individual school level in changing the organizational and structural nature of secondary schools. Block timetabling, increasingly evident in the UK, not only decreases the daily student/teacher class changes but is forcing teachers to develop alternative teaching strategies from those presently employed for the 40-minute time zone and, furthermore, enables teachers to utilize community resources more effectively. The use of structures such as the vertical nongraded line system (Middleton 1981) not only permits pupil choice and negotiation but acknowledges that achievement is not directly related to year level as well as appearing effective in removing the relative status accorded subjects by means of time allocations. Replacement of subject specialists by general class teachers or by a small team of teachers assigned to a stable group (either vertically or horizontally organized) ensures both teacher responsibility and continuity for the pupils as well as facilitating increased and effective pastoral care. For example, in a Canberra school, the Year 8 students are taught mainly in the one (owned) area by a small team of teachers, each of whom is responsible for one group of students for a number of subjects, usually mathematics, English and social studies.

Attempts to decrease the bewildering array of secondary school subjects are evident in the provision of integrated studies, such as the World Studies offered to Years 8 and 9 in an Inner London school, in place of English and separate humanities subjects. In Exeter, status teachers such as deputy-headteachers have assumed responsibility for developing, teaching and assessing innovative courses for low achievers. Two Australian states have formalized the position Deputy-Principal, Curriculum, which facilitates development of the school curriculum by a person who has the authority to implement changed school structures. At the teacher level, schools in Victoria provide teachers with three curriculum days per year to be used as deemed appropriate by the individual school staff. Whereas it would be simplistic to suggest that changed school structures guarantee more effective teaching for low achievers, nevertheless retaining such structures will maintain the status quo.

Another area of much individual teacher and school effort has been in the development of appropriate materials for low achievers. In Australia such materials have been confined mainly to English and social studies. However, in the UK a wide variety of materials have been developed specifically for low achievers in the areas of mathematics, science, English and the humanities. It seems that here the teachers have had widespread support in the development of such materials from the Schools Council, tertiary institutions and local education authorities. Unfortunately, such materials do not appear to reach the vast majority of low achievers (or their teachers).

Administrative and organizational changes will be negated unless teachers' views of teaching change. Secondary teachers committed to intellectual pursuits of 'subjects' will have to become committed to all students, including low attainers, learning skills other than passing examinations. This, of course, will require quite radical changes not only in schools but in pre-service and in-service teacher education.

It seems that school-based curriculum development and evaluation, carried out by the whole school staff with student, parent and community input, is the most effective way of in-servicing secondary teachers, headteachers and senior staff. Starting with the context of the local school, such a process not only will demand greater responsibility by the individual teacher but will require teachers to work with colleagues, outside their subject areas, who may approach teaching and learning differently. Hopefully this exercise may assist teachers to recognize their responsibilities towards low achievers and to develop, with the assistance of their colleagues, more effective ways of teaching these (and other) students. Unless in-service activities equip teachers with the required competencies, there is little hope of changing their attitudes towards those they feel incompetent to teach. Ideally, local education authorities and tertiary institutions should be providing supportive services, skills and knowledge to assist this development.

Unfortunately, pre-service reeducation of secondary teachers poses great problems, for secondary teacher education proceeds according to the same structural and organizational model as secondary schools, that is subject specialization. Content is the major focus and secondary student teachers gain confidence and self-esteem through content competence. Whereas teacher educators espouse mixed-ability grouping, student teachers are not given adequate skills to teach these classes, and so, on entering schools, gravitate towards academic classes. Secondary teachers are the successes of the secondary school system and, rarely having left the system, have little experience to become effective teachers of low achievers.

How, then, should pre-service teacher education change? Entry requirements should be based on nonacademic criteria, student teachers should be required to complete community service or nonteaching work experience, and lecturers (and students) should be required to justify the content, learning experiences and assessment. Teaching practice should provide student teachers with appropriate experiences in teaching both mixed-ability and streamed low-achieving classes and enable them to use appropriate resources for all pupils. Student teachers should be equipped to teach as generalist teachers as well as developing expertise in a specialist area. The teacher education institutions must establish a learning and teaching rather than content priority and this will necessitate departments working in close liaison, particularly with the professional education and psychology studies which secondary student teachers too often ignore. Finally, the use by teacher education institutions of normative graded assessment for student teachers can only reinforce the stranglehold assessment has on curriculum as well as ensure the failure of low achievers at school.

The evidence overwhelmingly demonstrates that schools and teachers are not achieving their stated goals with these students. The challenge and responsibility for such students must now be taken up by innovative schools and teachers firmly supported by government authorities and teacher educators.

References

Blachford, K. (1982) Self esteem and the school, *Curriculum and Research Bulletin*, 17, 4, pp.2–14.

Bunday, J. (1982) *An Organizational Analysis of 16 Comprehensive Schools*, Doctoral Thesis, University of Bath.

Cohen, D. (1982) What are curriculum decisions really like? *From the Lighthouse*, 7, 2.

Crittenden, B. (1981) The identity crisis in secondary education, *Australian Journal of Education*, 15, 2, pp.146–165.

Department of Education and Science (1981) *The School Curriculum*, London: HMSO.

Education Department of South Australia (1980) *Timetabling in South Australian Schools*, Adelaide.
Evans, G. (1983) *Imperatives for Teacher Education in the 80's*, SPATE Conference, Brisbane, July.
Hargreaves, D.H. (1982) *The Challenge for the Comprehensive School*, London: Routledge and Kegan Paul.
Middleton, M. (1981) Towards the adaptive school, *New Directions in School and Community Studies*, 2, pp.1–15.
Minister of Education in Western Australia (1981) *Review of Educational Standards in Lower-Secondary Schools in Western Australia* (Priest Report), Perth: Education Department of W.A.
Central Advisory Council (1963) *Half our Future* (Newsom Report), London: HMSO.
Parliament of NSW (1981) *Report from the Select Committee of the Legislative Assembly upon the School Certificate* (McGowan Report), NSW: Government Printer.
Plaskow, M. (1983) *Pupils and Curriculum Change*, Curriculum Evaluation: An International Seminar, London: British Council.
Power, C.N. (1981) *The Purdah Experience: A case study of alienation from school*, Report to Education Research and Development Committee, Canberra.
Raven, J. (1980) Bringing education back into schools, *in* Burgess, T. and Adams, E. *Outcomes of Education*, London: Macmillan.
Schools Commission (1980) *Schooling for 15 and 16 Year Olds*. Canberra: AGPS.
Secretary of State for Scotland (1977) *Truancy and Indiscipline in Scottish Schools* (Pack Report), Edinburgh: HMSO.
Skilbeck, M. (1982) *What is a relevant curriculum?* Centre for the Study of Comprehensive Schools Conference on Schools for the Next Generation.
Walsh, P.D. (1978) The upgrading of practical subjects, *Journal of Further and Higher Education*, 2, 3, pp.58–70.

CHAPTER 7

EDUCATION FOR INTERNATIONAL LIFE – A NEGLECTED AREA
Helen Connell

International life

The term 'education for international life' is a useful way of referring generically to a number of current strands of thought and activity in schools.

Central to education for international life is a recognition of the unity of mankind in a commonly shared world. Diversity and variety are real factors, but so too are similarities in human cultures and situations worldwide, and the continuing growth of contacts, linkages and interdependencies between people on a world scale. As a matter of course we buy items in our shops made in countries thousands of miles away. We watch live TV broadcasts from distant countries and read in daily newspapers of overseas sports events, different areas of tension and warfare, unemployment, of new foreign governments, oceanic pollution scares, local concerts by visiting foreign companies. Rock music has a strong following worldwide within a wide array of youth cultures. We may meet tourists to our country, or know migrants who have settled locally from various places. Day-to-day living has in practice become international in character, even though we ourselves might live in the same locality for our whole life, and not perceive or know about the international networks of which we are a part.

Social and economic studies of the contemporary world – from whatever ideological standpoint they are undertaken – share a common awareness of serious issues confronting the world as a whole: peace and security, existing and growing disparities between rich and poor, prejudice and discrimination towards various minority groups, and providing basic needs of clean water, adequate food and shelter for all citizens are just a few.

Looking to the future, the interlinkages, interdependencies and commonly experienced conditions appear likely to increase. This extended frame of reference marks an important social change during this century, with its roots deep in the past.

It is obvious that increased contact does not necessarily bring increased harmony, peace and prosperity for all. Indeed, through closer contact, some people merely find better reasons for disliking or remaining indifferent to others (Anderson 1964). As contact increases, so do the areas of potential conflict. As world citizens, then, we need to ask such questions as: What are the desirable and undesirable aspects of international life? How can we build on the desirable aspects? In what ways can we change or modify undesirable aspects? What roles, rights and responsibilities do individuals and different groups have? What is the role of school education in relation to these? How should and can the curriculum of the school respond to this challenge?

What is education for international life?

Education for international life should seek to go beyond a simple study of the world as it is, and challenge students to construct their own image of the world as it might be. This image should be grounded in the realities of present life, but look beyond them. Students should learn more than just how to operate effectively in the international world as it is. They should become involved in critical and creative forward-thinking, gain a sense of participation in and responsibility for their own future, and come to understand the processes through which planned individual and group action can bring about various sorts of desirable changes in the world. This brings them into areas of social controversy and value conflict.

Achieving an international outlook, or perspective, has several aspects. It is a perspective which seeks to take into account and understand the points of view of different peoples, particularly in relation to their national, cultural and social differences. It seeks to foster positive attitudes between these different groups, in relation to each other. It seeks to make this understanding the basis of actions contributing to the welfare of different peoples and to developing closer cooperation between them.

The capacity for informed reflective action in relation to international life should provide students with clear goals to be attained, appreciation of appropriate actions they as individuals can take within their day-to-day lives, and capacity and willingness to take these. Difficult as all this may seem, we need to build it into school-based curriculum development as one of the key – and often neglected – dimensions.

Teachers and schools interested to strengthen their activities in education for international life, will encounter a surprising array of terms in the relevant literature, denoting identifiable, but often overlapping, fields of study: peace studies, education for international understanding; citizenship education; world studies; development education; environmental education; multicultural education; human rights education; global education; and various regional studies, such as European, Commonwealth or Pacific studies. These fields share much in terms of educational aims and diagnoses of the world situation. Each, however, has distinctive origins and has developed distinctive traditions (Heater 1980). Often these fields have rather different groups of proponents, and address different parts of the school curriculum. Despite a variety of positions and views amongst individuals involved, the general orientation of each field is towards a future world characterized by peace, justice, fairness, greater understanding and cooperation, tolerance, care and respect for the different peoples and the different environments of the world. Substantial work has been undertaken over several decades, with particular stimulus and support from UNESCO (Scanlon 1960; Buergenthal and Torney 1976; Heater 1980).

Roles for schools

There are several roles for schools to consider in educating for international life:

a) establishing a school policy on education for international life;
b) mapping appropriate learning activities at the school;
c) supporting teachers in undertaking these activities;
d) monitoring and modifying these activities.

a) Establishing a school policy

A written school policy is useful even if in itself it does not bring about classroom changes. Teaching staff, school governors, parents and students can all be involved in the discussion and shaping of a policy document, or in reviewing existing documents. This could lay a basis for wide-ranging commitment and action to implement the policy, and could form part of the current process of school reviews in the UK (DES 1981).

An overall school policy on education for international life is important in helping establish a favourable school climate for student learning in this area. Students do not tend to learn cooperation in an authoritarian setting. Several writers emphasize that the ethos of the school, as well as the substance of the school curriculum, is important to international learning (Prescott 1930; Goodlad et al. 1974; Skilbeck and Connell 1983). Connell (1983) for example, identifies untempered individualism and competition as two major challenges to the development of peace and understanding.

A school should, then, be aware of, and possibly review, student responses to the pattern of relationships it maintains between staff and students, staff and staff, staff and community, and the expected student–student relationships. Sensitivity and skill are needed here, especially as school policies for education for international life are still relatively uncommon, experience is limited, and there are areas of potential conflict with other school policies.

b) Mapping appropriate learning activities

In considering mapping appropriate learning activities in education for international life at school, a situational analysis model of curriculum development is useful. Skilbeck, in the companion to this book *School-Based Curriculum Development*, suggests that analysing the particular situation of the school should be the first step. What are we looking for in a situational analysis of education for international life? Points which might be incuded are:

- students' existing knowledge and experience of the world;
- student and staff interests and attitudes in this area;
- staff knowledge and experience of teaching about international life;
- existing school teaching related to learning for international life;
- available resources (human, financial, material) both at the school and in the local community;
- how decisions are taken in the school, and changes implemented.

Bereday and Lauwerys (1964) discuss several commonly important contextual considerations.

In making curriculum decisions at a given school, there are three aspects of teaching which might be considered:

1. An international dimension in all areas of teaching

How is an international dimension evident in each timetabled area of the

curriculum of a given school? It could be useful to ask these questions about each area:
- What concepts are taught which could make a particular contribution to the structuring for students of a world frame of reference?
- Do examples come from only one's own culture and country?
- Do the questions asked of students encourage them to see other people's points of view and perspectives?
- Does teaching encourage students to be reflective about their own situation and to relate their situation to a world (or at least regional) frame of reference?
- Does teaching give students some understanding of the historical development of this area of study, in particular noting roles played by individuals from other countries?

2. Courses specifically focused on understanding international life
A number of schools have introduced courses or parts of courses specifically focused on understanding international life. These are usually the responsibility of a single teacher or a small group of teachers on a staff. Richardson (1977) has provided a useful review of five curriculum design strategies for studying world society:

- *places* – a traditional organizer in geographical teaching (e.g. desert lands, South America);
- *events* – a traditional organizer in historical teaching (e.g. World War I, the Meiji Restoration);
- *cultures* – a common organizer in topic teaching, and in social and religious studies (e.g. family, work, food, religion), which often emphasizes social science skills and draws on anthropological constructs;
- *actors and interactions* – uncommon in schools, though found in higher education (e.g. international organizations, networks of trade, jazz, literature, political ideas), where the stress is on the interconnections and interrelationships between individuals and groups in different parts of the world;
- *issues* – a common approach in social science and contemporary study courses, especially at secondary level (e.g. poverty, pollution).

A problem common to each of these models is selecting what to teach from the vast array of possible items. This has to be addressed and decided at the level of each individual school, according to local circumstances and resources including the particular interests and expertise of the teaching staff.

The organizers for the above models are conceptual, and focus attention on the substantive questions to be addressed by such courses. It is important, whatever model is used, also to consider what approaches to teaching are compatible with – and indeed foster – the goals of critical thinking and reflective action on the part of students, and promote desirable affective, moral, aesthetic and practical learning. Examples exist of student learning from courses dealing with sensitive value issues being markedly different from that intended by the teacher.

Courses and programmes focused on learning about international life show that individual schools have adopted a range of approaches. They also show that these programmes and courses are referred to by a considerable diversity of titles, and – at secondary school level – have been developed in relation to examination syllabuses in such varied areas for GCE and CSE as Modern Studies, Integrated Humanities, Geography, Commonwealth Literature, Environmental Science, World History and papers within the International Baccalaureate (Becker 1979; Heater 1980; Hicks and Townley 1982; *International Understanding at School*).

An important question in planning courses such as these is where they should be located within the school. The case of secondary-level European Studies exemplifies some problems. There has been an unfortunate tendency for European studies courses to be studied mainly by the so-called slow learners, as a 'soft option' for those not studying modern languages (SERC 1980). This means that only some students at any given age level might be exposed to such courses. *All* students of a given age group should have an equal opportunity to study and learn about international life.

Thought needs to be given also to how the international learning of individual students progresses as they move vertically through the school. It is desirable for all students to have at least one depth-learning opportunity in international life during each year of schooling, preferably in different curricular areas.

Research remains limited on the processes by which students actually learn about international life in different situations, and many questions remain unanswered (Buergenthal and Torney 1976; Pike and Barrows 1979; Heater 1980). There is scope for schools to plan modest action research programmes, to elucidate some of the issues in their own context. Evidence suggests students develop attitudes towards aspects of international life well before they have a firm factual basis for their beliefs. Thus, shifting any strongly or emotionally held beliefs which are based on false premises presents a challenging task for teachers. Children appear to develop a sense of national identity quite young, and the rigidity with which this is held is felt to influence children's views and understandings of other groups. The influential spiral model for primary social studies curriculum directs students' learning first to their immediate and local environment, and then gradually outwards through regional and national, finally to international studies. Is this widespread approach out of step with the needs of learning for international life, especially when young children are constantly exposed to overseas events and places from long hours of television viewing? In what ways can students learn meaningfully about life in countries other than their own at very early ages? How can these be structured into school curricula?

Are students always open-minded and interested in learning about international life? Torney and Buergenthal (1978) suggest that the middle years of schooling mark the stage when most students are most open and flexible in their thinking about other peoples, and some narrowing and hardening of views generally occurs during adolescence. Hence, unless students by adolescence have already developed an international base for their thinking, are they deprived?

3. Other areas of school life

Opportunities for learning about international life arise in many ways in the life of the school. Discussions of current international events during roll call periods, talks by casual visitors to the school, discussion of a popular TV series are only a few of the possibilities. Too often opportunities slip away without their full potential for international learning being realized. Assemblies, informal discussions, lunch-time films, homework assignments, stamp clubs, pen friends, school twinning, community projects are all activities into which small reinforcements and extensions of learning about international life can be simply built without major effort or major expense.

Some schools have run student exchanges and visits both at home and abroad. These have obvious potential for both structured and informal learning – although cost considerations make these difficult for many schools (Dunlop 1982).

c) Supporting teachers undertaking activities in education for international life

Once a school has a policy or the beginnings of a policy of teaching for international life, it needs to provide adequate support to those teachers involved – especially where this is a new undertaking for them. Two main areas of support might be considered:

1. Professional development

a) In-service activities and conferences In-service activities and conferences, both school based and outside school, can play a variety of useful roles. They can stimulate the interest of teachers uninvolved in educating for international life, and they can provide support and further development for those already involved. In school-focused in-service activities, specific teaching approaches for that school can be discussed and designed. Two World Studies Project publications give practical advice here (Richardson et al. 1979; Fisher and Hicks 1982). Some education authorities offer in-service courses through their advisory services or teachers' centres; a range of other agencies provide in-service support (Council for Education in World Citizenship 1980); some tertiary institutions offer short in-service courses and graduate degree work in this area as well as courses for initial trainees.

b) Suitable reference material Schools should ensure that staff have access to appropriate up-to-date journals and other publications, perhaps through local teachers' centres or tertiary institutions. Teachers should also receive relevant material from advisory services and other parts of the education system to help them in structuring and planning their teaching.

c) Visits and exchanges Schemes to enable teachers to visit overseas, or exchange positions with teachers overseas, should not be overlooked Although they cater for relatively small numbers, these experiences have proved valuable to many individual teachers involved in varied aspects of teaching, giving them a broader personal understanding of the world as the basis for their teaching (Young 1964). Such teachers can serve as resource personnel for their colleagues.

2. Teaching resources

The second type of support schools can offer is in the provision of adequate teaching resources. Three types of resources are important. *Human* resources can be found in the time and assistance of advisory staff, visits by staff of voluntary agencies, interested parents and community members etc. Allocation of *financial* resources can enable classes to go on trips and excursions – particularly valuable in helping give reality to situations often beyond the personal experience of class members. *Material* resources in the form of teaching/learning resources are now fairly extensive in their coverage of international life. Scope exists for teachers to exercise their traditional roles of selecting, adopting, adapting, and indeed creating their own resources in this area (Becker 1979; Council for Education in World Citizenship 1980; Hicks and Townley 1982). Teachers can also draw on students' out-of-school reading and TV watching.

d) Monitoring and modifying activities

The final key role suggested for schools to consider is monitoring and modifying school-level activities related to learning for international life. This does not have to be an onerous task, and can often be handled within existing arrangements. The key is to establish some regular system, such as brief reports at periodic staff meetings, plus, perhaps, a termly meeting for representatives of different groups on the staff. Such provision enables exchange of information on activities within the school as a whole, and coordination of forward planning.

Methods of evaluating the desirable aspects of student learning for international life need to be varied. While most teachers are familiar with different ways of assessing cognitive learning, attention could usefully be directed at methods appropriate to particular school situations in affective, aesthetic, moral and practical learning. This topic deserves further attention. As a start, schools might identify several specific purposes for evaluation, such as course improvement, assessment of student learning, student accreditation, and establishing the value of the course or activities within the school environment (i.e. legitimation to other staff, school governors, parents etc.). Once this has been done, the selection and application of particular evaluation procedures is a much more manageable task. There are several general guides to in-school evaluation that are useful here (Elliott 1981).

Initiating school-level activities in international learning

We hear constantly that the school curriculum is too overcrowded, and some embattled advisers and principals – not to mention teachers – cast apprehensive and besieged looks towards those demanding yet further change to it. Yet an increasing number of schools appear able and willing to meet the challenge.

As there is generally little reflection of international life in the examinations of England and Wales (Chalkley 1982), and no evidence of a widely held community expectation of teaching about international life (as there is, for example, of mathematics and English), external pressures on teachers to accept the challenge are not strong. Indeed, negative influences could be stronger – for example the lack of status conferred by internationally focused teaching, given the effort and uncertainties for individuals making any change from established teaching patterns. Also, the national and local organization of the UK school systems gives no natural international orientation.

In this situation, in decentralized education systems such as that in the UK, it appears to be the conviction, commitment, skill and persistence of particular individuals and groups within the education system which have generated the varied courses in schools today. Aucott et al. (1979) give a detailed account of the varied roles and tasks taken by four teachers to establish a World Studies course as part of the core curriculum of a new community college. Starkey (1982) illustrates how the initiative of a new staff member at another school led to an existing course being reshaped to stress study of world society. In discussing the introduction of development education into schools, Richardson (1982) refers to such individuals as the inside advocates. In fostering these changes, he identifies several roles – such as leading staff opinion and legitimizing the change – to be performed by different individuals in ensuring the success and take-up at school level of these changes. We come back, then, to the importance in the situational analysis discussed above of understanding the nature of the decision-taking process at each particular school.

Conclusion

In decentralized education systems, there is much that individual teachers and schools can do on their own initiative to foster understanding of international life amongst their students. A growing number of examples exist from which schools can draw inspiration, and support is available from a number of parts of the educational system. In view of the continuing integration of world experience, schools will do well to take seriously the challenges posed to them to participate in educating students for international life.

References

Abraham, H.J. (1981) *World Problems in the Classroom*, Educational Studies and Documents No. 41, Paris: Unesco.
Anderson, C.A. (1964) Sociological and educational constraints upon international understanding, *in* Bereday, G.Z. et al. (eds) *Education and International Life*, The Yearbook of Education, London: Evans, p. 67.
Aucott, J., Cox, H., Dodds, A. and Selby, D. (1979) World studies on the runway: one year's progress towards a core curriculum, *The New Era*, vol. 60, p. 212.
Becker, J.M. (ed.) (1979) *Schooling for a Global Age*, New York: McGraw Hill.
Bereday, G.Z. and Lauwerys, J.A. (eds) (1964) *Education and International Life*, The Yearbook of Education, London: Evans.
Buergenthal, T. and Torney, J.V. (1976) *International Human Rights and International Education*, Washington DC: US National Commission for Unesco.
Chalkley, B. (1982) *Education for International Understanding in the United Kingdom: A Study of the Syllabuses of the G.C.E. and C.S.E. Examination Boards to Assess their International Content*, London: Extramural Division, SOAS, University of London.
Connell, W.F. (1983) Curriculum for peace education, *The New Era*, vol. 64(1), p. 11.
Council for Education in World Citizenship (1980) *World Studies Resources Guide*, London: The Author.
Department of Education and Science: *Circular 6/81*
Dunlop, J. (1982) The Jordanhill Project in International Understanding, *in* Hicks, D. et al. (eds) *Teaching World Studies*, London: Longman.
Elliott, G. (1981) *Self Evaluation and the Teacher, An Annotated Bibliography and Report on Current Practice* in four parts, London: Schools Council.
Fisher, S. and Hicks, D. (1982) *Planning Workshops and Courses: A World Studies In-Service Handbook*, London: Schools Council.
Goodlad, J.L. and Associates (1974) *Towards a Mankind School: An Adventure in Humanistic Education*, New York: McGraw-Hill.
Heater, D. (1980) *World Studies – Education for International Understanding in Britain*, London: Harrap.
Hicks, D. and Townley, C. (eds) (1982) *Teaching World Studies – An Introduction to Global Perspectives in the Curriculum*, London: Longman.
International Understanding at School (Twice-yearly publication of the Unesco Associated Schools), Paris: Unesco.
Pike, L.W. and Barrows, T.S. (1979) *Other Nations, Other People – A Survey of Student Interests, Knowledge, Attitudes and Perceptions*, Washington DC: US Department of Health, Education and Welfare, Office of Education HEW Publication No. (OE) 78–19004.
Prescott, D. (1930) *Education and International Relations*, Cambridge, Mass.: Harvard University Press.
Richardson, R. (1977) Studying world society: some approaches to the design of courses, *The New Era*, vol. 58 (6), p. 175.
Richardson, R. (1982) Introducing development education in schools, *International Review of Education*, vol. 28 (4), p. 475.

Richardson, R., Flood, M. and Fisher, S. (1979) *Debate and Decision: Schools in a World of Change*, London: One World Trust.

Scanlon, D.G. (ed.) (1960) *International Education – A Documentary History*, New York: Classics in Education No. 5, Teachers College, Columbia.

SERC Schools Unit (1980) *Project Work in European Studies*, Sussex European Research Centre, Schools Unit, Teacher Fellowship Series.

Skilbeck, M. and Connell, H. (1983) WEF Seoul Conference, Part 2 – Ways and Means, *The New Era*, vol. 64 (1), p. 6 (see account by H. Röhrs of peace education in practice in a German pre-school).

Starkey, H. (1982) World Studies and the development of new resources, *in* Hicks, D. et al. (eds) *Teaching World Studies*, London: Longman.

Torney, J.V. and Buergenthal, T. (1978) The young person's view of world society: a review of research findings, *The New Era*, vol. 59 (2), p. 38.

Young, F.A. (1964) International exchanges of teachers and scholars: USA, *in* Bereday, G.Z. et al. (eds) *Education and International Life*, The Yearbook of Education, London: Evans.

SECTION 3

SCHOOL APPROACHES TO REVIEW, EVALUATION AND DEVELOPMENT

INTRODUCTION
Malcolm Skilbeck

Although the role of the school in curriculum development can be illuminated, analysed and assessed through a consideration of models of the curriculum, support systems and other external perspectives, it is ultimately in the school's experience that school-based curriculum development is to be understood. Relatively little research has been carried out in the form of schools systematically recording and evaluating their processes of curriculum review, evaluation and development. We may expect this kind of research to expand, as the teacher-as-researcher movement develops alongside institutional self-evaluation, action research and the pressures from external sources for greater visible school accountability and more public evidence of systematic self-appraisal. Nevertheless, the research and evaluative functions of schooling are limited: neither the actions of teaching and organizing teaching nor the resources available are likely to yield a major output of in-school research and evaluation. Doubtless, more experience by schools of self-conscious or deliberate curriculum review, evaluation and development will lead to greater sophistication in methodology: of project design, recording, observation and review procedures and analysis of findings. There is always likely to be, however, considerable emphasis on subjective and intersubjective procedures where such goals of the classical researcher as repeatability, canons of verification and the objective presentation of findings give place to the more personal and individual devices of case-study.

In this section, teachers and others working very closely with schools report individual projects which collectively illustrate many of the major trends and issues in school curriculum development. Examples are given of the tasks and problems confronting within-institution evaluators and developers from the primary, secondary and further education levels; the perspectives are those of headteachers, classroom practitioners, advisory and consultative personnel. Whilst no attempt is made to cover a representative range of school subjects or subject areas, there is an emphasis on whole-school approaches, even where individual contributors focus on a particular question, such as how to find an appropriate starting point, or the needs students have for guidance.

Colin Bayne-Jardine adapts A.A. Milne to his purposes: a school-based curriculum review is like the hunt during which Pooh and Piglet nearly caught a Woozle. This is perhaps the head's special dilemma: what is the purpose of a curriculum review and what results from it? In his case, as a new head of a large secondary school which for many years had been under a powerful and charismatic head, a review was a kind of test of Colin Bayne-Jardine's own role. On the basis of the experience of a successful, quite definitely limited review, he advises others in his position to find an understood and accepted task in which head and other staff can be involved together. It is perhaps comforting to the new teacher in the school to know that the new head, too, has problems of adjustment! The main thrust of this review is apparently towards a shift in a particularly contentious area: the school provision and student selection of fourth-year options. We see how the head, in close association with his director of studies and with the advice of a shrewdly chosen external consultant, is able to effect changes which, modest in themselves, have the potential for bringing in a major reorientation, towards a core curriculum. Such potential may or may not be explored subsequently: the immediate objectives, of a guided-options system and a means whereby the new head achieves a significant developmental role in the school, are attained.

For Elsa Davies, the head best sees her role in curriculum as a facilitator, a supporter and coordinator of innovation, not necessarily an initiator and certainly not 'the boss of the show'. The head must always state her case and even when it's not accepted, in the democratic environment of decision making that she envisages, that statement itself can be a positive force. The key to her analysis is to be found in a favourite curriculum term, 'improvement'. How can the head best release and support the springs of improvement which, she believes, belong in a natural and spontaneous way to any school? The answers she gives, which are drawn from varied experience including a particular project on language in the first school, place the onus very definitely on the head to join in, seeking out and fostering the positive aspects, as she sees them, of change and innovation. The head enjoys certain advantages but Elsa Davies argues that these ought to arise less from a traditional notion of the authority of the position than from access to knowledge and information both about the overall school situation and about strategies of curriculum change. The head's role in school-based curriculum development is seen as a function of knowledge and experience, themselves open to discussion in the open climate of the democratic school.

In his chapter Robert Crone shows how, among a group of Northern Ireland schools, primary as well as secondary, a bridge has been built between teachers working as curriculum critics and developers within their schools and a team of external consultants. The role of field officer, as he outlines it, combines in-school experience and knowledge with membership of a mobile team based in a university school of education. The 'outsider', playing this role, brings, in the words of one of the teachers, a divergent mode of analysis and a capability for solving problems. But the objects are to improve teachers' skills, to better achieve existing goals of schools, and to strengthen student learning in subject areas which are of concern to the public. This is an avowedly reformist stance: the Schools Support Service did not claim to innovate in a radical fashion and this proved to be a strength in the eyes of participants. On the other hand individual schools, and notably the one where Robert Crone reports the emergence of a core curriculum philosophy, were encouraged to strike out in ways that suited them. This Northern Ireland project, in a number of ways, shows how school-based curriculum development can be a practical, successful collaborative exercise which at one and the same time improves student learning and enhances teacher professionalism.

Chris Saville, formerly a primary head and now chief inspector in a local education authority, holds up a mirror to a school setting very different from those outlined by Colin Bayne-Jardine and Elsa Davies. His 'fictional' account, under the ironic title of 'communication and dialogue', illustrates all too convincingly a situation of stagnation and cynicism, where curriculum innovation exists as a succession of unrelated and meaningless events which seem to do little more than express the head's passing fads and provide scope for sardonic or opportunistic staff responses. Is this, as he suggests, the 'real world' of curriculum development, or is it a warning of the dangers attendant on ill-considered, nonparticipatory styles of school management?

A commonly used approach in reporting local development work is that of the case-study, conducted and written up by a participant-observer. As warden of a teachers' centre, Terence Joyes uses case-study method in a collaborative curriculum review in a first school. His account highlights several issues in contemporary curriculum evaluation: ways staff of a school can collaborate in what are essentially exercises in self and group critical reflection; building up confidentiality and trust; 'ownership' of evaluation data and negotiation of their release; the relationships of review to development and the question of audiences for evaluation reports. It is recognized that reviews and evaluation are intensely personal and interpersonal in nature. There is an interplay of roles, and leadership is a crucial consideration. The handling of leadership and participant roles is often a source of difficulty; it can also be, as Terence Joyes shows, the well-spring of staff cohesion, resulting in improved understanding and shared action.

From within-school evaluation, we turn to the question of how to relate curriculum to the interests and perspectives of students in school. Two papers on curriculum guidance, by Jean Cosslett and Carole Ann Eastgate, take as their starting point the difficulties students encounter in making sense of the curriculum. Jean Cosslett argues that students commencing secondary schooling need to understand and appreciate the overall rationale of the curriculum, the range and sequence of subjects, and the relationship of schooling to life. Much of this is, unwisely, taken for granted by schools or assumed to emerge naturally from the experience of subject learning. But students are frequently dissatisfied with schooling and resistant to studies which, while they are compulsory, are not thereby motivating and interesting. Curriculum guidance in the way Jean Cosslett outlines it, is a novel idea, which has value both in showing how the subject matter of learning can interrelate and in involving students in honest discussion of their own learning.

The focus of Carole Ann Eastgate's analysis is the widely decried practice of forcing subject choices on 13 and 14-year-old students on the basis of examination syllabuses and timetabling exigencies. A thoroughgoing reform of the secondary curriculum would bring into question the necessity for these option choices and the examination syllabuses in common use. Few schools and education authorities are, it seems, ready to undertake this kind of radical reappraisal even though many pay lip service to it. What, then, can teachers do to make greater educational sense of the options system? Carole Ann Eastgate's answer lies, like Jean Cosslett's, in reforms in student learning. These include the introduction of organized guidance programmes, individual tuition and explicit teaching of decision-making skills. Students, parents and teachers all need to be involved, through structured programmes.

The limitations of the options system provide the starting point for an in-school curriculum development exercise undertaken by Francis Fay and a group of his colleagues in a Liverpool secondary school. Their aim was to design, implement, monitor and evaluate a new course for fourth and fifth-year students, which would provide at least an introduction to areas of knowledge and understanding that the options system in practice is likely to leave untouched. The course was designed to pick up such topics as equal opportunities, sex education, politics and parentcraft. Francis Fay argues that on the one hand the group did select and use a wide repertory of curriculum development processes and, on the other, managed to avoid many of the difficulties encountered by in-school development groups. As he remarks, evaluation both of the effects of such courses and the processes of review, evaluation and development through which they are established cannot be completed except over a long time-span. What seems to be needed, therefore, is further work to elaborate a monitoring system for schools whereby long-term effects can be linked to short and medium-term indicators.

However, much of the change that occurs in schools results from factors and events over which the staff has very little if any control. Changes in school populations resulting from boundary changes, amalgamations and declining rolls are but one illustration of the scale of externally imposed change. Local authority encouragement or pressure leading to in-school curriculum review is a growing source of change; the introduction of new electronic equipment, or the incitement to a greater vocational emphasis through enhanced and earmarked central government subventions represents yet another external source of change. Indeed, it is doubtful whether more than a small minority of schools would, of their own initiative, undertake long-term and large-scale curriculum review, evaluation and development exercises, notwithstanding the growing professionalism of teachers. It is therefore necessary for us to examine closely the experience of curriculum change in, and through the effect of, these larger changes.

Allan Hodge provides a sobering account of how, in the transformation of a small, single-sex grammar school into an open-access, coeducational, sixth-form college, opportunities for significant curriculum development were missed. If, as is sometimes asserted, the most effective way to change the curriculum is to change school structure and organization, a great deal remains to be explained about the reluctance or inability of many comprehensive schools (organization) to produce a comprehensive curriculum. Pointers to this explanation are provided by Allan Hodge when he shows how, in a particular case, too little was done to involve and win over staff, to introduce staff development programmes, to build up confidence and capability in the face of new demands. Planning a new, whole-institution curriculum is a massive undertaking where not only participation but also training and confidence-building are essential. The onus falls very heavily on senior management, at school and local education authority level, to ensure that this kind of back-up is fully available.

It is questionable, however, whether in our education system we do indeed have a wide, high-level commitment to carrying the whole teaching profession forward through involvement in decision making, systematic staff development and engagement with central issues in curriculum. Institutionalized interests and roles, power blocs and system inertia resulting from the complex bureaucracies we have created in education combine to undermine the principle of the teacher as a collaborative professional. Arthur Donald points up the difficulties facing teacher developers in further education institutions dominated by college hierarchies, rigid and detailed external examination syllabuses, and a widespread commitment to behavioural objectives as a means of structuring vocational curricula. On this analysis, the choice seems to lie between individual tinkering with teaching methodologies at the classroom level, and concerted professional action to effect structural changes. This illustrates the point that school or institution-based curriculum development cannot always mean enlightened exercises of collaborative review, evaluation and development at the institutional level. A prior need is to determine the types of action appropriate to particular environments. This must be combined with a readiness to seek change on a variety of fronts.

We return to the point about collaborative development, made strongly by Robert Crone and Francis Fay, in a chapter by Agnes McMahon, who reports a successful Schools Council project, Guidelines for Review and Institutional Development (GRIDS). This project, at the pilot stage, brought together a number of schools, local education authorities and researchers and developers who jointly worked out a straightforward set of guidelines to foster school review. It was suggested that whereas local education authorities were well launched on guidelines for school review, they had less to say about just *how* a school is to proceed. GRIDS aimed to assist schools, primary and secondary, in the methods and procedures of reviewing, focusing on review not for accountability but for purposes of in-school development. The experience of this project confirmed that schools can undertake internal reviews, provided their reviews are well focused, outside assistance is drawn upon and rigorous reflection and analysis are given their place. Lacking these, reviews can be half-hearted and overhasty – a source of frustration and defeatism, not change and development.

Finally in this section, the case is made for grounding school-level curriculum review, evaluation and development in a consideration of students' engagement with learning materials and resources. This, in a sense, is a natural starting point for teachers since the most typical learning situation, by far, is one where a group of students are engaged in learning tasks, planned and structured by a teacher and centred on printed and other types of materials. Philip Waterhouse, after many years of experience in the field of resource-based learning and as leader of the pioneering Avon Resources for Learning Centre, is well placed to point up the needs and opportunities in resource management as a key to successful school-level curriculum making. It is resource *management*, not production, that he sees as crucial, at the school level. Thus, while teachers need design criteria and expertise in choosing a design for the use of resources, they ought not to give substantial attention to resource production. It is in the design of the learning programmes, and in the selection, organization and use of resources, that improvements are needed and can be expected. Philip Waterhouse thus helps to lay to rest one of the most common fallacies about school-based curriculum development: that the school and especially the teaching staff are assumed to create and make the curriculum in its entirety. It is precisely in determining an appropriate and manageable role and carrying it through successfully that the school plays its part in a wider system of curriculum decision making.

CHAPTER 8

CASE-STUDY OF SCHOOL-BASED CURRICULUM REVIEW
Colin C. Bayne-Jardine

Any newly appointed secondary head will understand the difficulty of getting to grips with the situation in the school. This is particularly true when the school is well established and successful. It is vital to find an understood and accepted task in which the head and the staff can be involved together. Under such circumstances the newly appointed head can begin to feel the climate (Halpin 1966) in the school and make informed judgements about the ways in which the organization operates. In 1976, upon my appointment to the headship of Henbury School, Bristol, I decided to embark upon a school-based curriculum review in order to feel my way into an organization which had developed over twenty-one years under my predecessor. I asked for, and received, help from the principal adviser, County of Avon, Alan Garnham; Grace Price, senior adviser for curriculum; the local HMI; Maurice Holt, formerly headmaster of Sheredes School, Hertfordshire, and, in 1976, a curriculum consultant. The governing body of the school were positive and supportive over the review and received regular reports. The staff also responded cheerfully and enthusiastically to the demands made upon them. The Northern Sub-Region of the South West In-Service Education and Training for Teachers Committee gave us financial support in order to run a number of in-service days at the school. This support is important because there is an expectation that a new head will play the part of the 'hero-innovator' (Baron 1975; Musgrove 1971) and outside perceptions will help to keep any review process in balance. In an established school the new head can very easily find that involvement in the internal politics hampers any serious review.

From the outset I was determined to approach the review in an open style

(Walton 1971). I outlined to all members of staff from the beginning the possible nature of any change. It is, after all, essential to maintain, service and improve the curriculum roundabout whilst it is still in motion. I wrote in my introduction to the review:

> 'Tracks,' said Piglet. 'Paw-marks.' He gave a little squeak of excitement. 'Oh, Pooh! Do you think it's a-a-a Woozle?'
> 'It may be,' said Pooh. 'Sometimes it is and sometimes it isn't. You can never tell with paw-marks.'
> (Milne 1926)
>
> A school-based curriculum review is like the hunt during which Pooh and Piglet nearly caught a Woozle. You never can tell where an analysis will lead and there is bound to be an ambivalence about any review carried out by those involved in the enterprise (Barnes 1982). Tony Becher and Stuart Maclure (1978) have sounded a warning against the way in which almost any curriculum outrage becomes a tradition if it can be nursed through infancy. They suggest that strange things have happened because any change in an established curriculum must be piecemeal. 'Like other forms of piecemeal development, school-based reform enables the system to change little by little, a boundary extended a few yards here, a quick strategic withdrawal to an earlier baseline there.' Yet a comprehensive school like Henbury which has been established for over twenty years can only consider such development as a viable method of curriculum change. Clearly there is a need for general guidance to give the changes direction and purpose.

This process continues still and the review undertaken eight years ago was not definitive. Such a review 'must, too, allow for future modification in response to new needs in the world outside schools: decisions cannot sensibly be taken once and for all' (DES 1980a). There has been an increased interest in curriculum on a national level and in many ways our review has been overtaken by events. A large and lively secondary school must be in a continual state of flux. School organizations are dynamic and living not static. However, there was one change made as a direct result of the review of the whole curriculum which illustrates how such planned change can arise from using the approach of rational interaction curriculum development starting with a situational analysis (see p.84). The importance of involvement in this initial analysis by all staff is crucial.

We took as general background to the situational analysis some notes I provided for all department heads:

Background discussion notes for school-based curriculum review
1. *Definition of curriculum*:
'All the experiences for learning which are planned and organised by the school' (Whitfield 1971). This definition is useful provided that we remember

that the whole of life provides experiences through which human beings can learn. The 'hidden curriculum' is important and is not planned. In addition it is probably unique for every person.

2. *The Educational Covenant*:
'In seeking a framework of principles for the whole curriculum we reached the view that the school's aims should start from an acknowledgement of the legitimate expectations of various groups of people who are involved in secondary education. We saw the aims of the school as emerging from an assessment of the balance of expectations to be met and thought of them as constituting a covenant, or social compact. This covenant defines the reasonable expectations and mutual responsibilities of the pupils, for whose welfare the school exists, their parents, the teachers, and such agencies as boards of governors, local education authorities and the Department of Education and Science. Seen as a covenant, the curriculum reveals what view the school takes of its pupils, what it regards as their legitimate entitlements, and what sort of people it thinks it should help them to become. Similarly in the ways in which its relations with parents and the wider community are conducted it will show, more eloquently than in any other way, what it regards as the proper place of the school in society. Finally, in its definition of roles and responsibilities, a curriculum incorporates a concept of teacher professionalism.' (Schools Council 1975)

3. *Seven stepping stones towards a coherent school curriculum*:
I suggest that we should try to clear our minds on seven counts (Warwick 1975). These stepping stones towards a coherent curriculum might be simplified as follows into a series of questions:
1. Have we an agreed general aim?
2. Do we accept the subject divisions?
3. Are we convinced that knowledge is studied at an appropriate level at the best age?
4. Do our teaching methods take account of the children's learning processes?
5. Do we ensure that all children gain basic and essential skills?
6. Do we develop desired attitudes?
7. Do we ensure that all pupils are given a full range of experience?

The curriculum design in 1976 was sophisticated and the director of studies, Michael Freeman, provided a clear descriptive paper containing some suggestions as to areas upon which to focus:

A. *STRUCTURE*
We are a nine-form entry school, with an annual intake (normally) of 270–285 pupils, roughly equally divided between boys and girls. Overall at present we have 798 boys and 774 girls.

In each of the first two years we choose to arrange this intake into seven mixed-ability forms each of (ideally) about 33 pupils, and two smaller streamed remedial classes. The lowest Reading Age normally acceptable for entry to the mixed-ability classes is about 9.0; Reading Ages in the remedial forms ranged this year (in September 1975) from 8.10 down to 6.0. In both mixed-ability and remedial classes the pupils have all lessons in their forms, and from September 1976 their Design lessons will be taught to eighteen groups each comprising half a form. Only in Games, therefore, is an opportunity provided to set by ability with units larger than one form. 'Withdrawal' systems operate in both mixed-ability and remedial areas for pupils with English problems of various sorts. On entry to the 3rd Year, the remedial band is normally reduced to about 35 pupils (13% of the intake). In the Middle School these pupils are defined as 'those for whom it is not appropriate to provide a curriculum determined by the requirements of external examinations'. (Some of them do usually take CSE in a few subjects.) The rest of the 3rd Year is broken into two exactly parallel halves – 3A and 3 alpha – each with 4 sets for all subjects except Design and Games, where the entire year is taught as a unit. The Languages, Maths and Science departments choose to set by ability in Year 3; English and Humanities retain mixed-ability sets, though English sometimes runs a 'bottom set' in each half, and the Humanities subjects have to accept what is in practice a top set because the introduction of German in Year 3 is done largely at their expense.

The curriculum structure in Years 4 and 5 is extremely complex, because our policy is to organize all 240 'non-remedial' children in a single band, to give each individual maximum flexibility and the widest possible number of options in compiling an examination course. Thus, we can and do provide courses ranging from those for students who achieve nine good O levels to those finishing with, say, four poor CSEs. Almost any combination of the subjects we offer is available, at either O level or CSE in most subjects. Supervised Private Study, and the non-examination 'Learning for Living' course, appear partly to enable us to cope within a single band with students taking eight or nine examination courses, and those for whom five or six are more appropriate.

The philosophy in the Upper School is very similar, catering for the three-A-level students, the six-retake students, and combinations in between. The LEA provides a more generous staffing ratio for the Upper School; we have tended increasingly to feed this into the rest of the school, and the Upper School receives less than its 'fair share' of staff.

Some Questions

In the Lower School, is the line between mixed-ability and remedial drawn in the right place? Should there be remedial forms at all?

Are we right to teach all Lower School mixed-ability pupils in forms all the time, thus compelling mixed-ability teaching in all subjects for two years? Has the move to parallel 3A and 3 alpha proved a success? Was it better when Year 3 had three streamed bands?

In Years 4 and 5, are we right to stress the requirements of each individual so much, when it causes such a complex curriculum structure and so much administration? (Many schools run systems of options within broad 'Faculties' and do not try to make all *subject* combinations possible.)

We think we have a genuinely comprehensive Upper School. What more could we do?

B. *CONTENT*
Remedial classes, at all age-levels, spend a good deal of time with specialist teachers, working on basic skills. Practical and semi-practical courses play an increased part in their curriculum as they move up the school.

In the Lower School, a common course is followed by all pupils in mixed-ability forms. In Year 1 they spend large amounts of time on Humanities (which includes English), Maths, French, Design and Physical Activities, and little time on Science and Music. In Year 2 English is taught separately from Humanity, and the Science element is increased by the introduction of separate Sciences. Otherwise, the pattern continues from Year 1.

In Year 3 there is again a standard course for all non-remedial children with two exceptions. The standard is English, Maths, French, three Sciences, three Humanities, Design, Physical Activities and Music; the 30 weakest at Science in each of 3A and 3 alpha take Rural Science and General Science instead of Biology, Chemistry and Physics. The other exception is that the opportunity is provided for the 30 or so ablest pupils in each of 3A and 3 alpha to start German in Year 3. This is an extra load for the students concerned, and is fitted in at the expense of one lesson of each of History, Geography, RE, Music and Swimming.

There is no point in listing here all the subjects offered in Years 4 and 5 and the Upper School. The policy is to offer only a comparatively limited number of subjects, but to allow great flexibility of subject-combinations and setting, so that specific careers or further education requirements can almost always be met.

Some Questions
Is French for all for three years the right policy?
Is the second foreign language for the few important enough to justify the dislocation of every student's curriculum arrangements in Year 3?
Are French and German the right two languages?
Do we put about the right emphasis upon Design, Drama, Music, and Physical Activities at every level? (e.g. Every pupil in Years 4 and 5 must take a Design subject, but only the less able can take more than one. Is this right? Games are compulsory up to and including Year 5 – is this right?)
Should we have more 'co-ordinated' work between Departments further up the school? Are we happy with the co-ordinated work we have got?
What other courses/subjects should we offer?

The subject departments within the school then carried out a detailed review of their work. This review was crucial and the response to a deadline at the end of the Christmas term was encouraging. I received twenty-five papers in which subject departments and curriculum teams, such as the lower school humanities teachers, analysed their position and outlined possible developments. I had played a small part in the school pantomime and the Mathematics Department addressed their review 'to the prettiest of the seven dwarfs'. In this review the department felt that their system of workcards, developed over the years to give each child in mixed-ability classes during their first two years a chance to progress at their own pace, could be improved. The request for sets for mathematics in the second year was made strongly and this became a timetabling priority and has now been introduced. Departments did not appear threatened by the review and following their own analysis of the existing situation some timetabling priorities were changed. Then we held an in-service day during which we challenged the subject-based framework. After this day, in which Maurice Holt was very closely involved, I produced a paper in September 1977 which attempted to pull together the discussion that had taken place at that date:

Position paper on school-based curriculum review
1. *Aims*
We should take positive action to encourage young people to share in an attitude of mind which through individual choice of personal experience enriches life inwardly and outwardly. The focus must be on helping the individual to develop their inward resources and to attain all possible excellence.

The aims of schools have been clearly set out in the Green Paper (DES 1977). 'Schools must have aims against which to judge the effectiveness of their work and hence the kinds of improvements that they may need to make from time to time. The majority of people would probably agree with the following attempt to set out these aims, though they might differ in the emphasis to be placed on one or the other:

  (i) to help children develop lively, enquiring minds; giving them the ability to question and to argue rationally, and to apply themselves to tasks;
  (ii) to instil respect for moral values, for other people and for oneself, and tolerance of other races, religions and ways of life;
  (iii) to help children understand the world in which we live, and the interdependence of nations;
  (iv) to help children to use language effectively and imaginatively in reading, writing and speaking;
  (v) to help children to appreciate how the nation earns and maintains its standard of living and properly to esteem the essential role of industry and commerce in this process;
  (vi) to provide a basis of mathematical, scientific and technical knowledge, enabling boys and girls to learn the essential skills needed in a fast-changing world of work;
  (vii) to teach children about human achievement and aspirations in the arts and sciences, in religion, and in the search for a more just social order;
  (viii) to encourage and foster the development of the children whose social

or environmental disadvantages cripple their capacity to learn, if necessary by making additional resources available to them.'

The curriculum pattern of any school outlines the way in which such aims are translated into classroom practice.

2. *Subject Departments*

Since a department cannot include all knowledge there has to be some selection. I am convinced that we should build on the strong subject department base in the school. The clear feeling that emerged from our in-service day was a desire amongst members of staff that they should be informed about the work being done by colleagues in various departments. There is a clear need to share classroom expertise and experience.

I suggest that departments consider these points:

a) The techniques of classroom management. The check list in our *Staff Handbook* may be helpful for this.

b) Ways in which their subject can mesh into the school curriculum.

c) The appropriateness of the level of the work demanded from groups (Curriculum Consultative Committee 1977). I would hope that we can respond to J.S. Bruner's challenge: 'We begin with the hypothesis that any subject can be taught effectively in some intellectually honest form to any child at any stage of development. It is a bold hypothesis and an essential one in thinking about the nature of a curriculum. No evidence exists to contradict it; considerable evidence is being amassed that supports it' (Bruner 1966).

3. *Developments*

The general framework of our curriculum then is sound. The individual is certainly given every opportunity to develop his or her own resources. A number of refinements have been suggested and these should be considered carefully before departments report to heads of schools. Mike Waters, director of studies, is providing a paper suggesting possible detailed developments.

Year 1: This is a sound and satisfactory year. The bridge year from primary to secondary school is clearly helped by the English/Humanity link. No changes recommended. The two parallel remedial groups will be carefully monitored during this year to check whether or not they are more effective than setted remedial groups.

Year 2: There is a feeling that some setting would be useful at this stage. Both Maths and French would like a split along the lines of A and Alpha in Year 3. This would make setting possible but would have to be done along with a simplification of Year 4.

The Science Department plan to introduce an integrated course in Year 2 and it might be worth considering ways in which the time released could be developed to stretch the able and give additional basic skills to those in need of such support.

Year 3: Provided the new approach to the introduction of German is successful no changes recommended.

Years 4 and 5: It is unlikely that the range of options can be maintained if we change the present general framework. At the same time we need to introduce some additional non-examination options and if possible greater opportunity for setting. Clearly an option 'communication skills' would be of value to youngsters weak in basic skills. The general studies programme is already undergoing review.

Upper School: It would seem to me that we have to reduce the minority studies in this area because of the Avon (LEA) cuts. I should be unhappy to see any further change until the examination pattern is settled nationally. We certainly offer a very wide A level combination of subject choices.

4. *Conclusion*

I am aware that this paper is far from revolutionary. I am also aware that departments have already spent a good deal of time on curriculum review. However, I am sure that all will appreciate the value of a tough-minded look at our curriculum. It is not surprising that a good comprehensive school like Henbury has developed a sound working curriculum. It is a tribute to all who teach and have taught at Henbury that the refinements required are fairly small. Provided we can hammer out these improvements we must have an excellent framework within which the individual can be helped and encouraged to develop to the full their potential. I am sure that we will all respond to the challenge of translating our aims within the broad school framework into classroom practice.

The school curriculum committee, composed of all heads of department, has become the forum for discussion of the ways in which improvements can be made. An effective idea has been the occasional meeting at which a head of department has presented the work of their subject department to their colleagues. Many colleagues have been invited to attend lessons following such a presentation and this has undoubtedly increased awareness of issues across the curriculum. Without doubt the key area for the review became the fourth-year curriculum – the segment of the curriculum which, as Maurice Holt pointed out, exposed most baldly the order of priorities which determine a school's strategies. Henbury had always taken pride in its ability to fit the curriculum to the individual rather than the individual to the curriculum. The price paid was an increasingly complicated process of negotiation over fourth-year choice so that the majority of pupils could be offered choices within a range from those taking nine GCE 'O' levels to those struggling to achieve four CSE Grades. Private study had been introduced as a positive option to make this complex pattern possible. This had been introduced by the deputy (curriculum), Peter Dines, in 1967, following a lecture given at Bristol University by Dr Lloyd-Trump (Lloyd-Trump 1968) on the role of the teacher in educational change. By 1977 it had become a curriculum mechanism as the situational analysis showed.

Maurice Holt put forward various suggestions as to the way ahead and one of his suggestions was for a common curriculum pattern.

A real root-and-branch job
It needs a strong stomach to face this. It is a question of grasping the nettle of the whole curriculum very firmly, and following through its implications for a broad curriculum centred on a selection from our culture rather than a collection of separate subjects. I have yet to be convinced that this can be done with conventional core + option schemes. The unmistakable implication, I think, is a much bigger core with far fewer option columns; and the core, because it is based on a holistic view of education, is bound to have the lineaments of a genuine faculty structure. (As opposed to one which has been introduced to facilitate administration, or make timetabling easier.)

Providing the staff could establish a consensus on such an approach, the necessary planning could go ahead in and between departments with a view to initiating a curriculum along these lines in the first year in, perhaps, September 1979 or 1980. There is no doubt that basic issues about curriculum aims and pupil choice are bound to arise, even if reform is confined to a less daring strategy. Whole-hoggers might therefore be tempted to push the argument further and advocate a more drastic reform. In the long run, my own view is that this would have great advantages; but in the short and medium term, the problems generated would call for a distinct shift of attitude in many camps.

I put forward an additional strategy in response to these suggestions:

Individual strength through curriculum diversity
1. I suggest that we move towards a more consistent blocking of subjects. This might mean a slightly narrower option choice.
2. I suggest we explore teaching the core subjects in two populations – A and Alpha.
3. I suggest we explore the possibility of providing an option across two columns which would be made up of integrated science + a craft.
4. I suggest that we build on the Bruner hypothesis and explore the levels at which subjects are offered in the columns. Such a move would mean that the 'Learning for Living' enclave could be phased out.
5. I suggest we take a very firm approach to private study as a positive learning situation.

I then followed this up with a paper (Figure 8.1) which suggested a way in which we could move the remedial groups into the main options and so make more effective use of teaching staff. By the fourth and fifth years the groups in the remedial area were small in numbers and correspondingly costly in staffing terms.

In practical terms this led to the change on the fourth-year option sheet shown by comparison between the option sheet of 1977 (Figure 8.2) and that of 1978 (Figure 8.3). A planned piecemeal change thus arose out of the curriculum review and was implemented.

In 1978 I produced a short paper on Henbury School and the 1980s. This

Figure 8.1 Operational Fourth-Year Breakthrough – suggested fourth-year options 1978

1	2	3 HUMANITY	4 SCIENCE	5 DESIGN	6	7	8
ENGLISH LANGUAGE & LITERATURE	MATHS						

One of:
History
Geography
RE

One of:
Chemistry
Physics
Biology
Integrated Science*

One of:
Home Economics
Dress
Art
Technical Design
Technical Drawing
Motor Engineering
Music

One of:
French
Commerce
Computer Science
A Science
A Humanity
Typing

One of:
German
Commerce
Computer Science
A Science
A Humanity
Technology
Drama
Art
Dress

One of:
German
Latin
A Science
A Humanity
Private Study
Integrated Science*

Notes

1. I propose that the section left of the double line be regarded as the section in which we allow students to make clearly *guided* choice. Those taking 'integrated science' must also take integrated science in column eight.
2. Right of the line is the option sector. Constraints will only be:
   (i) the number of places available
   (ii) a realistic assessment of a student's capacity
3. Integrated science will include four periods in which a good course could be developed from the experience gained by the 'Learning for Living' team.
4. This breakthrough is possible only because Mike Waters, director of studies, has ingeniously devised an eight-period block in which we can place technology, drama, art and dress.
5. Detailed costing in teacher periods will be our next move but I believe the scheme can work provided that we accept the principle of guided choice left of the line!

Colin Bayne-Jardine 24.1.1978

paper was intended to encourage a continuing review of the curriculum along the lines outlined by Douglas Barnes (1982).

Henbury School and the eighties
With this general background and the piecemeal changes that have been made during our curriculum review it is possible to suggest the areas in which future developments will take place.

1. *The curriculum framework*
Changes will make it possible to arrange two sections in Years 1, 2 and 3. These sections will follow parallel courses and not only ease timetabling but also bring the pastoral and academic organizations more in line.
The fourth-year programme will become more clearly a common core with a smaller elective area.

2. *The horizontal curriculum network*
Subject teachers have clearly expressed an interest in learning about the subjects taught to a year group by colleagues. It is intended to encourage this interest and so develop a more coherent curriculum year by year.

3. *The pattern of the curriculum*
The curriculum committee plans to set up a working party to report upon the overall pattern of the first-year curriculum. Parents and the community to be encouraged to give their views.

4. *Classroom management*
Clear interest in improving effectiveness in the classroom suggests that subject teachers will be reviewing their subject matter and their methods in the classroom. An in-service day is being devoted to this area in July.

5. *Sixth form*
'N and F' proposals are under discussion as is the Avon staffing policy for one-year sixth formers. Changes in the curriculum will emerge from this debate.

6. *Pupils on roll*
The decline in numbers on roll has not yet hit us at Henbury but we are joining with officers of the LEA to calculate the impact upon our present curriculum of a shrinking school in the eighties.

The process had completed one cycle but during the cyclical process other cycles had started. In many ways this process is untidy. With hindsight it can be made to appear more carefully planned than it was in reality. Importunate demands are made on schools. Declining numbers on roll are the obvious change factor for the immediate future. In many ways the most important result of this particular curriculum review was that we explored ways of working together as a staff in an open climate and this has given us a more flexible way in which to respond to change (Gray 1982). We are now making regular situational analyses, reviewing objectives, and designing plans for implementation. The weakest point in this process is still the evaluation as we find we have little time to do this, particularly as the show

Figure 8.2

FOURTH-YEAR OPTIONS FORM, MARCH 1977
(For pupils in 3A and 3 Alpha)

Name.................................. House..................

1	2	3	4	5	6	7	8
ENGLISH LANGUAGE & LITERATURE	MATHEMATICS	HUMANITY	DESIGN	SCIENCE			INTEGRATED SCIENCE / LEARNING FOR LIVING

Column 3 — *One of:* History, Geography, RE

Column 4 — *Leave blank now. Choice to be made in May from:* Home Economics, Dress, Art, Technical Design, Technical Drawing, Motor Engineering, Drama

Column 5 — *One of:* Chemistry, Physics, Biology

Column 6 — *One of:* French, Commerce, Computer Studies, A Science, A Humanity, Music, Technical Drawing, Road Science, Dress

Column 7 — *One of:* Latin, Commerce, Computer Studies, A Science, A Humanity, German, Music

Column 8 (Integrated Science) — *One of:* History, Geography, PE, Dress, Technical Drawing, Road Science, Typing

Column 8 (Learning for Living) — *One of:* Private Study, Typing, German, A Science, A Humanity

Career intention (if known)................................ Parent's signature ....

Date Returned	Checked by Tutor	Approved by Head of House	Interview with parents	Interview with pupil	Course entered
			Date:	Date:	Date:

Figure 8.3

FOURTH-YEAR OPTIONS FORM, FEB/MARCH 1978

Name..................
House..................

1	2	3	4	5	6	7	8
ENGLISH LANGUAGE & LITERATURE	MATHEMATICS	HUMANITY	SCIENCE	DESIGN			
				1st Choice............ 2nd Choice............			
		One of: History Geography RE	*One of:* Chemistry Physics Biology Integrated Science	*1st and 2nd choice to be made from:* Home Economics Dress Art Technical Studies Technical Drawing Motor Engineering Music	*One of:* French German Commerce Computer Science A Science A Humanity Typing	*One of:* French German Commerce Computer Science A Science A Humanity Typing Art Cookery Needlecraft Drama Technical Drawing Woodwork Technology	*One of:* Private Study Integrated Science* German Latin Typing A Science A Humanity Art Cookery Needlecraft Drama Technical Drawing Woodwork Technology

Career intention (if known) .... Parent's Signature..................

Date Returned	Checked by Tutor	Approved by Head of House	Interview with parents	Interview with pupil	Course entered
			Date:	Date:	Date:

must go on. Perhaps we can only evaluate by listening for the applause whilst counting the box office receipts! The curtain has certainly been raised on the curriculum process and developments must be made openly during the next decade. This account is an attempt to outline a review made in one secondary school in the hope that it may help others engaged in a similar process.

References

Barnes, D. (1982) *Practical Curriculum Study*, London: Routledge and Kegan Paul.
Baron, G. (1975) Some aspects of the 'Headmaster Tradition', *Management in Education Reader I*, London: Ward Lock.
Becher, T. and Maclure, S. (1978) *The Politics of Curriculum Change*, London: Hutchinson.
Bruner, J.S. (1960) *The Process of Education*, Cambridge, Mass: Harvard University Press.
Gray, H.L. (ed.) (1982) *The Management of Educational Institutions*, Lewes, Sussex: Falmer Press.
Halpin, A.W. (1966) *Theory and Research in Administration*, New York: Macmillan.
Hargreaves, D.H. (1982) *The Challenge for the Comprehensive School*, London: Routledge and Kegan Paul.
Holt, M. (1978) *The Common Curriculum*, London: Routledge and Kegan Paul.
Hoyle, E. (1969) *The Role of the Teacher*, London: Routledge and Kegan Paul.
Lawton, D. (1973) *Social Change, Educational Theory and Curriculum Planning*, London: Hodder and Stoughton.
Lloyd-Trump, J. (1968) *The Role of the Teacher in Educational Change*, University of Bristol Institute of Education paper.
Milne, A.A. (1926) *Winnie the Pooh*, London: Methuen.
Musgrove, F. (1971) *Patterns of Power and Authority in English Education*, London: Methuen.
Walton, J. (ed.) (1971) *Curriculum Organisation and Design*, London: Ward Lock.
Warwick, D. (1975) *Curriculum Structure and Design*, London: University of London.
Whitfield, R.C. (1971) *Disciplines of the Curriculum*, Maidenhead, Berkshire: McGraw Hill.

The school-based review took place against the background of the following government and Schools Council publications given in chronological order:
Schools Council (1975) Working Paper 53: *The Whole Curriculum 13–16*, London: Evans.
Department of Education and Science (1977) *Education in Schools, A Consultative Document*, London: HMSO.
Department of Education and Science (1977a) *Curriculum 11–16*, Working Paper by HM Inspectorate.
Consultative Committee on the Curriculum (1977) *The Structure of the Curriculum in*

the Third and Fourth Years of the Scottish Secondary School (Munn Report), Edinburgh: HMSO.
Department of Education and Science (1980) *A Framework for the School Curriculum*, London: HMSO.
Department of Education and Science (1980a) *A View of the Curriculum*, London: HMSO.
Department of Education and Science/Welsh Office (1981) *The School Curriculum*, London: HMSO.
Schools' Council (1981) Working Paper 70: *The Practical Curriculum*, London: Methuen.

CHAPTER 9

THE ROLE OF THE HEADTEACHER IN THE MANAGEMENT OF CHANGE
Elsa Davies

School improvement The dynamic nature of education subsumes the existence of a natural and spontaneous force for improvement. This constant and continuing drive for change needs positive encouragement and support, yet it is more often impeded by other forces at work in education. These obstructive forces manifest themselves in many ways from rigid examination systems to the habit, tradition and ritual associated with formally organized learning. In order to overcome these forces schools need first to become aware of them and their debilitating effect upon improvement, and secondly to devise strategies for nurturing the in-built desire to improve practice. As the urgency for major change in education increases, teachers need to acquire expertise in examining current practice, in responding constructively in areas where shortfall is revealed, in building new, purposeful programmes, and, most of all, in questioning critically the quality and relevance of experiences presented to the learner. Although it is important for all teachers to be involved in questioning the educational status quo, the main responsibility for managing school improvement lies with the headteacher, who holds a key position within the school's authority structure. This chapter sets out to take a serious and practical look at some of the issues facing school administrators involved in managing change and in doing so, aims to draw out positive factors significant in supporting successful change.

Can the headteacher be an effective manager of change? Before embarking on an analysis of the positive influences a headteacher can have on the change process, it is worth while looking at some of the limitations pertaining to the role of the head as a manager of change. These limitations are evident at two stages in the innovation process, that is, at the time of adoption of the new idea or practice and also during its implementation within the school.

(i) One of the most common assumptions in the literature on educational change and also in practice, is that the headteacher can be an effective change agent (Bolam 1974) successfully introducing an innovation to a school. The essence of this assumption is correct providing the lasting success of the innovation is not under discussion. It has always been open to headteachers to use power-coercive strategies to achieve change but few would deny that change by these means, without the involvement and commitment of the teachers, is shallow and transient. As democratic procedures grow within schools, staff groups are more likely to respond critically to innovative ideas, judging them on their merits, where once they might have acceded publicly to an authoritarian decision only to ignore it in the privacy of the classroom. Such openness is healthy but it can lead to difficulties for the headteacher in initiating ideas personally. This was so at one school where the headteacher wished to involve parents more in school decision making. After the idea had been tentatively broached that staff meetings might be opened to parents, a well-justified and professional case was made by the staff for retaining the privacy of staff meetings. However, providing positions are not allowed to become entrenched, such an innovative style can have a positive effect. It can create a situation where compromise is acceptable and, following through the example given, it led directly to the formation of a 'School Policy Group' with open membership (Davies 1983).

(ii) The question also arises regarding the effect of a headteacher's negative response to a proposed scheme. An interesting incident arose at a meeting of the previously mentioned 'School Policy Group' when the matter of school sports was raised on the agenda. Despite the explicit reservations of the headteacher regarding competitive races for young children, a policy decision was taken to proceed with a sports event. Not only did the sports turn out to be a notable improvement on previous events but it was so sensitively organized that it was instrumental in convincing the head and the staff that it was a worthwhile and enriching experience for the children. If, despite or instead of the policy decision, the headteacher had taken an autocratic decision against the sports, there could have been no improvement. As it was, the head's clear concern acted as a spur in ensuring that the whole event was organized to enhance the children's educational experience. Although this particular issue concerned an area which was relatively easily negotiable, it remains to be seen whether a deliberate policy of headteacher opposition to innovation is an effective method for encouraging improvement in other possibly more delicate curricular areas.

(*iii*) The second limitation of a school administrator's ability to innovate occurs at the implementation stage of innovation. When a headteacher is involved in operating the innovation it can lead to a position where staff members may find it difficult to initiate the necessary adjustments to the plans for improvement as the change proceeds. The net effect of this is to reduce teacher enthusiasm which, in turn, leads to a token approach and eventual unsuccessful change. Evidence of this phenomenon is illustrated by the gradual failure of a cooperative scheme involving a primary and secondary school in liaison over a child care and development course. One reason for the failure was undoubtedly the primary teachers' perception of the programme as being outside their sphere of control. Despite careful planning by the primary headteacher, through whom the liaison was arranged, and despite efforts to involve the primary staff as tutors to the secondary school pupils, the course never achieved more than marginal success and eventually foundered. Similar evidence of the effect of a headteacher's involvement in operating an innovation is revealed clearly by Shipman (1974) in his evaluation of the Keele Integrated Studies Project.

The more positive aspect of the headteacher's role in relation to the process of curriculum improvement is that, by virtue of not engaging too closely in the initiation and operation of projects, the head can become a balancing factor between the supporters of change and the negative reactions resulting from confusion in other teachers; the important point being that the headteacher is acting as the manager of the change process rather than as the change agent.

Factors contributing to success As a background to studying the positive action which a headteacher can take to encourage and support improvement, it is worth while looking briefly at three factors which can contribute to successful change.

(*i*) The first factor it is helpful for the school administrator to appreciate is the linkage between effective school improvement and the context within which the innovation occurs. The successful introduction of a major change in the language development programme of one primary school was aided by a relatively long period of stability and a shorter period of organizational and small-scale change. During the stable period an impetus for change was created and the brief but busy period of minor changes encouraged staff confidence in adopting and adapting new procedures and practices to suit the needs of the school.

(*ii*) Secondly, the school administrator needs to be aware of the inhibiting nature of major change in a specific area of school life, and of the influence of other simultaneous changes taking place within the school. The particular example of a major change in a school's language development programme illustrates both these features. Not only did the large-scale language development change inhibit any successful innovative activity in the academic curriculum for a number of years, but the change itself was considerably complemented by other changes, for example in the school's policy towards parental involvement and in the attitudinal and organizational changes in pupil assessment procedures.

(*iii*) In addition to the contextual issues, it is useful for the school administrator to realize the effect exerted by the nature of the change itself. Where the innovation is relatively vague, unstructured or ill-defined, such as the adoption of a policy of subject integration or of collaborative teaching, it is more difficult for teachers to transform it into a practical reality in the classroom. On the other hand, structured schemes, such as published skills teaching programmes in language or mathematics, have greater chance of success because they can carry more criticism without failing. The feedback mechanisms, which it is frequently easier to build into structured schemes, enable the continuing adjustment of the innovative practice to the learner's needs. Where this happens and teachers perceive the innovation as a valid and relevant learning device, their confidence in coping with the criticism and interest of those outside the programme is enhanced and the possibility for improvement in practice is increased.

More positively, the role of the headteacher in relation to change is to create conditions within the school which will welcome, nurture and support change. An extensive literature exists on ways in which change enters schools, but personal experience supports Gray and Coulson's explanation (1982) that major change happens unexpectedly rather than according to plan. The aforementioned language development programme provides an apt illustration of this point on two counts. The new scheme was introduced to the school through an accidental misunderstanding consequent upon the head and the deputy-headteacher seeking to increase their professional knowledge in a particular curricular area. It also brought with it, unknowingly, a major change in the school's approach to the teaching of reading. The adoption of the new scheme was natural and spontaneous and the new philosophy flourished as a result of favourable conditions within the school.

As a key role holder in the school, the headteacher is in a prime position to affect two areas of school organization which are vital in supporting natural change. The first of these areas concerns the structure of the school, which may be broadly defined as the framework within which people interact for a specific range of purposes, one of which is the improvement of practice. Schools where rigidity exists in areas such as timetabling and pupil grouping, allow little freedom for teachers to reorganize the environment to embrace and experience change. Where a more flexible school structure is found, teacher initiative can flourish. The opportunity for this to happen is crucial, for change is introduced to schools through people and is sustained by their interaction (Esland 1972). In a school which had a relatively high proportion of pupils with emotional difficulties, timetables were adjusted, class groups temporarily reorganized and additional teaching space explored on the initiative of one teacher sensitive to the needs of these particular children. This initiative in the field of educational counselling was sustained with the cooperation of the staff group and proved valuable to the pupils concerned and, in the longer term, extremely effective in relation to the attitude and response of the staff to pupils with special needs. Had the flexibility to organize such a group not been present, the impetus and enthusiasm for this worthwhile project might have been dampened and extinguished through delay. However, as much as it is the responsibility of the administrator to arrange for flexibility within the school, it is equally important to balance flexibility with both the stability and participatory decision-making strategies needed for successful change.

The other area of school organization significant in a headteacher's management of the change process is the nature of authority within the school. Strong hierarchical patterns of authority, which limit an individual teacher's scope for innovative action, are less conducive to large-scale school improvement. Where schools are organized along more participative and democratic lines, the authority placed in the group of professional equals creates greater opportunity for change. A headteacher can work to develop the quality, interaction and expertise within this staff group. Alongside a policy of individual career review and prospect in a staff development programme, a headteacher can arrange professional enrichment experiences for staff individually or in groups. One such scheme involved a headteacher in exchanging roles with a classteacher for up to a week. Although not designed for specific school improvement, it complemented change through the background of experience it provided within the staff group. Another scheme involved teachers in structuring classes for each academic year. Serious attempts of this nature to equalize the authority within the school encourage creativity, independence of thought and extended professional responsibility for the work of the school. Important advantages of collaborative policy making include the nourishment of individual talents through collegial support and the development of professional confidence. This greater professionality in outlook generates the constructive self-criticism needed to spur teachers into examining and improving practice. In one school this self-critical approach resulted in a questioning of the purpose of its pupil assessment procedures. As a consequence, individual assessment was changed to increase its relevance to the learner and the pupil record system was reorganized as a working document involving teachers, pupils and their parents.

In aiming for a position where mutual interpersonal respect is found amongst staff, the headteacher provides opportunity for opinion leaders to emerge in various areas of school life. It is from these internal change agents that spontaneous change often springs and upon them that it depends during its early period in the school. Although external change agents may offer expertise in a certain area of education, internal change agents offer a greater chance for innovative success. This is because an internal change agent's position is determined, not by expert subject knowledge, but by influence within the staff group and through the quality of interpersonal relationships built up. Consequently, it is more appropriate to regard an internal change agent as a person able to influence staff opinion – an opinion leader. In the case of the language development change, two strong opinion leaders emerged during the pilot study period and supported the innovation during its early years in the school. Another example concerned the successful introduction of a new approach to music teaching which resulted from the influence of a respected teacher on the staff group. However, the important emphasis needs to be placed on the role of the headteacher in laying the foundation for successful curricular improvement through providing conditions suitable for opinion leaders to emerge and to work effectively.

It has been shown that self-examination – of its procedures and practices – is an important activity for every school. To encourage such activity, many local education authorities have followed the lead of the Inner London Education Authority in using some formalized framework for structuring review. In some authorities, it takes the form of a series of questions arranged in sections on broad areas of school activity. In other authorities, it is a more subject-oriented curriculum report coupled with external oversight. Although it can be helpful to look at a school's activity with the aid of a structured framework, these formalized procedures may not be effective as instigators of major educational change. Their summative nature and external origin are unlikely to engender the degree of enthusiasm, commitment and involvement necessary for significant innovation. Their real value lies, first, in the opportunity created for teachers to think in depth about their work and, secondly, in the arenas provided for the release of tensions and exchange of ideas. The latter was precisely what happened when a particular primary school tested part of a school review document for one local education authority. After considerable discussion and an apparent will for improvement in the areas of nonteaching staff and home–school relationships, no significant improvement on current practice occurred. However, provided headteachers are aware of the danger of structure stifling flexibility, sensitive use of such devices may promote some change. It remains to be seen whether the incremental nature of the minor changes which may result will contribute to major educational improvement.

Often omitted from studies of educational change is a consideration of the headteacher's need for support, in a moral rather than in a practical sense, from colleagues and nonprofessional persons associated with the school. This moral support is vital because any new scheme or practice has an element of risk attached to it. External support affects the structure of the school through its influence on the headteacher's leadership style. Where a headteacher lacks this support from other colleagues, such as local authority advisers, and from school governors and other lay persons, little or no risk will be taken with innovation.

The vast literature on the management of change aims to help teachers understand the nature and process of innovation. Although in some areas the emphasis on the complexities of school improvement can be counterproductive, there are aspects of the literature which can support headteachers in managing change. A good example in this case is the description of the 'waves of difficulty' (Nisbet 1974) facing innovators. This theoretical background knowledge helped a primary school headteacher support staff through the difficult initial stages of a collaborative teaching project. They were helped to rationalize and come to terms with the confusion and chaos which the new scheme brought, on learning that these were naturally occurring stages on the way to improved practice. Appreciating the need to build in evaluation from the outset can also help school administrators cope with situations where conflict arises over the effectiveness of change.

Professional learning In seeking to nurture and promote the natural force for improvement which exists in schools, an appropriate professional response for headteachers is to investigate the positive aspects of their role in the process of innovation. As managers of change, school administrators should aim to develop conditions which encourage teachers to be more self-critical in their approach to the task, and to give them the support and freedom to solve curricular problems as they perceive them. Such experiential professional learning (Gray and Coulson 1982) goes hand in hand with the headteacher's role as the facilitator, supporter and coordinator of the innovation process. If teachers learn through experiencing the process of change, their new confidence and increased professional approach will lead to a healthy and continuing questioning of the status quo. This in turn leads to the reappraisal, renewal and reorganization of the innovation and current practice within the school. In this way and as a result of sensitive administration and leadership, the creative school is discovered and the improvement of education becomes achievable.

References

Bolam, R. (1974) *Planned Educational Change – Theory and Practice*, A report on a project funded by the DES. Unpublished.

Davies, E. (1983) Parental involvement in school policy making, *Educational Management and Administration*, vol. 11, no. 2.

Esland, G. (1972) Innovation in the school, *in* Seaman, P. et al. *Innovation and Ideology*, Open University Course E282 Units 11–14, Milton Keynes: Open University Press.

Gray, H. and Coulson, A.A. (1982) Teacher education management and the facilitation of change, *Educational Change and Development*, vol. 4, no. 1, Summer.

Nisbet, J. (1974) Innovation – bandwagon or hearse? *in* Harris, A. et al. (eds) *Curriculum Innovation*, London: Croom Helm.

Shipman, M.D. (1974) *Inside a Curriculum Project*, London, Methuen.

CHAPTER 10

PROBLEM SOLVING VIA A SCHOOLS SUPPORT SERVICE
Robert Crone

Elmhill is an 850-strong coeducational secondary modern school situated in an industrial and dormitory town, ten miles outside Belfast. Since it opened in 1974, Elmhill has been involved in two school staff and curriculum development projects based in the Department of Further Professional Studies in Education, Queen's University Belfast.

The Northern Ireland Schools Curriculum Project 1973–1978 (Crone and Malone 1979) and the Schools Support Service 1978–1982 (Crone and Malone 1983), funded by the Department of Education and local education authorities, were directed by a former secondary school principal and notable figure in Irish education, the late John Malone. Both projects were staffed by practising teachers, seconded for periods of one to four years, full or part-time, from their posts as heads of departments or senior managers in local schools. The Schools Curriculum Project and Schools Support Service adopted a reformist ideology and saw their role as assisting teachers to realize goals already in the education system but which, for one reason or another, schools were having difficulty in achieving. The fact that both projects operated during a decade of unprecedented community violence and social upheaval intensified and made more urgent the tasks local schools faced in undertaking organizational and curricular renewal aimed at ensuring they remained significant institutions to, and influences on, the province's young people. The school-based action programmes undertaken by the Schools Curriculum Project and Schools Support Service staff in association with teams of teachers in local secondary schools may therefore be seen in the context of the wider school review and improvement movement which seeks to confront organizational and curriculum problems common to most education systems in the developed world (OECD/CERI 1982).

Elmhill, as a new school, whose principal had been senior master in the secondary school of which the projects' director had been headmaster, and which had seconded teachers to and appointed staff from the Schools Curriculum Project and Schools Support Service, identified closely with the ideas, practices and personnel of both projects. Malcolm Skilbeck, in his personal study of the Schools Support Service (Skilbeck 1982) described Elmhill as 'a model experimental institution' which tried out and created many of the action programmes disseminated more widely in schools across the province.

The practical tasks associated with school review were undertaken at the weekly timetabled planning meetings by teachers engaged in school-based action programmes in collaboration with project staff. Project field officers participated as colleagues and on occasions team leaders at these meetings, sharing in teachers' diagnosis of school needs and their review of relevant organizational and curricular issues. This collaboration between project field officers and school staff extended to actual shared participation in the processes of implementation, including syllabus-building activities, team teaching in the classroom, assistance with design and reprographic facilities, and conducting pupil and teacher opinion polls on planned innovations as part of ongoing formative evaluation and the projects' commitment to action research.

The field officers may therefore be seen as:

- colleagues sharing with school staff responsibility for all the stages in curriculum development from design to evaluation, as well as for outcomes achieved in terms of pupil learning;
- change agents able to respond flexibly, urgently and imaginatively to individual teachers' current classroom needs and school organizational patterns;
- representatives of an external school support service willing to provide the continuous long-term support required by major staff and curriculum development programmes – in most cases this support includes weekly participation by field officers in timetabled planning meetings for a period of three to four years;
- unthreatening, nonjudgemental catalysts for curriculum change – the field officers as members of a university-based action-research team are perceived as having an independent status quite distinct from power-coercive representatives of local education authorities or Department of Education inspectors.

The field officers' role as collegial, nonjudgemental change agents attempted to combine recognition of the teachers' central role in curriculum development, and the uniqueness of individual school situations, with systematic and regular access to the best of practice from other schools, insights from contemporary innovations in curriculum pedagogy, and greater awareness of relevant findings available in current educational research. This concept of the school-based educational worker was not without its antecedents in the history of school change and curriculum development. Martin Shipman (Shipman 1974), writing of the coordinators of the Schools Council Integrated Studies Project based at Keele University, commented on the overwhelming approval of the work of the coordinators by the teachers in the schools, noting that 'these seconded teachers rapidly adapted to the role of curriculum development change agents'. Maurice Holt, also commenting on the Keele strategies, noted 'the advantages of independence for the co-ordinators were not on the staff of the school, nor employed by an agency like the LEA or DES with a power coercive function however attenuated. Their allegiance was to the project, that is to the process of change in some established way.'

Elmhill's director of studies, and author of this case-study, worked as a field officer for four years with the Schools Support Service and its predecessor, the Schools Curriculum Project. The director of studies, in conjunction with the Support Service's director, had been responsible for piloting through a series of organizational and curriculum innovations including:

- intensive reading development and numeracy programmes in Years 1 and 2;
- school guidance and home liaison procedures whereby pupils' pastoral and academic welfare became the responsibility of a class tutor throughout their school career;
- a review of school reporting and assessment procedures on the basis of the personal achievement of each pupil taught in mixed-ability class groups.

Two major outcomes of the school's long-term involvement with the Schools Support Service had been (1) *the creation of an open organizational climate responsive to curriculum reappraisal and development and* (2) *the acquisition among a wide range of staff of the skills and expertise necessary for undertaking problem-solving tasks aimed at school improvement*, defined as 'an attempt by a school to implement an innovation with the ultimate aim of producing positively valuable changes in student learning outcomes, in teachers' skills and attitudes, and in institutional functioning' (OECD/ CERI 1982).

In the Christmas term of 1981 the writer and another senior teacher undertook a review of the school curriculum at the principal's request. For the purpose of this Chapter, *curriculum* will refer to the planned learning experiences offered to pupils on the timetable, and *organization* to the methods of grouping pupils for learning and the procedures adopted for pastoral guidance in schools. This involved interviewing all heads of departments about their perceptions of the curriculum and the specific needs of their subject departments. Heads of departments were also asked for their views on the planned curriculum in the light of:

– an educational climate which increasingly encouraged all children to pursue science/technology courses throughout their secondary education
  – comments from our own careers staff, former pupils and parents encouraged school-based attempts to remodel the 'cafeteria' option design – there was a growing commitment among staff to the idea of 'education for capability';
– dissatisfaction expressed by some staff about the discontinuity which existed between the broadly based courses offered to all pupils in the junior school and the narrow specialism encouraged by the cafeteria design of the fourth and fifth-year option system (Table 10.1).

This option sheet permitted pupils at 14 to specialize entirely, and often on sexist lines, in humanities, scientific, or vocational areas of experience. The option sheet made explicit the stereotyping of types of pupil and fostered sexist divisions in subjects studied – boys doing woodwork, motor vehicle studies, metalwork and graphic communication, and girls studying shorthand, childcare, commerce and home economics. This practice was at odds with the school's declared intention to offer all children throughout the five years of compulsory secondary schooling a 'comprehensive' education which included breadth as well as depth of study. (See Ch. 5)

As a first step towards creating a curriculum design that would permit pupils to follow a five-year, broadly based general education the fourth and fifth-year option sheet was redesigned (Table 10.2) to enable every pupil to choose one course of study from the following 'core' areas of experience: English, mathematics, humanities, science, technology, arts and design. A 'bias' group was included to permit pupils to choose an additional course of study from one area of experience of their choice.

A much more difficult problem thrown up by the curriculum review was the sexually differentiated experience offered to boys and girls throughout Years 1, 2 and 3. Boys studied CDT and graphic communication while girls

Table 10.1 Original fourth and fifth-year option sheet

ENGLISH (G)	MATHS (G)	GROUP I	GROUP II	GROUP III	GROUP IV
ENGLISH (S)	MATHS (S)	HISTORY (G) (S) PHYSICS (G) (S) WOODWORK (S) SHORTHAND MUSIC (S) ART (G)	GEOGRAPHY (G) (S) CHEMISTRY (G) (S) METALWORK (G) MOTOR VEH. ST. (S) CHILD CARE (S) TYPEWRITING PHYS. ED. (S)	RELIG. ED. FRENCH (G) (S) BIOLOGY (G) (S) TECH. DRAW. (G) (S) COMMERCE (S) ART APPRECIATION	SOCIOLOGY (G) (S) ADDTL. MATHS (G) WOODWORK (G) METALWORK (S) COOKERY (G) (S) ART (G) (S)
8 periods	7 periods	6 periods	6 periods	6 periods	6 periods

(G) GCE (S) CSE

Table 10.2 Redesigned fourth and fifth-year option sheet

Option Sheet: Areas of Experience Model: 140 Coeducational Year Group

ENGLISH (G) (S)	MATHS (G) (S)	HUMANITIES	SCIENCE	TECHNOLOGY	ARTS & DESIGN	BIAS
		HISTORY G.S. GEOG. G.S. FRENCH R.E.	PHYSICS G.S. BIOLOGY G.S. GEOLOGY GEN. SC.	TECH. G,S H. ECON. G,S COMP. ST. G,S TYPING	C.T.D. G ART G,S HIST. OF ART G G. COMMUNI- CATION S MUSIC	SOCIOLOGY G,S. CHEMISTRY G,S G. COMMUNI- CATION G,S COMMERCE

(G) GCE (S) CSE

Table 10.3 The original curriculum relating to forms 1–3 with a six-form intake
Subject/period distribution
(based on the figures supplied for the school year 1981/82 plus an additional form)

1st Form	English	Maths	Science	Soc. S.	French	Relig. Ed.	Graphics (Boys)	C.D.T. (Boys)	Home Ec. (Girls)	Craft	Music	Phys. Ed.
	7 +1 Lib	7	5	5	5	2	1	2	3	3	2	4
6 form	48	42	40	30	30	12	6	12	18	24	12	36
	12 TT	12 TT	(4T–3C)	(TT = team teaching)						12HE+		(3T–2C)
	+41R	12R		(R = remedial) (Lib = library)						12 Art		
Totals	101	66	40	30	30	12	6	12	18	24	12	36

Total curriculum periods form 1 = 387: Average distribution/form = $\frac{387}{6}$ = 64.5 periods – 44 period week
Reasons: Remedial work, team teaching, division of classes to accommodate ministry regulations i.e. Science, Art, P.E.

2nd Form	English	Maths	Science P.B.C.	S.S.	French	R.E.	G.C.(B)	C.D.T.(B)	H.E.(G)	Art	Music	P.E.
	6	6	6	5	5	2	2	4	6	3	2	3
6 forms	36	36	48	30	30	12	12	24	36	27	18	27
	12TT	12TT	(4T–3C)								1 TT	(3T–2C)
	15R	7R										
	63	55	48	30	30	12	12	24	36	27	18	27

Total curriculum periods form 2 = 382: Average distribution/form = $\frac{382}{6}$ = 63.66 periods

3rd Form	English	Maths	Science P.B.C.	S.S.	French	R.E.	G.C.(B)	C.D.T.(B)	H.E.(G)	Art	Music	P.E.
	6	6	6	6	5	2	2	4	6	3	2	2
6 forms	36	36	54	36	10 (2 groups)	12	12	24	36	27	18	18
			(3T–2C)		5 (groups) XM 5 A 5 CS 5 XE 10					(3T–2C)	1 TT	(3T–2C)
	10R	5R +5CS								+ 5		
	46	46	54	36	10	12	12	24	36	32	18	18

Total curriculum periods form 3 = 344: Average distribution/form = $\frac{344}{6}$ = 57.3 periods were block-timetabled for home economics and needlework. The school's senior staff in seeking to offer all subjects to all pupils in Years 1–3 thought of (1) a rotating timetable in these sexually differentiated subjects (2) one or two-year 'terminal' courses for boys and girls in each of the subjects concerned. However neither solution was satisfactory, either from a timetabling point of view, or in terms of adequate time for laying a foundation for boys and girls seeking to pursue any of the subjects to examination level in Years 4 and 5.

It was at this point the school's senior teachers called on the help of the director of the Schools Support Service. A former headmaster himself, the director was presented with the information contained in Table 10.3 concerning the curriculum design and staffing of Elmhill's curriculum in the first three years.

The Support Service's director noted how 'expensive' in teacher time the school's sexually differentiated curriculum was. For example, 64.5 teacher periods were needed to cover one first-form class in a 44-period week. This was due to a variety of factors including withdrawal groups for pupils with difficulties in basic skills, splitting of classes for practicals, and team teaching in English and mathematics. The director suggested senior staff carried out an investigation of the expense, in terms of teacher time, of offering a sexually undifferentiated curriculum to an *eight-form* entry of 180 first-form pupils. If this could be done then a class group could be taught as a unit and offered all subjects on the curriculum. This would strengthen class identity, reduce class size by one-third in English, maths, history, geography, music and RE, and bring the academic arrangements for teaching subjects into line with the pastoral organization (a form tutor responsible for a single class group). The senior teachers carried out this research and produced the curriculum design shown in Table 10.4.

What the Support Service director had done was to look at the curriculum problem from a new angle. While the senior teachers had attempted to solve the problem within the framework of the *existing* curriculum design, the Support Service director broke the mould. As one of the senior teachers commented, 'It's rather like deciding how to get a brazil nut from its shell. We, thinking convergently, would apply pressure from outside, smash the shell and run the risk of crushing the nut inside. The Support Service's director, on the other hand, thinking divergently, might solve the problem by drilling a hole in the shell, and applying pressure from inside to break the shell without damage to the nut.'

The outcome of this particular curriculum review, initiated by the school

Table 10.4 The proposed curriculum relating to all pupils for forms 1–3 for a pupil intake of 160–180 pupils Subject/period distribution

1st Form	English	Maths	Science P.B.C.	S.S.	French	R.E.	G.C.	C.D.T.	H.E.	Art	Music	P.E.
8 forms	8	7	6	4	3	2	0	3	4	2	2	3
	24TT	16TT										
Totals	88	72	48	32	24	16	0	24	32	16	16	24

Total curriculum periods form 1 = 368: Average distribution/form = $\frac{392}{8}$ = 49 periods — 44 period week

2nd Form	English	Maths	Science P.B.C.	S.S.	French	R.E.	G.C.	C.D.T.	H.E.	Art	Music	P.E.
8 forms	7	6	6	4	3	2	2	3	4	2	2	3
		16TT										
Totals	72	48	48	32	24	16	16	24	32	16	16	24

Total curriculum periods form 2 = 360: Average distribution/form = $\frac{368}{8}$ = 46 periods

3rd Form	English	Maths	Science 2 from P.B.C.	S.S.	French	R.E.	G.C.	C.D.T.	H.E.	Art	Music	P.E.
8 forms	6	6	6	5	3	2	2	3	4	3	2	2
					(2C+3T)							
					9 + 18							
Totals	48	48	48	40	27	16	16	24	32	24	16	16

Total curriculum periods form 3 = 355: Average distribution/form = $\frac{355}{8}$ = 44.4 periods itself, supported by an external change agent at a critical point, was the creation of a five-year curriculum design which offered a common curriculum experience to every pupil for the first three years of secondary schooling and permitted pupils to pursue a course of study in Years 4 and 5 based on the following broad areas of experience: English, mathematics, humanities, science, technology, arts and design.

References

Crone, R. and Malone, J. (1979) *Continuities in Education*, Slough: NFER.
Crone, R. and Malone, J. (1983) *The Human Curriculum*, Belfast: Farset Press.
Organization for Economic Cooperation and Development/Centre for Educational Research and Innovation (1982) *Strategies for School Improvement*, Paris: OECD.
Shipman, M. (1974) *Inside a Curriculum Project*, London: Ward Lock Educational.
Skilbeck, M. (1982) *Schools Support Service Evaluation*, Belfast: Department of Further Professional Studies in Education, Queen's University.

CHAPTER 11

COMMUNICATION AND DIALOGUE IN THE SCHOOL SETTING
Chris Saville

'If the observer focusses his attention on specific hypotheses, or questions, or categories, he will see meanings within the framework of these preconditioning factors, but he will miss other meanings . . . which could be more important to people in the context of a culture' (Bruyn 1966).

During the past two decades teachers have been assailed by a plethora of curriculum developments and shrill calls for standards and accountability. As a local education authority adviser I have found myself attempting to be a change agent on the one hand and accountability agent on the other. This Janus-like existence has caused me to raise questions about the nature of curriculum development as I observe activity on the ground. For the sake of clarity this description takes the form of a fictionalized case-study leaving you, the reader, to interpret or render judgements. What follows is an attempt to describe a sequence of events or what I would describe as the real world of curriculum development.

The scene is set in and around a fictitious primary school with characters as fictitious as the school.

1. In the staff room

HEAD Mr Widdit our local friendly Adviser called this week with an offer of some free material for teaching history. I have been concerned for some time about how we teach history. In fact, I have come to the conclusion that some of us haven't been teaching much history at all. Now,

Communication and Dialogue in the School Setting

	I have put all the materials out on display in the staff room and I should be grateful if this was looked at before the end of term. I am suggesting that next term we make a point of including at least an hour of history in the curriculum. Of course, Mrs Jones, the infants won't be involved in this, you can carry on as usual. Any questions?
Mr SPROGGIT	(*mature teacher holds a scale 2 for resources*) I have been doing history with my lot for years now. Have I got to change?
HEAD	Well Jim you have a look at the stuff and see what you think. I don't want to force this on anybody but I do think we ought to include some real history and this project looks pretty good stuff to me and anyway the HMIs say we ought to do more.
Mrs ASPALL	(*scale 2 teacher*) What am I going to give up? I have hardly enough time to do all the things now and I have only got started on the science thing you gave me last term.
HEAD	I don't want you to give up anything but I am sure that we could fit it in somewhere if we all look very carefully.
Mr GETTUM	(*scale 2 teacher for PE*) Have we got to buy the materials? The games equipment is in an appalling state and we did decide to reequip that first at our last meeting.
HEAD	With respect Mr Gettum, I think that the history has got to take priority this time. Mr Widdit has promised me half the cost and it seems too good an opportunity to lose.
Mrs NICELY	(*scale 1 teacher*) I think it's a good idea Headmaster. I am ashamed to say that some of my children don't even know the date of the Battle of Hastings and it would make a change from the SRA cards.

(*The head has left the staff meeting*)

Mr SPROGGIT   You know why he's doing this, don't you? He's after that job in the new school. Well I for one am going to carry on as before. I've seen these projects come and go. You mark my words, in two years the whole thing will be forgotten and we shall all be racing round doing inter-galactic studies or something daft like that. Me, I've seen 'em all. Look how crazy we went on Fletcher.

Mrs NICELY   (*knitting*) Well, I think it's a good idea.

Mr SPROGGIT   I bet you, if you look at the stuff your kids still won't be able to tell you the date of the Battle of Hastings.

Mr GETTUM   (*lighting his pipe and leaning forward*) Well, if my games stuff isn't improved I'll tell him I can't take games any more.

2. The following term

The materials have been bought and some of the teachers have tried to use them. They have hit snags. First, the material is very reference-based and relies upon easy access to reference material. Secondly, some elements in the course involve drama and the teachers have had very little experience of teaching drama and there have been complications about using the hall. Thirdly, the material requires a group teaching approach and some of the teachers do not agree with this method. Fourthly, the project is very environmentally-based and asks for considerable local knowledge by the teacher.

3. In the meantime

A letter from Mr Jones to the Head:

Dear Sir,
My daughter Annabel Jane tells me that she no longer has music at school. The reason she gives me is that her teacher (Mr Gettum) is too busy doing history. I should be grateful for an explanation.
Yours faithfully,
Fred Jones

Communication and Dialogue in the School Setting 137

(*At home*)

| HEAD | (*sipping his coffee before 'Coronation Street' begins*) That Gettum is nothing but a blocker. |
| WIFE | (*meekly*) Why not apply for that Adviser's job? |

4. Visit from Mr Widdit, the History Adviser

| Mr WIDDIT | Well, Basil, how's the project going? |
| HEAD | Great. Mrs Nicely's our leading light. Come along and see her classroom. |

They get to the classroom which is bedecked with pictures and posters. Mrs Nicely explains how the project has revolutionized her teaching and expounds the theory that children don't need to know dates but understand the feeling of living in Victorian times.

The Head and the History Adviser return to the Head's room.

| Mr WIDDIT | I'll send you along some film strips and maps. I'm glad it's going so well. It's a credit to your enthusiasm. |

5. Staff room – later in the term

| Mr SPROGGIT | I went on a smashing maths course at the weekend. Just my kind of material, a good balance between formal skills and experimental work. I'm going to ask the Head if I can get some of the materials. |
| Mr GETTUM | I'm going to apply for the PE post in the Middle School. I've had enough. I'm fed up with this place. I think I'll go on a course run by the PE Adviser and get him to visit this place. Might help with the job at the Middle School too. |

6. Letters

A letter from the secretary of the Local History Association

Dear Headmaster,
At our meeting last week Mr Widdit told us of the interesting work being

done at your school. We have a number of original local documents that might be of interest to the children. We also run a series of history trails through the town with supporting colour slides and museum packs for classroom use. Can we help in any way?
Yours faithfully,
A.G. Taylor

A letter from the Headmaster of the local secondary school

Dear Basil, (*he's the Head*)
At a recent meeting of Secondary Heads concern was expressed over our lack of understanding and knowledge of primary school work. I know we receive your record cards and very comprehensive they are, but some of my Heads of Department would like to forge better curriculum links. The Head of Maths and the Head of English are particularly concerned over the basic standards. Perhaps we could meet to discuss matters!
Your sincerely,
J. Greatonix

7. At the next staff meeting

HEAD	I have been concerned for some time about the standards of basic literacy and numeracy. I think the answer is to increase the amount of time spent on these vital and necessary basic skills, perhaps at the expense of some of the frills.
Mr SPROGGIT	Like history?
Mrs NICELY	Certainly not! In my new job at the Middle School the Head has asked me to introduce the project and it would be a shame if it didn't carry on here.

Reference

Bruyn, S.T. (1966), *The Human Perspective in Sociology. The Methodology of Participant Observation*, New York: Prentice Hall.

CHAPTER 12

SCHOOL SELF-EVALUATION
Terence B. Joyes

Introduction
This is a brief description of the process experienced by a group of teachers undertaking a limited self-evaluation exercise. Although hard data were not collected, this exercise was self-evaluative, since the participants considered their own practice in deciding how an internally generated evaluation exercise, aimed at self-improvement, might be carried out.

The context (in 1981)
Denebrook First School[1] is a two-form entry (NOR 320), plus two-times-twenty-place nursery class, situated in a London-overspill area within a shire-county LEA. Separate junior and infants' schools had reorganized ten years previously as a single 5–9 year olds' establishment under one head-teacher. Four teachers are involved in the upper unit (7–9 year olds): the deputy-headteacher; a probationer; a scale 2 recently transferred from teaching infants; and a scale 2 experienced with older first school children. All but the probationer had participated extensively in in-service education and the deputy-headteacher in particular had collaborated frequently in my teachers' centre courses.

The role of the writer
As the local teachers' centre leader interested in conducting research into self-evaluation, I considered schools where I had enjoyed close professional relationships. Denebrook was an obvious choice since its staff had worked with me on curriculum and professional development for over a decade. I

negotiated with the headteacher who supported the proposition provided the upper unit personnel were in agreement. I agreed to act as participant/observer within the group. Although fully supportive, the headteacher chose not to participate. Importantly, the headteacher agreed to discuss the project with the upper unit teachers and to report their reactions – which proved favourable. No coercion or subtle persuasion took place: the teachers were interested, ready to confer, and willing to cooperate with each other. Nevertheless, I pointed out that while the exercise could bring self-improvement and benefit to the school, I could not guarantee the outcomes.

Hypotheses[2]

For the research plan I formulated general hypotheses/propositions:

– Self-evaluation requires leadership and management.
– Such leadership is facilitated by knowledge of group dynamics, chairmanship and management style.
– Certain management styles relate closely to particular evaluation models.
– Ethical and procedural guidelines are fundamentally important.
– A base-point of common perception of a self-evaluation exercise is fundamentally important.
– A self-evaluation exercise passes through critical stages, some of which are universal.

Conduct of the exercise: the case-study

Space here permits only a highlighting of certain aspects: brevity brings loss of detail and close argument to support the description.

By 1981 LEAs were beginning to produce school self-evaluation guidelines.[3] Some documents were tightly constructed, others more open-ended in question structure. All were in some degree responses to the accountability call. For Denebrook there was no LEA initiative. Using a process model, which evolved from their considerations and developed through their activity, Denebrook upper unit staff devised their own guidelines for self-evaluation.

Prior to the exercise I had decided to employ a case-study methodology approach. Case-study[4] is eclectic: it draws upon a variety of methodologies and allows for the action to be described as it is seen, so that evidence otherwise ignored or omitted can be admitted. In assuming the role of participant/observer during the exercise I was able to provide the group with an added 'reference point', while the deputy-headteacher assumed the role of convenor/chairman/secretary. The case-study approach also allowed the chairman to adopt various leadership/management styles in group discussions, according to situation requirements.

At my first meeting with the group of four teachers, I was aware that they held varying perceptions of self-evaluation. I sought to use that first meeting to discuss these perceptions so that we could all begin at the same base-point of understanding. I impressed upon them that there were no predetermined views of results or conduct of the exercise, and that it must develop according to their influence. I was to learn in later meetings that one member could not reject easily the notion that I or the deputy-headteacher had some 'grand plan' for the exercise. Noticeably, the conviction weakened as group members became mutually supportive and more willing to receive each other's criticism.

If members were to have common information about each other's working context, they could not rely upon what they all *thought* they knew. I gave them a specially constructed Situational Analysis Form to be completed in time for copies to be made and distributed prior to the next meeting. The Form asked them to consider the working context under seven headings: staffing; pupils; school plant; school climate; curriculum provision; aims of the school; other relevant factors. It was prefaced by the words 'A personal perspective' and by two overriding considerations: (1) 'What sort of establishment are we?' (2) 'What sort of establishment would we want to become?'[5] I analysed the completed Forms by listing recurring issues. I invited group members to inspect and amend the list.

This occurred at the first meeting proper. I had prepared an agenda for their agreement before proceeding. Thus I initiated a negotiating procedure which would be important in coming months. Much later the group said that this strategy had been helpful since the formal agenda had provided something firm when they were feeling unsure.

One agenda item asked group members to commit themselves initially to two sessions, after which further projection of the exercise would be negotiated by the group. Such a 'trial period' seems valuable since it allows members to discover more about that to which they are committing themselves, and to understand that they can opt out. Paradoxically, a negotiated 'trial period' tends to tie members in more strongly. Having opportunity to shape the events in which they are participating, they become committed to the eventual contract.

Information derived from the Situational Analysis Forms convinced the group that there were issues to which they could all relate. The Forms also demonstrated individual anxieties and concerns, which were formalized under seven headings of ethical and procedural guidelines: confidentiality and trust; judgemental factors; career aspects; professional self-exposure; professional 'restoration'; procedural negotiation; audience factors. The group's overriding concern related to the issue of judgement – both by themselves of others and by others of themselves. The Analysis Forms identified these issues and they were tabled for open discussion.

Consequently, group members – with myself – grew in mutual trust and in respect for confidentiality. They came to understand that we were collecting judgements, not passing them, that we were concerned with the strengths, not just the weaknesses, of individuals and the school. Crucially, insight occurred when group members recognized that they could start from the base-line of strengths and not feel threatened by scrutiny: that insight deepened when members recognized that to inspect weaknesses and not feel threatened is in fact a strength. A critical moment occurred subsequently when one member said 'Ouch!' in open, almost involuntary response to a revelation that a classroom practice to which she had long subscribed unquestioningly was highly questionable when under close scrutiny. Encouragingly, she was able to confirm immediately that through that revelation the seeds of self-improvement were sown. She could now see that self-inspection and evaluation could bring improvement, whereas her earlier, preexercise view of evaluation had been one of destructively pointing out poor practice.

A related issue is that of audience. To whom, if anyone, should one address an evaluation report? How will it be read? Should one use a jargon-free style to facilitate universal comprehension? Should one report the same facts in a variety of formats with varying language according to the status, understanding, potential influence of the recipient? Many ethical questions arose through consideration of audience and the group decided their audience would be the school's headteacher. Involvement of other staff members at Denebrook would stem from renegotiation.

The group felt it important to limit their exercise. They knew that they were to work within a timescale of a school term, and they felt confident in handling the workload of inspecting in depth one aspect of the upper unit's work. They came to recognize that a limited exercise might identify certain processes applicable to other aspects of the school's work. Thus a rolling programme, rather than a 'once-and-for-all', could be initiated.

The group decided to inspect mathematics and wrote a set of five key questions. Aware that some LEAs had produced somewhat restrictive self-evaluation guidelines, the group resolved to construct 'open' questions to ensure a process of critical inspection.

A model for sequencing was devised: it became known as the 'walking-through' model since it proposed a beginning of consideration outside the school (parents and local environment), and a progressing through the school to the classroom and the pupil.

Using this model group members found a cohesion and a common reference point in their work. By now they had determined to extend their exercise and to meet throughout the whole term. Between meetings individuals broke down the key questions, making them gradually less abstract. At each meeting each member's work was discussed and synthesis drawn through skilful chairmanship. Significantly, the chairman understood that to concretize too quickly could be to miss out important levels of consideration and possibly to neglect unexpected evidence. Furthermore, to work systematically from the abstract to the concrete would help ensure that appropriate questions would be written and checked against classroom practice.

As questions became more concrete and operational, a technique for testing their effectiveness was employed: the prepositions 'by' or 'through' were prefixed to the question's response. In this way the appropriate level for operating each question in a classroom situation was determined so that data and evidence could be elicited.

A generous mix of practice and theory was discovered, but that mix was subjected to rigorous scrutiny in discussion. The process of evaluation is an intellectual one: in developing their powers of questioning, group members came to accept the limitations of the wholly 'practical' approach which they might formerly have adopted.

Throughout the group's meetings I found interest not only in how the group developed its self-evaluation exercise but also in the leadership/management of that exercise. One can trace styles of leadership/management on a consultative–participative continuum, and match them with models of evaluation:[6] e.g. classical (agricultural-botanical), research-and-development (industrial-economic) and briefing-decision-makers (political) models tend to be matched by leadership/management styles at the consultative end of the continuum, where edicts and authoritarian directives are symptomatic; whereas illuminative (socio-anthropological/responsive) and teacher-as-researcher (professional) models tend to employ leadership/

management styles at the participative end of the continuum, where there exists a joint leader-member commitment to initiate, discuss, decide and enact together. The Denebrook self-evaluation exercise employed a case-study approach which owes something to these models, particularly to the illuminative since it portrays in thick description the widest possible view of what occurs and the subjective views of the actors. The case-study approach would seem to involve a maximally participative style of leadership/management. As it draws upon evaluation models so it involves a range of matching leadership styles along the consultative-participative continuum.[7]

My observations led me to conclude that anyone leading a self-evaluation exercise should have relevant training and should be aware of the appropriateness of various leadership styles.

Conclusions

Of the hypotheses/propositions formulated initially, three referred to leadership/management. Comments above indicate conclusions. Another referred to common perceptions of self-evaluation: its fundamental importance was highlighted late in the exercise by the individual who demonstrated that we had been wrong in assuming her understanding. Her enduring belief in a predetermined 'grand plan' made us all aware that her early anxiety had not been completely dispelled.

Another hypothesis/proposition referred to ethical and procedural guidelines. In the exercise these guidelines arose from completed Situational Analysis Forms. When formalized the guidelines would seem to have universal applicability – an important conclusion in providing reference points for others. With such reference points and with the fundamental understanding that we can begin with strengths, others can confront their anxieties and perhaps convert them into productive self-evaluation.

In developing their exercise the Denebrook group identified certain critical stages which are possibly transferable to other self-evaluation exercises.

After initial interest and knowledge had been gained, issues were raised enabling the anxieties within the group to be laid bare. The formalizing of ethical and procedural guidelines, the establishment of a negotiated contract for action, and the recognition of strengths as base-points went far in reducing anxieties. The definition of a model provided a reference point for ordering questions, while a commitment to write open-ended questions for gradual refinement gave the group the opportunity to move from generalities to action proposals, to maintain consideration of process rather than content. Throughout the exercise the group worked towards practicalities through gradual abstractions so that the maximum possibilities could be reviewed. In summary one could note that nothing occurred without negotiation within the group. 'Negotiation' was the key word in the whole process.[8]

After the exercise I asked group members about the values of the exercise and about changes in attitude which it might have induced. Two particular responses are worth quoting in summary of views generally expressed:

> I have learnt to question what I am doing in a way which I have never done before, and to do something about what I'm finding.
>
> It was extremely valuable and I think I now have a positive way of looking at what I am doing in my classroom and of improving it for the children.

These comments demonstrate that teachers beginning self-evaluation anxiously can move to fresh awareness of themselves as professionals and to improvement of their classroom provision. Arguably it is up to the leader of an exercise to be aware of difficulties and problems, of the critical stages ahead. It is wholly inadequate to leave such matters of leadership ability to chance: as a profession we must ensure that leadership is adequately trained through consolidated programmes of in-service education.

Notes and references

1 The anonymity of the school and its staff has been preserved throughout.
2 In the original study other hypotheses were formulated in relation to evaluation as innovation – an aspect for which there is no space in this article.
3 The group of teachers found particular value in studying contrasting presentations in LEA self-evaluation documents produced by:
ILEA (1977) *Keeping the School Under Review.*
Oxfordshire LEA (1979) *Starting Points in Self-Evaluation.*
Avon LEA (1980) *In-School Evaluation.*
Solihull LEA (1980) *Evaluating the Primary School: A Guide for Primary Schools in the Metropolitan Borough of Solihull.*
4 a) Adelman, C., Jenkins, D. and Kemmis, S. (1976) Rethinking case study: notes from the second Cambridge conference, *Cambridge Journal of Education*, 3.
b) MacDonald, B. and Walker, R. (1977) Case study and the social philosophy of education research, *in* Hamilton, D. et al. (eds) *Beyond the Numbers Game*, London: Macmillan.
  Both provide illuminating descriptions of the case-study approach, including its limitations.
5 Elliott, J. (1979) Self-accounting schools: Are they possible? *Education Analysis*, 1, p. 71.

146 Readings in School-Based Curriculum Development

6 See Lawton, D. (1980) *The Politics of the School Curriculum*, pp. 112–26, London: Routledge and Kegan Paul, for a clear analysis of the models noted as well as of the case-study approach.
7 A tabulated summary of models of evaluation as well as case-study approach alongside appropriate leadership/management styles could be given:

Table of Evaluation Models. Underlying Assumptions, and Appropriate Leadership/Management Styles

EVALUATION MODEL	STYLE	SOME UNDERLYING ASSUMPTIONS	APPROPRIATE LEADERSHIP/ MANAGEMENT STYLE
CLASSICAL	Agricultural–botanical	An item sown, manured, fed & watered will grow & can be measured	Minimally Consultative/ Minimally Participative
RESEARCH & DEVELOPMENT	Industrial–economic	Find need, construct a solution, implant solution & measure reception	Consultative
BRIEFING DECISION-MAKERS	Political	Exercise reported with selected audience in mind	Consultative/ Minimally Participative – or Consultative/ Participative
ILLUMINATIVE	Social–anthropological/ responsive	Explore widest possible situation/context of exercise/scheme – rely on subjective views of 'actors'	Consultative/ Predominantly Participative
TEACHER-AS-RESEARCHER	Professional	Evaluation as action–research–monitoring & improvement of item as it progresses	Participative
CASE-STUDY	Eclectic/ portrayal	Thick description of limited situation/ context – cf. Illuminative Model – outcome prob. for internal consumption only	Maximally Participative

The first three columns (left to right) are freely adapted from the analysis in Lawton (op. cit.). The final right-hand column is my own addition.

8 cf. Simons, H. (1979). Suggestions for a school self-evaluation based on democratic principles, *Classroom Action Research Network Bulletin No. 3 – School-Based Evaluation*, Cambridge: Cambridge Institute of Education.
Simons' thesis is that self-evaluation should be based on democratic principles including: impartiality; confidentiality/control; negotiation; collaboration; accountability. It has clear links with 'democratic evaluation' defined by: MacDonald, B. (1978) Accountability standards and the process of schooling, *in* Becher, T. and Maclure, S. (1978) *Accountability in Education*, Slough: National Foundation for Educational Research.

CHAPTER 13

CURRICULUM GUIDANCE AND THE ROLE OF PUPILS IN THE LOWER SECONDARY SCHOOL
Jean Cosslett

What is curriculum guidance?

A few years ago I returned to the classroom after a period of full-time research. I took up supply-teaching in order to observe and analyse pupils' responses to all the subjects of the timetable. This was essential experience because the brief I had chosen for myself, following the inspirations of an earlier educator, was this – 'Find ways of explaining to pupils the purpose, and the process, of education' (Ellis 1852; Royal Commission 1861; Cosslett 1977).

This case-study is not strictly part of the discussion on how to change the curriculum. It is about a form of guidance which teachers could use to change pupils' responses to the curriculum. Curriculum guidance explains the purpose, and the process, of education; it involves pupils by discussion of various topics and themes. The curriculum guidance scheme which resulted from my experiences as a supply-teacher will be briefly outlined. By use of the scheme we can give much more information to young people about their schooling and how learning could be of benefit. The full development of the scheme will be discussed at the end of this chapter for I believe that we should use the technological resources available to give a lively presentation of the main points. My intention here is to give sufficient information on the scheme for teachers to consider, perhaps even practise, certain elements in the role of curriculum guide.

Bringing the scheme to its present form was not an easy task. Pupils' responses to lessons are extremely varied and we all have to deal with youngsters who are restless, ebullient and apathetic. Would guidance help to alleviate some of the stresses of the job of teaching? I hoped so. The problem was – just how could those ideas of 'purpose' and 'process' of education be translated into a language which could be understood by pupils? The scheme needed a shape and a structure; I needed to choose themes and perspectives which would help pupils to understand the curriculum. Talking to pupils, observing their responses to the subject matter of lessons helped me to find a framework.

I took what opportunities I could to practise curriculum guidance, especially when I was supervising some difficult lesson material. In some instances I was learning with them – a common experience for supply-teachers! The guidance which I found most useful was to discuss with pupils the 'human perspective' on the contribution to knowledge. This will be found in the second-year scheme.

When the scheme was in outline form I received some helpful comments from my colleagues which assisted a fuller development of the ideas. I thank them and I hope that some of the ideas will be useful to others. The intention is to improve pupils' responses to lessons. We need to do this and I believe that in order to achieve better responses we should begin to give curriculum guidance as soon as pupils enter the secondary school.

As an overall theme for the two-year scheme I have chosen: 'Finding our way in this complex world'. In a very general sense this is what teachers hope pupils will be able to do as a result of education. How does schooling help young people to find their way in this complex world? This question is explored and discussed by the use of a number of topics. The structure and the framework for giving explanations makes use of four key words – Aims, Content, Benefits and Attributes.

First-year guidance scheme

1. The courses of study in the school: Aims, Content, Benefits.
2. A proper environment for learning: Attributes.
3. Social cohesion – learning how to get on with others: Attributes.
4. The specialists – how teachers help pupils: Aims, Content, Benefits.

Under the first topic the key word 'Aims' covers the question: 'Why do young people have to attend school?' The aim of vocational preparation is acknowledged first because this is the pupils' understanding of the purpose of education. Their restricted view is then enlarged by discussing the aims of self-development in terms of intellect, aesthetic responses, physical prowess, manual dexterity in various crafts and skills.

'Content' is the next key word and it covers explanations and describes the character of the different subjects on their timetables. The subjects are organized under four main areas – teachers know them as faculties – Humanities, Sciences, Languages, Creative/Expressive Arts.

To help pupils to appreciate the 'Benefits' of learning, the guidance begins by examining each pupil's need to understand – and respond to – the environment in which they live. We then take the discussion further. Global events, so readily described and covered by the media, almost to a point of confusion for young people, are part of the wider environment. What pupils need is some help to relate the lessons in school to their awareness of the world; we explain that formal schooling does help them to 'find their way in this complex world'. It is, therefore, very much in their own interest to learn what they are taught because their studies are intended as a preparation for living.

'Attributes' is the key word used to explain what teachers understand as social/moral education. The scheme directly relates the development of personal attributes to the learning situation. We explain that teachers and pupils are in a social situation where good relationships are important; our work is teaching, theirs is learning. Cooperative behaviour, receptivity to lessons, involvement with activities, learning how to relate to others in school – all these are needed so that we create the kind of environment in which successful teaching and learning can take place. Classroom teaching and social/moral education need to be much more closely linked. The guidance starts from the situation in schools where social skills are needed and explores more aspects of social cohesion later. Two sections are devoted to guidance on 'Attributes'.

How do experts in the timetabled subject help pupils to acquire knowledge and develop skills? This is the final part of the first-year scheme. Each subject is located under the appropriate faculty. Using the framework of Aims, Content and Benefits, teachers explain and discuss:

Why is this subject part of the timetable?
Has this subject any special features?
What are the benefits of studying this subject?

Guidance in the first year is directed to the individual pupil – taking the approach: 'You, the pupil. How lessons help you to find your way in this complex world'. This approach capitalizes on their natural self-interest. However, in the second year the approach changes to: 'You and others. How lessons teach you about other people's responses to living in this world'.

Second-year guidance scheme

In order to persuade pupils to consider themselves in relation to 'others' and to 'other people's responses to living in this world', I have used a particular focus, a new perspective, in order to give guidance. I referred to this earlier as the 'human perspective'.

Pupils tend to view some subject matter as rather 'dead'. How could curriculum guidance put a little 'life' into lessons and change their views that learning was of little relevance to their needs? I realized that they had not thought about where the subject matter of lessons had originated. I made the link to human action, to human endeavour and explained how lessons – at their root – could be traced back to a human source. We discussed how people have responded to the environment, how they made discoveries, communicated ideas, thoughts and feelings. I then explained how useful skills and certain areas of knowledge are then handed on to the younger generation. Using this perspective helps pupils to understand their part in a long process. The above points were incorporated into the scheme and the idea of a human response appears in the structure of the second-year guidance:

1. Why do teachers believe that it is necessary to learn about other people's responses to the environment? Aims.
2. What are the courses of study and the activities in the school which deal with the various human responses? Content.
3. How is this learning of use to pupils? Benefits.
4. How do we respond to each other? Are we learning how to make relationships with other people? Attributes.

The 'human perspective' is also used when the subjects of the timetable are examined more closely.

There is a particular advantage in using the 'human perspective'. It will, I believe, help us to guide pupils about the complexities of modern life. To illustrate this I shall use the example of one of the subsidiary topics of the scheme – 'Work and Leisure'. This introduces to second-year pupils the evidence of changing patterns of work today and the increased leisure time. The mass media have given young people an awareness of technological developments and their possible effects, not only in relation to work but also to their far more fearful possibilities. We do not want them to be overwhelmed by such information and we should try to help them to be more confident. Each pupil has a unique individuality and it must be emphasized that they are far more marvellous creations than the computers already at their finger tips. Guidance needs to have a strong focus upon people, upon human interaction in many different roles and tasks. The use of the 'human perspective' helps to emphasize what people have done in many fields of knowledge and that the application of their findings has often had positive effects. Many pupils – and some are very young indeed – are fearful about the future. What about nuclear war? What about unemployment? Uncertainty is affecting their view of schooling and it is interfering with their responses to the curriculum. Guidance can, at least, reduce some of their uncertainty about the purpose, and the process, of education.

Implementation

The most effective way to implement the scheme would be to have a series of video films. These would cover the main points and a lively presentation would set the tone for the discussions to follow. In the first year, the groups viewing the films should be small so that the appeal to each individual pupil is maintained. Existing tutorial time could be used for follow-up discussions; possibly an hour a week would suffice. Lesson time would be used for subject guidance but, if the result is improved responses to lessons, then the sacrifice of some instruction time would probably be considered worth while. In the second year, much larger groups could watch the films, dividing into smaller discussion groups. It would also be possible to give subject guidance to larger groups, perhaps on a team-teaching basis for each of the four faculties. Once formal guidance has been introduced it would be a question of letting the principle and the practice of guidance permeate our methods of teaching. Many points of the above suggestions could be used if teachers wished to use guidance techniques without introductory video films. We have, of course, existing visual resources which could illustrate the 'human perspective'. Other topics of the scheme could be given in classrooms, with discussions of aims and showing the organization of timetabled subjects under faculties. Linking social/moral development with the learning situation would be an important area to include.

Following the introduction of a fully developed scheme of curriculum guidance in schools I hope there would be two main results. First, I believe that if we give pupils more information about the purpose, and the process, of education we shall increase their motivation. This may very well lead to improved standards of attainment. Secondly, I believe that guidance will improve relationships between teacher and pupils. Young people would appreciate being taken into our confidence about our intentions and would begin to understand the teacher's role, their own, and the roles of all other learners. If improved learning and improved relationships were achieved we would have a much better ethos in schools. Changes in the curriculum could then be more easily accommodated and we could look with more confidence to improved pupil responses to lessons.

The topic of this rapidly changing world and its effects upon the young is a main talking point in the world today. Why not carry the discussion into the classroom in the form of curriculum guidance? In the first instance we would be preparing pupils for the changes they face in the new secondary school. The complex and rapidly changing world is by no means ignored in the themes and perspectives of the guidance scheme but acknowledged and discussed. It is when these young pupils grow and develop that we can expect more lively and critical responses, but encouragement to respond to the curriculum must be given in early years. From the beginning of secondary education the use of curriculum guidance places a strong emphasis upon the important tasks of teaching and learning. It is an emphasis which is very much needed.

References

Cosslett, J. (1977) *Opinions regarding the theory and practice of imparting information to the lower orders*, M.Phil. Thesis, University of London.

Ellis, W. (1851) *Education as a Means of Preventing Destitution*.

Ellis, W. (1852) *What am I? Where am I? What ought I to do? How am I to become qualified and disposed to do what I ought to do?* (William Ellis was founder of the Birkbeck Schools which practised his principle of guiding pupils).

Royal Commission (1861) *The State of Popular Education in England and Wales – The Newcastle Report*, Volume 6 (Oral and written evidence given by W.A. Shields, Master of Peckham Birkbeck School).

CHAPTER 14

CURRICULUM GUIDANCE AT 14+
Carole Ann Eastgate

Subject option choice has become a major feature of the school calendar for the third-year secondary school pupil because it leads to a major change in the curriculum for such pupils in their fourth and fifth years. It is at this time, when they have a say in their choice of studies for the last two years of compulsory schooling, that pupils, probably for the first time in their school career, have an opportunity to participate in major educational decisions which will affect their future life chances. Consequently, the impact of the optional subject choice process is such that it may be considered 'the beginning of an important sequence of decisions' (Hurman 1978). At this time, too, the school has an important function to fulfil and faces a major challenge in helping children to make realistic, well-informed decisions relating courses of study to individual capabilities, interests and future plans.

Today, so that pupils can make informed decisions at 14+ there is the demand for organized guidance programmes which are not only concerned with giving relevant information but also include elements dealing with the development of self-awareness and decision-making skills. Despite this demand, however, the whole process of pupils' choosing their optional subjects is still, in many cases, an ad hoc one. Although some schools provide a comprehensive programme followed throughout the third year, in other schools pupils come to option choice 'cold' with little preparation for the important decisions they have to make. Instead, therefore, of optional subject choice being conceived of as a 'continuing and integral part of day to day education' (Benn and Simon 1972) it becomes a crisis in school life. In some schools, too, staff seem ignorant of how the process operates and are unclear about the part they are expected to play.

Although research has been carried out relating to factors affecting pupil subject choices at 14+ (Reid et al. 1974; Hurman 1978), and although the necessary characteristics of a guidance programme at 14+ have been well documented (Law and Watts 1977), very little attention has been paid to the identification of those features of the process which are seen to have been of most value in helping pupils to make their choices. This is probably because the idiosyncratic way that option choice procedures are conducted by individual schools in relation to their local circumstances and ideals makes it impossible and undesirable to make any generalizations.

In an attempt to identify such features I examined the subject option systems operating within two schools and their effectiveness from the point of view of the third-year pupils and a cross-section of teachers (Eastgate 1982).

The schools were two 11–16 comprehensives of 889 and 632 pupils respectively in an outer London borough. Their curricular organization fitted into the traditional pattern (DES 1979; DES 1980; DES 1981) of a broad common curriculum in the first three years replaced at 14+, that is in the fourth and fifth year, by a 'common core' and choice of optional subjects. Both schools had established option choice procedures and both gave guidance to pupils to help them make their decisions. However, the nature and emphasis of the guidance varied.

Two instruments were used in the survey. Pupil opinion was sought by a questionnaire divided into two sections, the first section of which was subdivided into questions concerning a) fact and b) opinion. For the purpose of analysis questions were categorized into those concerned with a) option organization, b) preparation for choice, c) teacher advice, d) pupil perception. The second section consisted of multiple choice and open-ended items. A semistructured interview schedule composed of eleven questions was given to option coordinators, heads of careers and a sample of third-year form tutors and heads of departments. Both instruments were validated in a pilot study held in another comprehensive school in the same borough.

I am well aware of the limitations of such surveys and realize that findings cannot be widely generalised. However, in essence, my purpose was to identify features which prove salient and pertinent in helping pupils to make well-informed and realistic choices so that the whole process is meaningful to them. At the same time it was hoped that the findings could be used by the two schools when operating their option systems in subsequent years.

Evidence from the case-study survey suggests that the following considerations can play an important part in providing positive, effective and realistic guidance at 14+:

1. The option blocks must be carefully constructed with a rationale behind their composition. Greater pupil satisfaction and ease of choice seems to come from a system where blocks relate to core fields with additional blocks heterogeneously composed allowing a free choice. Such:
    a) helps to provide a balanced timetable for individual pupils;
    b) genuinely allows for a free choice in the heterogeneous blocks.
   Wherever possible, pupils should be made aware of the reason for the make up of (rationale behind the composition of) the blocks so they can more readily appreciate the inevitable constraints.
2. The pupils need a clear, repeated explanation of how the option system works in their school. They need to know:
    a) what the procedures are;
    b) how to fill in the option form correctly.
3. Individual interviews *with each pupil* are desirable. They should include:
    a) discussions of *all* choices in relation to each other;
    b) linking of choices to future aspirations.
4. A school report relating to present effort and performance in school studies should be available before choices are made.
5. An option booklet describing the courses on offer is desirable. It should include:
    a) a description of the courses indicating their content, the examinations to which they lead, the type of work expected from the pupils (familiar subjects can change in nature and presentation in the fourth and fifth year);
    b) a list of the core areas;
    c) an explanation of the constraints on choosing;
    d) a list of suitable subject combinations for certain jobs/careers.
6. The content and expectations of *new courses* must be carefully explained.
7. It is desirable for appropriate teachers to describe the courses orally to pupils either in assembly or in lessons.
8. There should be a *guidance programme* during the third year centred around option choice. Such a programme should include:
    a)   development of pupil self-awareness;

b) practice in decision making;
c) a vocational element.
9. In setting up the vocational element the following factors need to be considered:
   a) pupils should know who the careers teacher is;
   b) children should know what careers facilities and resources exist and when they might use them;
   c) as well as having careers as part of the guidance programme, there should be an opportunity for children to browse through books and leaflets on their own, other than in lessons;
   d) the careers teacher's role needs to be clearly defined and he/she should take an active part in helping pupils to relate courses to career/job opportunities;
   e) the vocational course content element in the guidance programme needs to be structured.
10. All teachers are involved in guidance at 14+ to a lesser or greater extent. They need to work as a team. They need to know:
    a) how the system operates;
    b) their role in it;
    c) to whom to refer the pupils for specific problems.
11. Form teachers (third year) need to be involved. They:
    a) need to be aware of the courses on offer;
    b) should listen to the explanations given by subject teachers as to course content;
    c) should listen to the option organizer's explanation to the pupils about the option choice procedures.
12. Before option choice there should be a briefing for all teachers by the option coordinators.
13. Parents appear to have more influence over pupil choices than do teachers. Therefore:
    a) links must be established between home and school;
    b) parents should be aware of how the system operates, the courses available and the nature of the examinations;
    c) there should be a parents' evening to discuss pupil choices, and pupils should have the option of coming with parents if both desire it;
    d) a careers officer should be present at the parents' evening.

Many of the suggestions listed above may appear to be matters of common sense. However, such considerations can be taken for granted and unless made explicit may not be considered or utilized during option choice.

Although curriculum guidance needs are idiosyncratic to individual schools, as much as possible needs to be done to make the pupils' process of choice as easy as possible. Whatever features are considered by individual schools to be important to effect this and however individual schools direct the process of choosing, there needs to be a structured plan of action with which both pupils and teachers are familiar. I hope, albeit in a small way, that my case-study survey has pin-pointed from within two schools components which are considered important in meeting these ends in a concrete, realistic way.

References

Bardell, G. (1982) *Options for the Fourth – the report of an exploratory study in ten schools*, London: The Schools Council.
Benn, C. and Simon, B. (1972) *Half Way There*, Harmondsworth: Penguin.
Department of Education and Science (1979) *Aspects of Secondary Education*, London: HMSO.
Department of Education and Science (1980) *A View of the Curriculum* (HMI Series: Matters for Discussion), London: HMSO.
Department of Education and Science (1981) *Curriculum 11–16: a review of progress*, London: HMSO.
Eastgate, C.A. (1982) *Curriculum Guidance at 14+: Teacher and Pupil Perspectives*, MA Dissertation, University of London Institute of Education.
Hamblin, D. (1978) *The Teacher and Pastoral Care*, Oxford: Blackwell.
Hurman, A. (1978) *A Charter for Choice* – a study of option schemes, Slough: NFER.
Law, B. and Watts, A.G. (1977) *School, Careers and Community*, London: CIO Publishing.
Reid, M.I., Barnett, B.R. and Rosenberg, H.A. (1974) *A Matter of Choice* – a study of guidance and subject options, Slough: NFER.
Ryrie, A.C., Furst, A. and Lauder, M. (1979) *Choices and Chances* – a study of pupils' subject choices and future career intentions, London: Hodder and Stoughton for Scottish Council for Research in Education.
Schools Council (1972) Working Paper 40, *Careers Education in the 1970's*, London: Evans Methuen.
Schools Council (1975) Working Paper 53, *The Whole Curriculum 13–16*, London: Evans Methuen.
Woods, P. (1979) *The Divided School*, London: Routledge and Kegan Paul.

CHAPTER 15

CURRICULUM CHANGE IN A CATHOLIC SECONDARY SCHOOL
Francis Fay

The thinking which lay behind the setting up of the curriculum group at the Red School is well summarized by A. and H. Nicholls (1972) when they say:

> We live in a changing society in which new knowledge is constantly being discovered and in which old knowledge is being proved wrong . . . With the realisation that pupils must be prepared to cope with the demands of a society which is changing so quickly, teachers need to reappraise what they are offering to their pupils.

The Red School was opened in 1959 as a secondary modern. By 1971 it had grown to an eight-form-entry school, serving an area on the northern outskirts of Liverpool comprising three large council estates and a smaller amount of private housing. The school became an 11–18 comprehensive school in 1975 under the LEA's scheme for reorganization. In 1982 there were approximately one thousand pupils on the roll with a full-time staff of sixty-one teachers. The school, like others in the area, has experienced falling rolls over the past few years. It is organized into year groups for pastoral care and administration; and for teaching purposes the children are divided into two broad bands, though setting does occur in some subjects. A high proportion of the staff are graduates and the staff room contains its share of innovators, enthusiasts, cynics and time servers.

In October 1981 an invitation was given, first to heads of departments, and then to all members of staff, to participate in a curriculum group, which would be looking at the existing curriculum offered by the school and attempting to improve it. By curriculum I mean those subjects, skills and learning experiences that are offered to the pupils by the school. The group was the idea of Mr Grundy who had been appointed the previous year as Deputy-Head Curriculum.

The group eventually comprised fifteen members of staff, including Mr Grundy and myself, of whom eight were heads of departments. The group decided that a course was needed for the fourth and fifth-year pupils to cover aspects of modern life not at present covered or inadequately covered in existing courses. The options system allows some pupils to miss out completely on certain areas of knowledge which were considered most important to their development. It should be pointed out that the 'areas of knowledge' were considered 'most important' by the group members and not necessarily by the pupils. Below is a list of topics which were to be included in the course:

1. The contemporary world
2. Politics
3. Sex education
4. Equal opportunities
5. Health education
6. Computer studies
7. Economics
8. Parentcraft

In order to establish whether or not the pupils' perceptions of need were in any way similar to the group's perception, a questionnaire was devised and given to a random sample of 50 pupils taken from each form in the third year. The responses to the questionnaire showed that most pupils regarded the course as interesting and/or relevant.

A considerable amount of time was devoted to discussing the overall aim of the course. Some staff were quite happy to let an aim emerge, but a majority insisted on formulating an aim. It was finally decided that this would be, 'to prepare children for leaving school and entering into the local environment as it exists'. My own opinion is that this was such a high-order aim as to be meaningless. Nevertheless the group seemed happy to accept it. In producing the course the group attempted to tailor it to our school in the following ways:

1. It took the school situation as its starting point.
2. It identified a need.
3. It took account of available teacher expertise.
4. It took account of the resources available.

5. The method of teaching could be geared to a known group of children.
6. The course could be evaluated by those concerned (teachers and pupils) and modified accordingly. This seems to me to be a good example of school-based curriculum development as defined by Eggleston (1980).

The course was introduced in September 1982 and at the time of writing has not completed a full year. No evaluation has so far been attempted and I feel that a course with an aim such as this one has would be extremely difficult to evaluate, since its success or failure could not be judged until after the pupils had left school. I rather think, too, that any long-term evaluation would be beyond the capacity of our small group. On a more practical level, the compilers of each unit of the course have defined their own objectives and suggested methods for assessment. This, at least, should provide us with feedback and enable a formative evaluation, and perhaps even a summative evaluation can be attempted in a group situation at the end of the first or second year of the course.

I would like now to make a brief reference to the problems which Skilbeck (1976) suggests face school-based curriculum innovations, and say to what extent our group confronted and coped with them. The list is too long to reproduce in this article and so I will refer only to those items which I consider significant. Information for this section of the article was collected by me by means of questionnaire and interview. I will state briefly each problem suggested by Skilbeck and relate the group response to it;

1. Low esteem and inadequacy in staff and lack of relevant skills – most of the group claim to have had little difficulty in formulating their objectives and preparing contents for their unit.
2. Lack of interest or conviction in staff in sustaining change processes – most of the group have indicated a willingness to modify their units if they are not successful; and nine of the original group are involved in another curriculum development whose planning commenced in September 1982.
3. Inadequate allocation of resources – only half the staff felt that extra ones would be needed to run their courses. The significant point here was the time element. All planning sessions took place in the lunch-time or after school and materials preparation was done in the group members' own time. The staff were divided about the adequacy of time devoted to formulating aims and objectives of the course and the content of the units; and even more significant I feel is the fact that four of the staff felt inclined at some time to give up their curriculum development because

of the pressures of their normal teaching. This was reflected in the less than 100% attendance at all meetings and the cancellation of at least one meeting because of group members' other commitments.
4. Failure to appreciate the subtleties of group interactions – as far as I know the group is not perceived as a threat by anyone. It has the blessing of the headmaster who has been kept informed about each stage of development. In addition the meetings have all been open and the general invitation to staff to join the group has made it possible for anyone to participate.
5. Neglect of the diversity of the different teaching styles – very little thought was given to this. It was agreed right at the start that the teaching groups would be of mixed ability, but, that apart, it was generally assumed that a person responsible for teaching a unit would adopt a style to suit him/herself.

I believe that the curriculum group at the Red School has got off to a good start. It has, sensibly in my opinion, not tried to be too ambitious. As Stenhouse (1975) says, ' . . . schools are a going concern and to try wholesale change rapidly is not advisable.' The innovation we are attempting has several merits for a group just embarking on curriculum development. It is not too demanding of either teaching time, money or other resources, and will not therefore attract criticism from heads of departments. It is not very controversial in that it does not interfere with pupils' examination prospects, indeed it may even enhance some pupils' chances in some of their subjects. Consequently we do not anticipate opposition from either governors or parents. The innovation has allowed staff to make contributions in areas which they know well and in which they feel comfortable, and to participate in group discussions. Finally, it has established a framework within which the curriculum at the Red School can be developed. This, I think, is very important. As Owen (1973) says,

> Within a framework which both the assistant teachers and the head can see and understand, decisions about the curriculum become both intelligible and defensible. . . . Everyone will know when it was he had the opportunity to take the initiative, or to make some formative contribution. He will know too when the chance will come again, how the progress of an idea will be assessed, who is to assess it and when.

When the course was introduced in September 1982 it did not mark the end of the curriculum group's work, but the start of a group of teachers' attempts to become problem solvers in their own school. We hope that this experiment will benefit both teachers and pupils.

References

Eggleston, J. (1980) *in* Eggleston, J. (ed.) *School Based Curriculum Development in Britain*, London: Routledge and Kegan Paul, p. 7.

Nicholls, A. and H. (1972) *Developing a Curriculum*, London: George Allen and Unwin, p. 15.

Owen, J.G. (1973) *The Management of Curriculum Development*, Cambridge: Cambridge University Press, p. 83.

Skilbeck, M. (1976) School based curriculum development, *in* Walton, J. and Welton, J. (eds) *Rational Curriculum Planning*, London: Ward Lock Educational, pp. 164–165.

Stenhouse, L. (1975) *An Introduction to Curriculum Research and Development*, London: Heinemann, p. 171.

CHAPTER 16

SIXTH-FORM CURRICULUM CHANGE
Allan Hodge

This case concerns the dynamics of sixth-form curriculum change in the transition by one institution from small, single-sex grammar school to open-access, coeducational sixth-form college. In particular, it focuses on the management of the change process by those charged with responsibility for implementing it, and draws on the insights of organizational analysis in identifying the reasons for their success or failure. General conclusions are drawn about the optimum means for managing curriculum change on an institutionwide basis. During the transition period the author was a head of department in the institution concerned.

During the 1960s and 1970s the sixth form became a more heterogeneous body than before. The Crowther Report (Central Advisory Council 1959) had been the last, great expression of support for the 'traditional' grammar school sixth form, with its essential 'marks' of close university links, subject-mindedness, independent work, intellectual discipleship and social responsibility; and while one could still find many examples of this type – predominantly academic, specialist, selective institutions – changing considerations of who should receive what kind of education at this age took the sixth form in a new direction. In this study, the same problem that had exercised the minds of educational thinkers for more than half a century – that of whether, or how, to broaden the curriculum – became a reality and demanded an organizational response in under two years.

Factual evidence of the changes that occurred was obtained mainly from documents. The other main source of evidence on curriculum, and particularly on the social aspects of change, was questionnaires and interviews. The choice between written replies and audio recordings came down in favour of the former, the reasoning being that deliberation was wanted rather than spontaneity. The comprehensiveness of the written replies seemed to justify this choice, and they were followed up by oral interviews where necessary.

Ratification of the scheme to change the school into a sixth-form college came early in one year, the college to open in the autumn of the next. Curricular questions that had to be addressed included planning for girls, in so far as these might demand subjects not provided in a boys' school; for greater numbers; and for the less able 'new' sixth former for whom the grammar school A level diet would be inappropriate. The first two questions were to be tackled relatively easily, the third less so. In addition, and most importantly, there were to be the social problems associated with institutional change, particularly with respect to the reaction of the grammar school staff to the demands that were now to be made on them. Evidence will be put forward to show that planning for this did not receive sufficient attention, with consequent detrimental effects on the efficiency of the change.

Initially, the planning period was beset with difficulties. The Headmaster resigned in the summer of the first year, and there was an interregnum until the January of the second. Before the resignation, some thought had been given to the question of the college curriculum, in a document drawn up for heads of departments only by the Headmaster. It considered the expected intake, and made proposals for the duration and type of courses to be offered. There was an air of *fait accompli* about it, not surprisingly since the basic diet of O and A levels proposed found ready acceptance amongst the staff consulted, none of whom had had experience of sixth-form colleges, and few of teaching students of lower ability. This document, with all its limitations, was to provide the main thinking on the college curriculum for some time to come, there being a virtual halt to progressive thought on curriculum matters during the autumn, with the result that staff entered the new year, just nine months before the scheduled opening, scarcely better informed or prepared than they had been a year earlier.

The Vice-Principal (Curriculum), who had been appointed internally late in the first year, produced three planning documents before the college opened. The first, 'A strategy for producing a balanced curriculum at the sixth-form college', was a highly theoretical exercise in categorization which remained private and which drew heavily on the current theory and practice of curriculum building for its inspiration. Later evidence was to suggest that the curriculum that did emerge owed little to these initial thoughts, and although not ever meant as a 'blueprint' plan as such, it serves as a reminder that grand schemes which proceed from theoretical bases may be rendered inoperable by the practicalities and constraints of the actual planning process.

The second document, 'Thoughts on the development of the sixth-form college', also remained private, and was described as a 'campaign document'. It was much wider in scope than the first, going beyond curriculum, reflecting an aims-and-objectives, problem-solving approach, with a clear expression of relevant contextual variables but little indication of possible interaction between them. It still expressed the not-to-be-realized commitment of a 'broad' education for all.

The third document, 'College curriculum: statement of theoretical position', was presented to the whole staff early in the second year, the first and only explicit thinking on the curriculum that most of them were to see. Curriculum examples illustrated 'essential subjects' expressed in terms of five areas that could form a 'common core', and a 'balance of curriculum'. As with the document presented to heads of departments by the departed Headmaster, this received general acquiescence, and it is difficult to know to what extent staff felt constrained from commenting constructively by lack of adequate conceptual background and prior involvement.

This early history of the development of the college curriculum suggests that nearly all the background work on its total structure had been undertaken by the Vice-Principal without reference to heads of departments and other teachers. There had been no 'Working Party on the Whole Curriculum' that might have been given the brief to go back to first principles, nor had there been the opportunity for background discussion on post-Crowther thinking on the sixth-form curriculum. This is not to imply that a working party would not have come up with exactly the same curriculum as was, in fact, adopted for the college's opening, since many constraints of time and finance were operating which limited the scope for innovation; but it remains true that there existed an opportunity for self-education and participation amongst staff that was not taken. There was a positive need to reeducate, especially among the grammar school stalwarts who were to form a major and entrenched element in the expanded staff, and to enlist their support through active involvement in planning.

With hindsight, the actual basis for the selection of curriculum content seems to have had less to do with elaborate planning schemes, and more to do with reliance on the familiar and reaction to events. As the Principal stated, in describing this 'contingency' approach:

It was regarded that the O and A levels would be the mainstay of our curriculum here, but that we would have to accommodate the lower-ability students that we thought were coming in . . . We didn't really know what the proportions would be of the A level, the O level, and the other students . . . A lot of it (i.e. planning) had to be ad hoc from one time to another . . . really to see what happened and then to accommodate it as best we could.

Later evidence showed a lack of knowledge of, and ability successfully to plan for, these 'nonacademic' sixth formers who were to arrive in such large numbers. As late as five years after the college opened, the Vice-Principal could express concern about the '. . . mismatch between students and courses below A level . . .' The problem itself, of course, has not been one peculiar to the institution studied.

The social aspect of the change was an important part of the study. The grammar school staff had the right to transfer to the college, with all its differences of purpose and clientele; and organization studies (Hoyle 1964/65; Bidwell 1965; Davis 1973) indicate that this was a situation likely to contain major problems in terms of reaction to innovation.

As Davis (1973) reminds us, we can never assume congruency between the 'formal', publicly stated aims of an organization, and the 'informal' motivations and preoccupations of those who work within it. Even within an established institution, '. . . activities and aims are generated whose purposes have less to do with official goals or the specification of the organisation's "charter" than with the interests of members or groups of members themselves'. A major managerial function is to achieve convergence of formal and informal, and this is particularly crucial when the formal is itself being redefined, as with a change in institutional function.

In this case, the Vice-Principal thought that a great deal of time had been spent on staff preparation for change, while the Principal thought the opposite. This divergence may simply reflect a different approach by each, but if this is so, it must mean that the question of individual preparation for change had not received sufficient attention at the time for it to be resolved into a unified approach – either this, or that agreement could not be reached. Yet, as indicated above, our understanding of social reaction to change would lead us to believe that this should have been one of the most important areas for action. The Principal admitted some failure in this area, saying that he had spent much time setting up 'structures', and not enough listening to the anxieties of individual members of staff.

With regard to the authority structure of the college, the Principal described the 'deliberate decision' to change it from that which had characterized the school, where all lines of authority were vertical, to one which had positions of major devolved responsibility and a greater emphasis on horizontal communications and decision making. At first sight, this might appear to have been a conscious decision to move, at least for the period of change, from a 'mechanistic' to an 'organismic' structure (Shaw 1971). The 'mechanistic' model assumes a rigidity of organization, with specified roles and role relationships within a rigidly defined, hierarchical authority structure – it approximates, in many respects, to the classical bureaucracy. The 'organismic' model represents a more flexible, adaptive, dynamic structure, or 'system', as Shaw prefers to call it. Role definitions become blurred and the authority structure is based on knowledge and expertise rather than position. Shaw's basic premise is that democratic, participatory methods of effecting change are both morally preferable and ultimately more profound and successful than authoritarian ones. The difficulty is that they require a large measure of knowledge, skill and confidence on the part of the planners, and the dividing line between organismic pattern and anarchy can be a thin one. In the case under review, however, the main stated reason was not to establish a more 'organismic' structure but to improve communications and spread decision-making powers, in the interests of greater efficiency in the developing college.

Staff reaction to change was a mixture of apprehension and excitement. There was a perceived change in leadership style from 'authoritative/ inspirational to managerial', and a sense of movement into a world of unknowns and relative insecurity. There was a general feeling, even among the older-established staff, that school structures had become rather rigid and in need of modification, and so little sense of deep-rooted hostility existed. Apprehension expressed was in terms of the individual's lack of confidence in his ability to adapt to the change.

Involvement of the staff in the change process was seen by them in terms of particular subsystems within the college, rather than in the area of total curriculum. Many expressed a feeling of separation between themselves and office-holders above head of department level, and had misgivings about the latter's curriculum planning procedures. They were unhappy about neglect of individual preparation for change, and lack of involvement in planning the whole curriculum. As one said:

> There have been, from time to time, many occasions when closer consultation would have been a great help, and only now [i.e. some five years later] are we getting a much more uniform appreciation of the need for all-round agreement about the curriculum.

The major point that emerges from this study is that institutionwide curriculum change has two components, the organizational and the social. To neglect either, or both, of these is to court failure. With respect to the organizational aspects, reference has been made to the restricted nature of curriculum planning for the college opening – restricted in terms of both participation and vision of practical requirements – and it was suggested that greater involvement of staff from an early stage might have proved beneficial in addressing the task of structuring the curriculum in the most appropriate way for the needs of the new student clientele. As for the social aspects of the change, the evidence of this study suggests that not enough was done to *educate* the teachers about the coming changes, nor to *enlist* their support, with detrimental effects.

The two components of institutional change are not, of course, independent of each other. One of the major constraints on change in curriculum structure is entrenched staff interest, and this stresses the primacy of staff preparation as a prerequisite for successful innovation. Conversely, a curriculum proposal which is seen to be inappropriate or unacceptable itself engenders staff dissatisfaction. It appears that what is needed is a coherent vision of curricular requirements and a carefully planned and sustained exercise to get the staff behind it. The art of progress will be to accept modifications, and even casualties, without losing the essential vision in a disruptive fragmentation. Devolution of responsibilities, by itself, is not enough. It may imply the formation of obstructive, semiautonomous subgroups. Successful curriculum change requires the *majority* to participate in a plan that they have helped to evolve. The task of the leadership is to direct the development and implementation of the plan, and to be aware of the social problems that change brings with it. The price of unpreparedness is disarray and disharmony.

References

Bidwell, C.E. (1965) The school as a formal organization, *in* March, J.G. (ed.) *The Handbook of Organizations*, Chicago: Rand McNally.
Central Advisory Council (1959) *15–18* (Crowther Report), London: HMSO.
Davis, B. (1973) On the contribution of organisational analysis to the study of educational institutions, *in* Brown, R. (ed.) *Knowledge, Education and Cultural Change*, London: Tavistock.
Hoyle, E. (1964/5) Organisational analysis in the field of education, *Educational Research*, vol. 7, no. 2.
Shaw, K. (1971) Management and innovation in education, *in* Walton, J. (ed.) *Curriculum Organisation and Design*, London: Ward Lock.

Tyler, W. (1973) The organisational structure of the secondary school, in sociology and teaching, *Educational Review*, 25/3, June.

CHAPTER 17

THE ROLE OF THE TEACHER AS AN AGENT OF CHANGE IN FURTHER EDUCATION
Arthur S. Donald

The distinction between further education and adult education has its origins in Section 41 of the 1944 Education Act which differentiates between those courses directed towards 'full-time and part-time education' for (vocational) instruction and those concerned with 'leisure-time occupation'. However, to delineate such interest so definitively would be to deny the interwoven fabric of the further education sector. Nevertheless, in the interests of brevity this chapter focuses on non-advanced further education (NAFE) found in further education institutions, and excludes all leisure-time activities such as one would expect to find mostly in evening institutions.

This difficulty of defining the role of further education precisely is not new and was very aptly, and prophetically, recognized in 1959 by the Crowther Committee:

> Further Education will, we believe, be the next great battleground of English education, however, any attempt to map the terrain of further education renders it difficult to focus on the exact location of the 'battlefield'. (Central Advisory Council 1959)

While the battlefield may remain fluid, the front line at present must surely be found in NAFE and the conflict arising from the competing interests and policies of government, LEAs, the Manpower Services Commission and the design and implementation of new initiatives. Of fundamental importance amidst such change is the role of the teacher within further education to influence the direction of such change, and it is with such parameters in mind that this chapter is written.

In reviewing provision within further education the dominant theme which emerges is the complexity and diversity of curricula existing under the umbrella of this sector. Nevertheless, within the wide spectrum of this provision the central examination and validating bodies are a principal unifying factor, providing some degree of cohesion.

The extent to which such bodies influence various levels of staff within a college obviously differs with the degree of influence they are able to exercise over the curriculum. One example could be courses of the Technician Education Council (TEC) and Business Education Council (BEC) – and now Business and Education Council (BTEC) – in which a college has an opportunity to influence the composition of the curriculum while acknowledging the existence of central guidelines. Examinations are the responsibility of the college although subject to external moderation. It is also interesting to note the apparent dichotomy integral to the official TEC policy of 'developing a unified national system of courses while also encouraging college based curriculum innovation in the design of such courses'.

The origins of such policy and the inception of both TEC and BEC can be found in the Haslegrave Committee's (1969) criticism of the courses and examinations which existed in the late 1960s and the subsequent 'bewildering picture of complexity to employers and students'. This complexity was further compounded by the uncoordinated involvement of too many agencies in technician courses, and highlighted the need for a new pattern of courses under the supervision of two new national councils covering technician and business education, whose task was the creation of a national structure of provision. From October 1983, these two councils combined to form the Business and Technician Education Council (BTEC) and, while there are obvious administrative advantages, it remains to be seen how the council proposes to meet the very different demands from those existing at the time of the Haslegrave Report. To succeed, the new council must reflect in its aims those changes brought about by unemployment, the demise of the apprenticeship system, the broadening concept of craftsmanship and the impact of microtechnology.

The need for a coordinated national policy in education and training was not, however, restricted to technician education but was reflected also in the 1964 Industrial Training Act. It was this Act which gave rise to the Industrial Training Boards with the objective of creating 'an adequate supply of trained men and women at all levels' and of improving the quality of training throughout industry.

The subsequent curriculum model on which many industrial training board courses was based reflected an explicit and centrally imposed curriculum structure reminiscent of the systems design (Hamilton 1976) approach. This model is significant because it is quite possible for the teacher on some courses to have imposed upon him/her:

a) a curriculum design which he/she has never been involved with or consulted about;
b) learning objectives which are behavioural and highly specific;
c) little opportunity to exercise autonomy at classroom level which, at best, is reduced to selection of suitable methodology while all other constraints are predetermined by an external agency: i.e. topics, materials, project design, standards demanded, assessment procedures and, ultimately, both the design and marking of examinations may well have been conducted externally.

Such an approach may be exemplified by the notes for teachers issued by one of the training boards which stated:

> The most efficient route to a destination can only be selected when the destination is known. Without clearly defined objectives there can be no sound basis for selection, training methods and terminal assessment.

Surely one must view with some suspicion any reference to educational processes in terms of reaching a 'destination'? Is it not possible that our concept of the inquiry under review may well change as a result of what takes place en route? (Pring 1973) Unquestionably this must be so and yet there appears little provision for this if we are restricted to a specific destination by a predetermined route. Indeed, is there not a danger in pursuing greater specificity and organization of intended learning outcomes that we run counter to the very notion of what education is about?

A further constraint imposed by the use of behavioural objectives in vocational education lies in the need to produce only those results which can be measured and which, therefore, tend to reflect industry's concept of what is educationally worth while (Further Education Unit 1980). It must, however, be made clear that recognizing the constraints imposed by such an approach does not necessarily ignore the advantages which can also be gained. There is no need to impale oneself on the artificial dichotomy of whether one is 'for' or 'against' behavioural objectives but rather to recognize that this approach lends itself admirably to some learning situations within the broad notion of what constitutes education and is totally inappropriate, if not counter-productive, in others. (Skilbeck 1984, ch. 8)

In further education the career structure is such that promotion in most cases reflects an inverse proportion of administrative duties to class contact. This means that not only is one required to fulfil fewer teaching hours but, in keeping with promotion in the hierarchical structure of a college, a teacher is better able to influence curriculum change the higher the level or promotion attained.

The difficulties facing staff on the lower rungs are compounded by the fact that they must function within vertical working relationships (Bernstein 1974) through the hierarchy while senior staff enjoy both vertical and horizontal working relationships. In addition to this there is a tendency for strong subject loyalties to exist within departments, and the interaction of staff is often restricted to shared specialist interests (Tipton 1973). The head of department having reached a position of some authority, albeit invested in his/her position, may cultivate loyalty and cohesion within the department and see his/her role as that of projecting, improving and safeguarding the position and resources of the department. There is, therefore, a danger that academic boards may become a platform for little more than departmental infighting rather than the initiation of curriculum change or analysis in keeping with some agreed collegewide corporate policy.

To effect significant curriculum change is difficult for any teacher when working within the constraints imposed by external examination agencies or when the curriculum demands adherence to a behavioural objectives approach. The active teacher's task of influencing change within a college-based curriculum may prove no less daunting when the vertical working relationship referred to is strictly imposed.

Within such constraints even a proposed change in methodology involving the adoption of team teaching techniques or cross-modular assignments involving staff from differing disciplines may well be vetoed when submitted to senior staff. It thus becomes clear that the power of the teacher to publicize the need for innovation internally may well be negated by the power of his/her head of department to actually sanction such change. This is not to suggest that senior staff or boards of study should not have the power of veto, but rather to acknowledge the limited ability of the teacher to effect significant change.

Indeed, it is not unknown for innovative ideas to be squashed on the grounds that 'they' (external validating/moderating agencies) would never agree with such suggestions. This reference to the nebulous 'they' is dangerous on two counts since not only does it place the teacher in a position in which he is unable to verify the validity of the claim, but it can invest an

The Role of the Teacher as an Agent of Change in Further Education 175

external agency with an authority which in reality it does not possess.

The model shown in Table 17.1 is of interest in illustrating the relationship between power and influence within colleges, and therefore also largely reflects where the power behind curriculum innovation really lies.

Table 17.1

Initiator	Unit	Example	Power/Influence ratio
Government	National System	Raising school leaving age	POWER
LEA Committee	LEA	Tertiary reorganisation	
Principal	College	Allocation of resources	
Head of Department	Department	New syllabus	
Teacher	Class	Learning	INFLUENCE

Source: Hoyle (1970)

A traditional approach to the implementation of any specific curriculum innovation within colleges is often the setting up of a working party or some similar group. Such a group may face the task of preparing college units for TEC or BEC programmes, foundation or vocational preparation courses and, most important, the dissemination of proposed curricula to college staff. It is interesting to note that in a survey (Further Education Unit 1980a) concerned with curriculum dissemination, half of the respondents claimed to be involved in such working parties. Perhaps even more significant was the fact that a considerably higher proportion of staff so involved were from the senior levels, that is 96% were heads of department, 83% vice-principals, while only 41% of lecturers (Grade I) claimed to be involved.

What becomes apparent is that the opportunity for lower levels of staff to influence curriculum change is frequently reduced to tinkering with teaching methodology within the autonomy of the classroom. While teachers can, and do, influence change within college-based curricula, such change tends to emanate from working parties whose responsibility is often directed primarily towards the design and content of specific course curricula.

To be able to influence decisions affecting the curriculum the message for those at or near the bottom of the lecturer scale is clear: direct your energies towards involvement in those committees and working parties set up to consider curriculum design but understand that it is likely the composition of the working party will reflect a preponderance of senior staff. While association with such groups may well assist the career development of some lecturers, it is unlikely they will be able to influence significantly any radical change in an environment which places so much emphasis on recognizing the influence of individual staff by virtue of the authority invested in the position they hold.

However, I do not intend to project an image of all teachers constantly being obstructed in the pursuit and implementation of innovative ideas. Indeed, there is evidence (Kaneti Barry 1974) to suggest that even when new craft courses have been introduced in further education there has been a tendency to adhere to old practices with the only significant change taking place largely restricted to a change of course title.

Nevertheless, there is little doubt that involvement in working parties can prove most beneficial in understanding and fulfilling the needs of new curricula. What is more questionable is whether there is a sufficient representation of teachers who will actually implement the curriculum decided upon. Furthermore, it is self-evident that the ability to influence change is largely dependent upon access to relevant information, yet such access may well be denied since responsibility for the dissemination of information may be seen by some as a means of establishing or maintaining power and authority (Pettigrew 1972). There is no reason to believe that information control as a device for exercising power and authority is any less prevalent within the departmental structure to be found in many colleges than in other organizations. Indeed, it may well at times account for the failure of information to be disseminated downwards through the hierarchy. In an interview (Further Education Unit 1980a) with a BEC representative concerning curriculum dissemination the officer made public what many staff have found through experience, that 'the dissemination of information within college institutions leaves a great deal to be desired'.

In terms of curriculum change the departmental structure is seen by many as a constraining influence, ill-equipped to respond to rapid change and the adoption of interdisciplinary courses or courses requiring cross-modular assignments. In this respect it is interesting to note Abbott's (1969) claim that 'it is unreasonable to expect any radical departure from traditional educational practices so long as we insist on placing undue emphasis upon hierarchical status'.

Such structures, however, are not without advantages and the charge of empire building may be countered by pointing to the growth of some departments as recognized centres of excellence as a positive advantage. Nor is the narrow specialism associated with many departments to be seen only in negative terms since it can also reflect high professional standards and a strong sense of purpose.

Nevertheless, it would appear that there exists limited opportunity for lecturers at the lower levels to influence curriculum change significantly. This lack of opportunity may lie within the nature of the departmental or hierarchical structure to be found in most further education colleges. This factor along with a general disquiet has resulted in recent years in a 'significant move in further education to find an alternative to the traditional hierarchical structure based on departments' (Ferguson 1979). Such an alternative, however, need not be identified with the extremes of a full-blooded matrix system nor the strict management by objectives approach.

Like many problems facing education there is a danger of reducing solutions to a choice of two extremes when in reality the dynamic nature of education imposes a mixture of methods and a combination of solutions which have been adopted by virtue of the decentralized nature of provision. This autonomy of institutional development is reflected in the way in which some institutions have moved from the traditional departmental system in varying degrees towards a matrix system with a greater emphasis on horizontal communications.

The problems associated with organizational structure have a direct bearing on curricula and the speed with which innovation can respond to social, economic and political developments. It is, therefore, inevitable that conflicting views will abound concerning the influence of structure upon curriculum change and, perhaps, the situation will remain largely one of academic discussion unless much more is done to achieve widespread evaluation by teachers throughout further education.

References

Abbott, M.G. (1969) Hierarchical impediments to innovation in educational organisations, *in* Carver, F. and Sergiovanni, T. (eds) *Organisations and Human Behaviour*, New York: McGraw-Hill.

Bernstein, B. (1974) Classification and framing of educational knowledge, *Class, Codes and Control*, vol. 1, London: Routledge and Kegan Paul.

Central Advisory Council for Education (England) (1959) *15 to 18* (Crowther Report), London: HMSO.

Ferguson, C. (1979) Alternative organisational structures in Higher and Further Education, *Aspects of College Management*, part 1, Coombe Lodge Report, vol. 12, no. 12, 1980.

Further Education Curriculum Review and Development Unit (1980) *Day Release – a Desk Study*, P.R.2, Project Report, London: DES.

Further Education Curriculum Review and Development Unit (1980a) *Loud and Clear*, a study of curriculum dissemination in Further and Higher Education, London: HMSO.

Hamilton, D. (1976) *Curriculum Evaluation*, London: Open Books.

Hoyle, E. (1970) Planned organisation change, *Research in Education*, May.

Kaneti Barry, S.M. (1974) *Engineering Craft Studies: Monitoring a new syllabus*, Slough: National Foundation for Educational Research.

National Advisory Council on Education for Industry and Commerce (1969) Report of the Committee on Technician Courses and Examinations under the chairmanship of Dr H.L. Haslegrave, London: HMSO.

Pettigrew, A.M. (1972) Information control as a power resource, *Sociology*, vol. 6, no. 2, July.

Pring, R. (1973) Objectives and innovation: the irrelevance of theory, *London Educational Review*, vol. 2, no. 3.

Skilbeck, M. (1984) *School-Based Curriculum Development*, London: Harper and Row.

Tipton, B. (1973) *Conflict and Change in a Technical College*, London: Hutchinson Educational.

CHAPTER 18

REVIEWING AND DEVELOPING THE CURRICULUM: THE GRIDS PROJECT*
Agnes McMahon

School self-evaluation or review occurs when the staff of a school meet together to review and assess their work. The underlying and major purpose of such activity is to improve the process of teaching and learning in the school. In practice a self-review exercise may lead to changes and improvements in the curriculum, the organization of the school or, indeed, any aspect of its work. It can also have direct benefits for the teachers since participating in an exercise of this type is a very valuable form of staff development. A school may decide independently to undertake a review or alternatively it may be requested to do one by the local education authority for accountability purposes but whatever the motivation, once the decision has been taken, the staff have to agree upon a working procedure. Since by the early 1980s local education authorities in England and Wales had produced schemes for self-evaluation or review there ought to have been plenty of suggestions available, but though the majority of the LEA documents include sets of prompting questions under various headings, few give any guidance about *how* the review process should be tackled. The project which is outlined in this article has attempted to fill this gap by producing process guidelines for schools wishing to conduct a self-review.

Project outline and aims

The Guidelines for Review and Internal Development in Schools (GRIDS)

---

* This chapter is adapted from an article by the author which was published in *Educational Management and Administration*, vol. 10, no. 3, 1982, pp. 217–222.

Project was a Schools Council Programme 1 activity based at the University of Bristol. The project was designed to help teachers who wish to review and develop the curriculum and organization of their school, and two practical handbooks, one primary, one secondary, have been produced for this purpose. The title of the project was carefully chosen. First, the materials are guidelines: they contain structured step-by-step advice about how to conduct a school review and development exercise; schools are not expected to follow these suggestions slavishly but rather to adapt and amend as required. Secondly, the focus is on school review leading to internal school development and not something that stops short at the review stage. Finally, the word 'school' emphasizes that GRIDS is directed at the whole school rather than individual teachers or small groups. These points are further spelt out in the list of key principles that underpin the materials and are central to the GRIDS method. These are that:

1. the aim is to achieve internal school development and not to produce a report for formal accountability purposes;
2. the main purpose is to move beyond the review stage into development for school improvement;
3. the staff of the school should be consulted and involved in the review and development process as much as possible;
4. decisions about what happens to any information or reports produced should rest with the teachers and others concerned;
5. the head and teachers should decide whether and how to involve the other groups in the school, e.g. pupils, parents, advisers, governors;
6. outsiders (e.g. external consultants) should be invited to provide help and advice when this seems appropriate;
7. the demands made on key resources, like time, money and skilled personnel, should be realistic and feasible for schools and LEAs.

Probably the most significant of these is the principle that all the teachers should be consulted and involved in the exercise as much as possible. The arguments for this are that it would be counter-productive for the head and senior management to initiate major changes without reference to the views of the staff and, secondly, that the more the teachers are consulted and involved in the process the more they will be committed to it and so the greater the likelihood that the school will benefit from the exercise.

The central practical recommendation in the GRIDS method is that schools should not attempt to review everything at once. Instead, the recommended procedure is to take a broad look at what is happening in the

Reviewing and Developing the Curriculum: the GRIDS Project 181

school, on the basis of this identify one or two areas that the staff consider to be priorities for specific review and development, tackle these first, evaluate what has been achieved and then select another priority area. The five stages in this cyclical process are outlined in Figure 18.1.

Figure 18.1 The five stages of the institutional review and development process

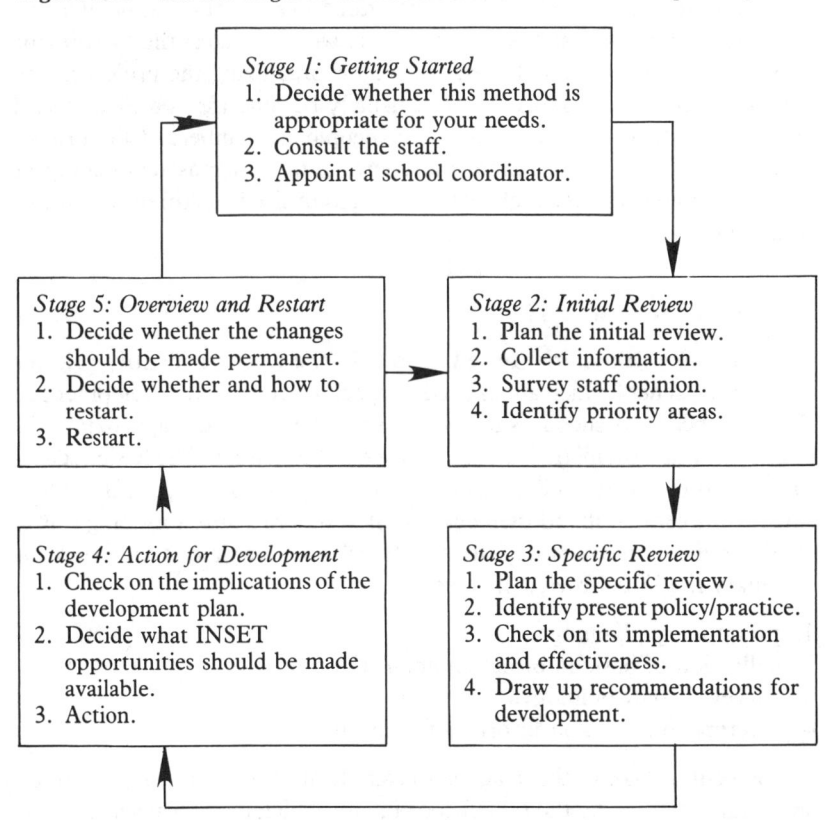

Stage 1: Getting Started
1. Decide whether this method is appropriate for your needs.
2. Consult the staff.
3. Appoint a school coordinator.

Stage 5: Overview and Restart
1. Decide whether the changes should be made permanent.
2. Decide whether and how to restart.
3. Restart.

Stage 2: Initial Review
1. Plan the initial review.
2. Collect information.
3. Survey staff opinion.
4. Identify priority areas.

Stage 4: Action for Development
1. Check on the implications of the development plan.
2. Decide what INSET opportunities should be made available.
3. Action.

Stage 3: Specific Review
1. Plan the specific review.
2. Identify present policy/practice.
3. Check on its implementation and effectiveness.
4. Draw up recommendations for development.

The GRIDS materials have been piloted in some thirty primary and secondary schools in five LEAs, Avon, Clwyd, Coventry, Essex and Leeds. Each authority appointed a project supervisor (a senior or chief adviser) with responsibility for overseeing the whole exercise and an LEA coordinator who was released from his/her normal duties for approximately one day a week to work on the project. These LEA coordinators all had school experience and positions of responsibility within the LEA either as teacher centre wardens, advisory teachers or college lecturers. Should an LEA afterwards decide to extend the project to other schools, these coordinators would be able to provide guidance and support.

All the pilot schools were asked to designate a school coordinator and a small team of people to be centrally involved in the project. The heads chose their coordinator but in the GRIDS introductory booklet it was pointed out that appropriate time, status and experience were needed as the coordinator would be the person mainly responsible for organizing the project in the school. In primary schools the head usually became the coordinator and she/he identified just one or two other people as members of the project team. In the secondary school the coordinator was most commonly at deputy-head level and the school team ranged in size from three or four to a much larger group.

The initial review

The purpose of the initial review is to help the teachers identify priority areas in the school which are in need of specific review and development in the year ahead. As such it is intended to be a fairly speedy (approximately one term) but systematic look at the work of the school. The basic recommendation is that the school coordinator and team should plan the initial review, implement it and then evaluate it. The procedure for doing this is spelled out in a series of key steps with tasks to complete at each step. In summary the initial review involves:

1. preliminary planning;
2. collection of basic information about the school;
3. survey of staff opinion;
4. meeting to decide on priorities for specific review.

The central task in this stage is to sample staff opinion using a survey sheet administered by the school coordinator which every teacher, including the head, completes. This survey sheet gives each teacher the opportunity to state what he/she feels are the priority areas. It falls into two parts: in section one the teachers are asked to say whether an area of the school is a strength or weakness and whether or not it is in need of specific review and development; in section two they are asked to identify three aspects of school life and rank them in order of priority for specific review and development over the next twelve months. To try and ensure that the teachers have access to information that will enable them to make an informed rather than superficial judgement about what should be the priorities for specific review, the school coordinator and team are recommended to collect basic information about the school and incorporate this into a summary report for the staff explaining what the school's position is on the various aspects highlighted in the survey sheet. This summary report should be distributed before the teachers complete the sheet. During their preliminary planning the school coordinator and team are also asked to decide when the exercise should take place, identify the resources that are available, identify the people inside and outside the school who should be involved and consulted, and draw up a timetable for the review.

Once the survey sheet has been completed, the school coordinator is asked to analyse the findings and present the results to the staff before organizing a meeting to agree on the areas to be selected for specific review. When some agreement has been reached about these priority areas, the school coordinator has the responsibility of drawing up a plan for the specific review(s) and moving the school forward into the next stage.

Specific review and development

A school may decide to undertake any number of specific reviews in a year. In practice, it is anticipated that a small primary school will probably only tackle one and a large secondary school possibly two or three. Once the teachers have identified particular aspects for specific review and development, it may become apparent that the school coordinator is not the most appropriate person to organize the specific review. Other people, termed specific review coordinators (SRCs), may take over particular coordinating tasks; for example, if the aspect being reviewed is the language policy, the teacher with a post of responsibility for this or the head of the English department may become the SRC.

The tasks of the school coordinator then change. He or she is responsible for overseeing the specific reviews, providing practical help and advice for the specific review coordinators, and for keeping the rest of the staff informed about what is happening. Once the SRCs have prepared their conclusions and recommendations for action, the school coordinator has then to prepare a plan for the development phase.

The guidelines for the SRCs and team incorporate the same three broad recommendations as are in the initial review: plan, implement and evaluate. Once again the procedure is spelt out in a series of key steps with tasks to complete at each step. In summary, this involves:

1. planning the specific review;
2. clarifying what is the school's present policy on the area under specific review;
3. establishing whether this policy is actually being implemented;
4. deciding how effective present policy/practice is;
5. agreeing conclusions and recommendations and judging the effectiveness of the review.

The planning tasks require the SRC team to clarify not just why the particular area was selected for review but also what aspect of the topic they should focus on first. They are recommended to consult existing school documents in order to establish what the school's policy is on a particular area and to question the other teachers about what they think happens if there is no documentation so that some fairly hard evidence can be collected. The next step requires them to consider whether this policy is actually being implemented in the school. Depending on the area being reviewed, a variety of methods can be used to establish what is actually happening, e.g. discussion groups, staff questionnaire, observation of practice, asking parents/children, etc.

The fourth step – 'decide how effective present policy/practice actually is' – is undoubtedly the most difficult. If institutional self-review is to be of benefit and if it is to have some credibility with outsiders, then it must be rigorous and systematic. There seems little point in embarking on an exercise which is essentially designed to preserve the status quo. The judgements that the SRC team make about the effectiveness of present practice are crucial since these may not only be the basis on which they will make a diagnostic assessment of the action that should be taken but, afterwards, they may well be the bench-marks against which the effectiveness of any development work is judged. The SRC team ultimately have to decide what criteria and procedures will be relevant and appropriate for assessing the effectiveness of present policy and practice. These can range from easily manageable measures which they collect themselves to more rigorous ones which may involve using standardized tests. It is at this point that help from an external consultant can be invaluable. It may, for example, be much easier to agree on appropriate criteria when maths rather than communication between staff is the area selected for specific review and development.

One of the pilot schools was a primary school in the middle of a town with a small playground and no playing field. The priority area that the staff selected was physical education which they felt was a weakness in the school since, as well as having very poor facilities, they had no specialist teacher on the staff. As part of their specific review they conducted a very detailed survey of their present practice and invited the local PE adviser into the school to talk about PE in the primary school and to discuss their particular problems. After this they drew up a list of questions that they used as their criteria for assessing the effectiveness of their present practice.

a. Do the children enjoy their PE?
b. Is there observation of the children by the teacher to see the skills acquired, and assessment made of future needs?
c. Is there observation of the social interaction of each child within a group?
d. Do the children respond to teacher direction?
e. Are the children developing the skills needed at the appropriate age?
f. Does the level of work match the needs of the children?

Another school which was examining its provision for less able children used a number of commercial tests to mark the children's achievement at that point and to establish a base line against which future work could be judged. Teachers are not generally accustomed to making rigorous assessments of the effectiveness of their work and they will need to experiment and use a range of different criteria.

Once this step has been completed the SRC team are asked to consider their conclusions and recommendations for development work, not only in the light of their assessment of the effectiveness of present policy/practice, but after also considering its appropriateness. One of the underlying principles of the project is that the demand it places on key resources should be realistic for schools, and the SRCs are asked to bear this in mind when they check out the feasibility of their recommendations.

Action for development

The fourth stage of the process is concerned with development and especially with providing support for the implementation of innovations – something that has been all too frequently neglected. The head and school coordinator must be centrally involved in any decisions about how to implement the recommendations from the specific review. The detailed work can be carried out by a specific development team who probably, but not necessarily, are the same people who were responsible for the specific review. The key steps and tasks for this stage are intended to make the development team aware of the factors that can hinder or prevent the successful implementations of innovations, and to draw attention to the need to provide any necessary in-service education. The procedure suggested is to:

- check out the implications of the development plan;
- draw up a timetable for the implementation stage;
- decide what in-service opportunities should be made available;
- judge the effectiveness of the development work.

Overview and restart

This stage is intended to help schools complete one cycle of the review and development process and start upon a second cycle. It is suggested that decisions have to be made about:

- whether or not the changes introduced during the development phase should be made a permanent feature of the school;
- whether this approach to institutional review and development should be continued or adapted.

Key steps and tasks were identified for both these issues. If a decision is made in favour of continuing the same style of review and development, three ways of restarting the cycle are suggested:

1. reviewing the remaining areas that the staff had identified as priorities;
2. consulting the staff using a limited survey sheet;
3. conducting a second initial review using the original survey sheet.

The final suggestion put forward for consideration is whether additional people inside or outside the school should be informed about the review and development exercise and what has been achieved during the first cycle.

The time-scale for the project has been short and the majority of the pilot schools are still in the development stage and have not yet taken decisions about overview and restart.

External support

In the pilot phase of the project a fairly strong support structure was provided both inside and outside the school. Each school was asked to identify both a coordinator and a small project team in order to promote ownership of the project within the school. In turn, the LEA coordinator provided a first line of support for this school team. The LEA coordinators did not adopt an interventionist role but they kept in close contact with the schools and helped with any problems that arose. The school coordinators were told that if they had any queries or difficulties they should contact their LEA coordinator in the first instance. The LEA coordinators organized regular (i.e. every half-term) meetings for the school coordinators and, though their main purpose was to exchange information and advice, they did have a partial 'training' function and this is something that could be developed more in any future work.

Three of the five authorities set up some form of local project advisory/steering committee and this helped to consolidate knowledge and experience of the GRIDS materials and the institutional self-review process.

The question of whether a school can quite independently conduct an institutional self-review must be problematic. In the GRIDS materials the issue is left fairly open though one of the underlying principles of the project is that 'schools should seek help and advice from an external consultant when this seems appropriate'. The pilot LEAs interpreted this principle in different ways. Three of them adopted a fairly low-key approach in that, though they were quite prepared to respond to requests for help from the schools, they did not make any deliberate attempt to involve the members of the advisory team, teachers' centre wardens, etc. in the project. In contrast, the remaining two authorities actively encouraged their pilot schools to use outside help. In one case, the pilot schools were all selected from one division of the authority and the LEA advisers for that division were asked to work closely with the schools. The second of these LEAs added a further dimension to the project by asking the schools to use a consultant during the institutional self-review and development process. The schools could select a teacher from another school or a member of the advisory team as consultant, and these people were then briefly trained for their new role by the LEA.

Support at national level was provided by the project Advisory Committee which consisted of one representative from each LEA plus a number of 'experts' in the field. This committee monitored the progress of the project and also commented upon and provided practical suggestions about the materials. In addition, there were a number of workshops and meetings for LEA supervisors and coordinators. The primary purpose of these meetings was always to discuss drafts of the GRIDS materials, to discuss particular strategies and to receive reports on progress. However, they did fulfil the secondary purpose of building up a network of people who have experience of this approach to institutional self-review.

The GRIDS materials are intended to be a low-cost, simple, do-it-yourself kit for schools wishing to conduct a self-review and development exercise. As such they are only one of several approaches that can be adopted. There is now a growing interest in school self-review, and as knowledge increases so a greater range of possible strategies should be made available to the schools. As they stand the GRIDS materials are not necessarily incompatible with other approaches. They are intended to be process guidelines and if the basic notion of selecting priority areas for specific review and development rather than reviewing everything at once is accepted, then the key steps and tasks which are essentially suggestions about procedure can be adapted to fit other schemes and conditions.

What has been learned

Experience gained during the GRIDS project has indicated that over a twelve-month period schools can use these materials to conduct a self-review and development exercise and that they can move successfully into the development phase. Secondly it is clear that it is extremely difficult for schools to undertake wholesale review and development without external support and indeed they would be unwise to attempt to do this if it can be avoided. The experience has also shown that many schools have an action orientation and tend to rush into the development phase without first establishing, and then making a detailed assessment of, their present practice. As anticipated, selecting criteria for assessment is extremely difficult. Finally, not enough is known about the practical strategies that schools can adopt to evaluate their development work. On all these points further research and development work is necessary.

In the meantime some practical suggestions for schools planning to undertake a school self-review would be: first, to try and ensure that the staff are in agreement and that external support is available; second, to make a realistic assessment of what can be done and not attempt to review all aspects of the school at once but select one or two priority areas and tackle these first; third, to appreciate that the exercise will take time, at least a year, but also recognize that unless timetables and deadlines are drawn up and adhered to, the review can lose all momentum.

References

Baker, K. and Sikora, J. (1982) *The Schools and In-service Teacher Education (SITE) Evaluation Project: Final Report*, University of Bristol School of Education.

Becher, R. and Maclure, S. (1978) *Accountability in Education*, Windsor: NFER.

Clift, P. (1982) LEA schemes for school self-evaluation: a critique, *Educational Research*, 24, 4, pp.262–271.

Elliott, G. (1980 and 1981) *Self Evaluation and the Teacher Parts 1–4* An annotated bibliography and report on current practice, London: Schools Council.

Hopkins, D. (1983) *School Based Review for School Improvement: A preliminary state of the art*, Paris: OECD.

McCormick, R. (ed.) (1982) *Calling Education to Account*, London: Heinemann.

Nuttall, D.L. (1981) *School Self Evaluation: Accountability with a human face?* London: Schools Council.

Open University (1982) Course E364 *Curriculum Evaluation and Assessment in Educational Studies*, Bletchley: Open University Press.

CHAPTER 19

THE DESIGN, SELECTION AND USE OF RESOURCES IN CURRICULUM DEVELOPMENT
Philip Waterhouse

The interest of teachers in learning resources derives from two convictions: first, that a good collection of learning resources can help provide for their pupils a richer and more stimulating educational experience; and second, that the sophisticated use of learning resources is a necessary condition for the successful individualization of learning.

The richness, the variety, and the stimulating nature of modern learning resources are due to advances in technology. Printed materials have improved enormously in the last two decades. Books are once again objects of great beauty, thanks to developments in printing technology and in graphic design. The development of the offset litho printing techniques has simplified and enhanced the quality production of home-made materials. Developments in photography, in broadcasting, in audio and visual recording techniques, in microelectronics, and in telecommunications are constantly revealing new horizons. All this is supported by increased sophistication in the skills of finding, storing, and retrieving of information. Already there are exciting combinations of the three constituent parts of information technology: information handling (finding, storing and retrieving); information transmission (telecommunications and broadcasting); and information transformation (the manipulation of information by manual or electronic techniques). Today's teacher operates with a resource capability that is already far superior to that enjoyed by his predecessor in the immediate postwar period; and the rate of improvement is increasing.

The commitment of the teaching profession to the individualization of learning seems to be as strong as ever. Individualization means that the teacher aims to adapt programmes of work to individual needs, capabilities and interests, thus contributing to the growth of personal autonomy. Resource-based learning with its emphasis on a rich and varied collection of learning resources helps to achieve that aim. It is not *necessarily* an individualized system, although that is the context in which it is most frequently used in practice. In a practical way it also allows different pupils to be engaged on different topics at the same time. This encourages cooperation in learning, resulting in meaningful choices within a disciplined framework, and in a more economical use of learning resources. There is also the argument that resource-based learning offers greater potential for a more personal and adult relationship between teachers and their pupils. The contact is usually individual and it is quiet, so that the work of others is not disturbed. And when challenge or reprimand or assessment are needed, the deed can be done privately, so lessening resentment and encouraging thoughtful response.

While there are undoubtedly some financial and organizational problems, it is difficult to find flaws in the pedagogical arguments for a greater use of resource-based learning. Dissatisfactions with class teaching, with 'chalk and talk', are frequently expressed. But it is too easy to exaggerate the case against it, and it is not wise to propose resource-based learning as a total alternative to it. Most teachers today recognize the value of a broad repertoire of styles and methods. This includes class work as well as small-group and individual work, not merely to 'ring the changes', but in order to use the most appropriate method at every point in the development of a programme of learning.

Another cautionary note must be sounded. Resource-based learning requires a greater degree of sophistication in classroom management than class teaching. Lots of resources and good intentions are not enough. Many of the earlier failures in resource-based learning can be attributed to the concentration on school-based resource production when the thought and effort should have been directed towards the development of better systems of classroom management.

The remainder of this chapter seeks to clarify the issues of design, selection, organization and use of learning resources *from the teaching point of view*.

The design and selection of learning resources
Sources
In the acquisition of learning resources three simple choices face the

teacher: to buy; to borrow; or to make. The busy teacher, short of both time and money, will nevertheless find the decisions difficult. Some suggestions follow.

1. Avoid school production as much as possible. Cost it carefully both in terms of materials and in terms of precious teacher time. Confine it to topics that are too local or specialized for the commercial producer.
2. Investigate the availability of low-cost and free resources, from a wide range of commercial, industrial, professional, and public sources.
3. Make full use of loan services, from the local authority's library, museum, and art services, as well as from other organizations.
4. Take advantage of opportunities to be involved in cooperative resource making in the local area.
5. When buying from commercial sources prefer resources that are small in size and format. This means, for example, going for the small topic booklet which can help towards an economical use of resources. (Contrast it with the situation where one pupil is working on one page of a 500-page textbook.)

Media

Of course it is wise to use a variety of media in the selection of resources. The simplest justification for this is that pupils welcome a variety of approach. But the teacher also needs to consider carefully the selection of the most appropriate medium for each learning activity. Some learning tasks are best performed with the help of the written page. Others demand copious visual illustration in diagrammatic or pictorial form. Others benefit from the moving images of film or television (live or recorded). Others depend on recorded sound.

The decisions are made more complex when the important considerations of cost and availability are taken into account. These can be paramount and as a result they are often taken first in the decision-making process: decide what is available within the cost limitations – consider the strengths and weaknesses of each available medium – select from the items available in the chosen medium.

A more systematic approach would be to carry out a thorough analysis of the learning objectives and then to consider the strengths and weaknesses of each possible medium.

Design

The design of learning resources is important to the teacher whether buying, borrowing or making. It is concerned with the major decisions about the composition and format of the resources, what they consist of and how they are arranged.

Two major components can be recognized: first, the data and stimuli which form the raw material for learning; and second, the guidance which helps the learner to process the raw material.

The former covers a wide range of materials: descriptive and explanatory text; evocative writing; statistical information; pictures in all media; diagrams and drawings of all kinds; sound recordings; film and television presentations. By itself the stimulus material does not constitute a formal educational programme. In the hands of a sophisticated learner, who is capable of formulating his own objectives, devising his own work programme, testing ideas, and making decisions about the form of the end product, this great diversity of resources can be powerful.

But for the younger and less experienced learner the guidance material provides essential support. This tells the learner how to set about the work. It provides guidance about the overall objectives, sets tasks, formulates problems, advises about the choice and use of resources, gives guidance about the form and style of the finished product, and makes clear statements about standards.

A fundamental design decision for the teacher is whether to use resource material that attempts to integrate the stimulus and guidance materials, or whether to deliberately plan that they shall exist separately.

There has been an assumption that the former decision is necessary or preferable. Programmed Learning materials made this assumption, as do many of the school-produced 'worksheets' which abound. This is a reasonable assumption where the amount of stimulus material is very small, and the amount of guidance is large. An example would be resource material developed to teach a particular skill in a craft subject, using a limited range of equipment and materials. The emphasis must be on the careful sequencing of small tasks, with small steps between them, with frequent short responses required from the learner, and immediate feedback about performance. This style can be extended into topics in mathematics, laboratory skills in science, graphic and statistical skills in the social sciences, and many other well-defined, self-contained topics in a wide range of subjects.

But it would be a tragic mistake to apply it to all situations. In literature, the humanities, the social sciences, and the pure sciences, there is a strong case to be made for separating the stimulus material from the guidance material.

First, the arrangement offers more flexibility. The teacher or the pupil does not feel bound by a predetermined sequencing. Adjusting the guidance material to allow for individual needs and preferences is a much easier task than trying to redesign a whole integrated package.

Second, it allows a given set of stimulus material to be used in many different situations with different learners for different purposes. It is not locked into one learning programme. Good stimulus material can have use and meaning for a very wide range of learners; pupils are not always as imprisoned by their own reading ages as some would have us believe. Adults often find books produced for young people intrinsically interesting; young people can acquire understanding and inspiration from material aimed at an adult audience.

Third, it allows the teacher a much wider choice in the search for good stimulus material; indeed, it opens it up completely. The school's own library/resource centre now comes into its own. The teacher, in cooperation with the librarian, can develop a course in a very flexible way. This contrasts sharply with preoccupations of the teachers who are always searching for integrated material, feeling the desperate need to produce their own 'worksheet' systems. These have been so common, but they tend to be 'closed' systems, and are rightly condemned.

Fourth, it is an economical system. Good stimulus material can be used in a variety of learning situations with a variety of learners. It can be acquired or produced as single copies or in small sets, rather than in complete class sets.

So the collection of stimulus materials is best separated from the prepared guidance material. The collection might be integrated, with all the elements combined within a single cover; or it might be loosely assembled as a 'pack' in order to give the user greater flexibility. Whichever arrangement is used the contents can be classified into five components: a structured course; a looser collection of unstructured materials; a list of background reference materials; a bank of test materials; and printed (or taped) guidance for the learner.

1. The *structured 'course'* is the heart of the collection. Its purpose is to provide a sound logical structure, a comprehensive coverage, and an effective sequencing of the learning material. It is the firm framework of

the resources collection. It helps the learner to keep his sense of direction, to review what he has previously learned, and to plan ahead for the next phase. It provides a discipline, and serves as a map and a guidebook to the learning programme. Characteristic features of such a structured 'course' are:
* clear statements of objectives for each section of the course;
* a clear logical structure in the text, made clear by the effective use of headings and subheadings, different typefaces, and various graphic aids to clarity such as boxes, and diagrammatic presentation of ideas;
* careful sequencing of information and tasks.
2. *Unstructured material* should be an additional component in any organized resource collection. By itself the structured course might seem to be a rather plain diet. The purpose of including unstructured material is to stimulate the pupil and to gain his interest, to make the learning experience more exciting, or more human. It might include:
* written material in an evocative style;
* well-chosen visual material;
* material that appeals to the heart as well as the head;
* material that suggests practical applications of the new knowledge;
* material that is people oriented.

This kind of material is far better left in unstructured form than packed tightly within the disciplined framework of a structured course. It lends itself to reflective browsing as well as systematic researching.
3. Whatever overall design has been adopted for the resource collection the learner will need a list of *background reference material*. The materials should if possible be multimedia, and they would normally be available in the school's library/resources centre. They would help the learner to set the new experiences into a wider context, by offering alternative explanations, different examples, and interesting extensions to the information and ideas presented in the structured course.
4. *Test materials* will help to determine the pupil's readiness for a particular learning experience, help the pupil to understand his own progress and performance, and help the teacher to make assessments of the pupil's work at various stages. Many designers of integrated resource collections include self-assessment questions as an important part of the structured course.
5. Finally, *guidance for the learner* is essential. It needs to be prepared in advance, because of the pressures under which the teacher in the classroom works. In a perfect world it would be possible to discuss each piece

of new work with each individual pupil, adapting all the time to needs, interests and capabilities. This is unfortunately not possible and we have to find ways of economizing in the use of time while not losing sight of the ideal. Prepared guidance is one such useful economy. Like any other packaged commodity it offers convenience in exchange for some loss of flexibility and individuality; but it can be remarkably flexible when used imaginatively.

In the design of an integrated resources collection, the guidance will almost certainly be incorporated with the structured course component. The aim will be to make the text genuinely interactive, and to increase the involvement of the pupil.

For the segregated resources collection a useful distinction can be made between the assignment which is short term and specific, and the study guide which is long term and more general.

An assignment should ideally set short-term objectives, specify the resources to be used, set tasks and problems, and give some idea of standards expected and how the end product should be presented. It is usually a fairly short document, and a collection of assignments for a course or part of a course can often be organized in card index form using standard A5 cards with tabbed dividers. Writing good assignments is an art, well worth a lot of practice. Well-designed assignments can be instrumental in lifting the quality of classroom work to new heights.

A study guide which may be directed at a more mature or more capable pupil might offer guidance on entry conditions (what previous knowledge is assumed), on the aims of the learning programme, on the methods of study proposed, on the resources that are available (distinguishing between the core material and the supplementary), and finally offer guidance on personal organization. It is usually written in more general terms than an assignment and leaves much more decision making to the learner. Clearly there is no rigid demarcation between a study guide and an assignment. Good designers of collections for resource-based learning will plan a unique product for each individual collection, bearing in mind the objectives of the course, the needs, interests and capabilities of the learners, and the availability of suitable simulus material and data.

The organization of learning resources

As resources for learning have increased in quantity, quality and variety, so have the problems associated with their organization. Much of the discussion about resource centres in schools, and about resources provision generally, has been about the choice between centralization and decentralization. Enthusiasts for the development of resource centres have sometimes been carried away by the logic of their own case. The arguments for centralization are that a learning resource may be put to a number of quite different uses within a school by different departments, that efficient storage for searching and retrieving is best organized by someone who is trained to do it, and that a well-organized library/resource centre is a stimulating and inspiring focus of the intellectual life of a school. The arguments are powerful ones, but they should always be set against the day-by-day practical concerns of the teacher. The arguments for decentralization stress the need for a department's specialized resources to be permanently available at the point of use, and the additional administrative work involved in running and using a complex system of loans from a centralized collection.

Associated with the debate about centralization has been a debate about the status of the qualified librarian in schools. The arguments have tended to focus on the roles of librarians and teachers: librarians are seen by many teachers as ancillaries who are solely concerned with the storage and issue of materials from the resource collection; teachers are seen by many librarians as narrowly preoccupied with what happens in their own classrooms and insensitive to the professional competence and contribution of the librarian.

In both these debates there is a natural tendency for the 'opposing' sides to polarize the arguments. Rather than allow this to grow, it is better to accept at the start that serious and thoughtful discussion must take place *at school level* so that policies and styles may be established. Both centralized and decentralized resource collections are necessary, and it should be fairly easy to define the main responsibility of each part of the school's resources system. The difficulties are those of definition at the frontiers, and these need to be resolved in a pragmatic way; there are unlikely to be any universal principles to invoke, just the practicalities and logic of the unique situation. Likewise, teachers and librarians must be encouraged to see themselves as part of the same team, to accept, as in any good team, that roles and functions will overlap in the interest of mutual support.

So the school's learning resources system must be thought of in terms of the classroom as a resource centre, the school's library/resource centre, and the links to sources of information and guidance from outside the school.

The classroom as a learning resource centre

The classroom resource centre is a most important part of the system. Each classroom may develop its own collection, or there may be a small centre serving a suite of classrooms. A good classroom resource centre is only possible where the school policy favours functional specialization of rooms. Many secondary schools still allow 'general purpose' classrooms that are expected, at different times of the week, to house a wide variety of subject teaching and a wide age range of pupils. This is not helpful to the teacher. Functional specialization, by contrast, provides substantial benefits: teachers can cooperate in the collection and management of resources required for a particular educational programme; responsibility for the room can be clearly assigned; pupils use one familiar classroom for all their work in one subject; the utilization of the resources can be organized in a cost-effective way.

The classroom resource centre should be thought of as a small, specialized multimedia library. Its resources will be mostly single copies or small sets of resource items; full class sets are not so useful in resource-based learning. The items will have been selected because they are directly relevant to the course, and because they match the capabilities of the pupils. They are mostly of small format and specific in content: the short topic booklet, the leaflet or broadsheet, the short tape and short filmstrip. Of course there will be more substantial reference books in the collection, those that are in frequent use in the subject.

Storage of resources within the classroom must take account of the varied shapes and sizes of a multimedia collection. The various kinds of pamphlet boxes and library boxes seem to offer the best prospects, although some teachers prefer to use conventional vertical or lateral filing.

The classification of resources within the classroom presents a problem. On the one hand the teacher who is preparing a unit of a course needs only the simplest system which can be set up quickly and used easily. A simple accession number system has a lot to commend it. Each item is numbered in turn as it is acquired; the number is nothing more than an identification tag within the collection of resources made for the particular unit. On the other hand, there is much to be said for having all resources on the school's central catalogue of resources, and this means classifying the classroom materials accordingly. In an ideal world, where there is a commitment to schoolwide resource-based learning, both systems should be used.

The school learning resource centre

In its most advanced form this can be a large and complex organization. In a smaller school things will be scaled down, but the principles are the same. So a perfect school learning resource centre might contain:

* A production service, including reprographic facilities, some simple graphic design facilities, off-air recording of both radio and television, copying facilities of all kinds (print, slides, audio and video tape).
* A multimedia library covering both fiction and nonfiction which has been carefully planned to meet the needs of the school, both in a general library sense, and in the sense of a specialist information service.
* A classification and indexing service for all the resources held in the individual subject departments.
* A loans service both for individual pupils and for subject departments.
* An equipment service for loan and maintenance of larger audio and visual equipment.
* An information and advisory service about resources within and beyond the bounds of the school, together with a cooperative involvement in course planning and design.
* A capability of giving support to individual pupils engaged in private study. This includes not only the necessary furniture and fittings, but also the advice and help of a knowledgeable adult.

The director of such an array of services carries a substantial responsibility. There are three important issues. First, there is the problem of the mutual incompatibility of some of the functions. Some of the activities are busy and even noisy, and need to be kept separate from the private study areas. It is wrong in an enthusiasm for these kinds of activities to allow the private study opportunities to be hampered. The use of the resources should be the guiding principle. Second, the arguments for centralization of resources should not be pressed with too great zeal. The benefits of convenience (all materials in one place), range (wide variety of materials), and economy (pooling of material and human resources) seem overwhelming if viewed from the school's resource centre. But it is important to remember that, even in the best-equipped school, the vast majority of learning will still take place in the classrooms, and substantial separation of resources from these work centres will result in inconvenience, time wasting, and a loss of personal control by the teacher. Coordination of a large central collection of resources together with a number of satellite collections is undoubtedly much harder work, but it seems to be the only reasonable solution. Third, the most important function of the director of a learning resources centre is the one that is often most ignored: that is, the job of helping departments (or individual teachers) in the design and planning of their courses. The reason why it is neglected is the jealously guarded autonomy of the individual departments. To break this down requires knowledge, skill and diplomacy. There seems to be a real need for all who take on responsibility for a school's resources collection, regardless of whether their initial qualifications were in teaching or librarianship, to be well versed in the design, planning, and preparation of school courses.

The area resources centre

This represents the outer ring of the resources services available to the classroom teacher. The ARC might be a teachers' centre or a more specialized centre serving a much wider area. It offers a similar range of services to the school resources centre. It can possess a more sophisticated production unit, employing graphic designers and print technicians, using offset litho for print work, an audio studio and a photographic studio. It may back up the school centre by providing specialist materials on loan. It may offer a centralized purchasing, processing and cataloguing service for books, and a purchasing and maintenance service for equipment.

There are three main issues for ARCs. First, to what extent should the staff of the centre offer consultancy to the school about course planning and resource-based learning techniques? Second, to what extent should a local authority centralize some of the functions that have been listed as belonging to the school resource centre? Both of these issues are similar to those for the schools' own resource centres. The third is somewhat different. To what extent should the ARC go for integration as opposed to separate development? Good arguments can be advanced for all the services and activities of the ARC to be under one roof and under one direction. There are the benefits for the school in only having one centre to deal with, and the benefits for the centre in being able to respond in a comprehensive way to requests for assistance. Against that there are good arguments for separate development: the schools library service housed where it can use the total service of the public library system; the schools museum service that can draw on the collections and expertise of the local museum; the schools art service that can similarly relate to the Art and Design faculty of a polytechnic.

Probably there is no best way to organize resources for learning, but it does seem desirable that no one of the three centres described above should be developed excessively at the expense of the others. Close cooperation can be of enormous benefit so that the three elements combine to form a truly creative system.

Using resources in the classroom

The organization of resource-based learning in the classroom demands special knowledge and skills. The teacher needs to retain all the traditional skills of exposition and class control, and at the same time develop new skills in management and in personal tutoring. The main problems of resource-based learning spring from the diversity of activities that result from the individualized approach. Success seems to depend on three essentials: the careful planning of group structures within the class; the establishment of a smooth cycle of monitoring and control; and the development of techniques of tutoring.

Structures

Many failures in resource-based learning can be attributed to a failure to give enough attention to the group structures in the class.ABandoning a total addiction to class teaching may be desirable, but it does not follow that the only alternative is to go to the other extreme in which every individual pupil is working entirely independently of the others. Such an arrangement puts too much pressure on the teacher; it is both mentally and physically exhausting. In addition it makes it difficult for the teacher to arrange any properly integrated group activities. A compromise must be found which will retain some of the benefits of a more individualized approach, while leaving the teacher with more discretionary time and in a more relaxed frame of mind.

A useful structure can be created by dividing the class into four 'divisions', each consisting of seven or eight pupils. The division is the administrative unit for classroom organization. The pupils within a division always work on the same topic and start a topic at the same time. The teacher thus knows that within one area of the classroom all the pupils are roughly at the same stage and on the same topic. For the actual work the pupils within a division are organized into pairs, and two pairs may occasionally combine for small-group work.

A structure like this is very flexible, and used sensitively it can preserve most of the benefits of an individualized approach.

The cycle of monitoring and control

Using the structure described in the previous paragraphs the teacher can now devise a monitoring and control programme. When topics are being studied that demand a big use of resources, the teacher needs to operate a cycle of events for each division, as follows:

1. The division is briefed. The teacher explains the objectives and content of the next unit of study, in very simple language, making sure that all the pupils have a good mental picture of the work to be done. Opportunity is taken, too, to arouse their interest and enthusiasm for the topic by the vivid portrayal of some of the key elements in the study. Finally, using the other pupils as witnesses and sounding boards, the teacher gives each pupil a short personal briefing, suggesting which prepared assignments to use and making sure that the pupil is ready in every way for the task. The division can then proceed to its tasks, working in pairs or in small groups according to the agreed assignments. This advance briefing is the most vital part of the cycle. To stress its importance is to reject totally the view of resource-based learning as a style in which the teacher only responds to questions or difficulties raised by the pupils. The younger the pupils the more they need high-quality advance briefing; they should not be set down cold in front of their learning resources; they need their teachers more than that!
2. The division is left to proceed on its own using the prepared assignments as guidance, but bearing in mind that during the briefing the teacher may well have modified the guidance to make it more attuned to each individual's needs. Resources are collected as and when they are needed from the classroom or departmental centre, or a visit to the school's library resource centre may be required. The teacher will, of course, respond to individual requests for clarification or help, but the object should be to keep these to a minimum. If the resources have been sympathetically chosen, the assignments carefully written, and the briefing thoroughly conducted, the pupils should not find too many difficulties. Rather than make a virtue out of constantly responding to short questions, the teacher would be wise to review the choice of resources, the wording of the assignments, and the conduct of the briefing. The teacher's time is better spent in constructive and imaginative tutoring.
3. As individual pupils come to the end of their assigned tasks some kind of

review is essential. This is usually done on an individual basis. Actual marking is probably best done outside class time, but a brief discussion with the pupil is very desirable when the work is returned.
4. Some simple arrangements need to be made for those periods of time when some members of a division are ready to proceed to the next briefing while others are still at work on the present tasks. Pupils need a set of 'standing orders' to cover this. Usually short additional assignments of an enriching kind, background reading, work on some long-term project, and so on, can convert what might seem to be a problem into a really useful opportunity.

Personal tutoring

Where the structure has been properly organized and a smooth cycle of operations established, the teacher will find frequent opportunities to spend more time on personal tutoring. This can be most economically accomplished in small groups of four or five pupils (a whole division is probably bigger than the optimum size for this activity).

Tutoring is an art that requires practice. It should be thought of as a 'learning conversation' in which each of the pupils is being helped to be aware of his own learning processes and development. It must be conducted with great sensitivity and with warmth. The teacher needs to spend a lot of time listening. There is a natural temptation to get things on the move and this can easily lead to the teacher dominating. The object is not to get the pupil to the teacher's level of understanding, still less to persuade him of the teacher's point of view, but rather to develop the pupil's confidence in himself as a learner, self-respect, and a sense of serious purpose. Of course, a lot will be accomplished in a purely cognitive sense, but tutoring in a personal style is a sound investment for the learner's future.

Conclusions

We have probably progressed a long way since the heady days when it seemed that truly individualized learning based on the use of resources was easily within our grasp. The setting up of competent resource support systems for teachers is a complex and costly business for the schools and their local authorities. But even more complex are the tasks of the teacher in the classroom. There are so many pressures and imperatives; it is not surprising that many teachers have turned back to simpler models of teaching.

But this should not be a time for pessimism and retreat. Advances in technology offer the teacher a quality and variety of resource material hitherto undreamed of. And the profession is slowly getting to grips with the management problems involved. There have been many mistakes and wrong directions, but a certain amount of trial and error is what development is all about. There are good grounds at the present time for some cautious optimism, and teachers who are engaged in development work in resource-based learning deserve encouragement.

References

Atherton, B. (1980) *Guidelines 8: Adapting Spaces for Resource-based Learning*, London: Council for Educational Technology.
Beswick, N.W. (1975) *Organizing Resources*, London: Heinemann.
Beswick, N.W. (1977) *Resource-based Learning*, London: Heinemann.
Davies, W.J.K. (1975) *Guidelines 1: Learning Resources? An Argument for Schools*, London: Council for Educational Technology.
Davies, W.J.K. (1978) *Implementing Individualised Learning in Schools and Colleges*, London: Council for Educational Technology.
Davies, W.J.K. (1980) *Guidelines 9: Alternatives to Class Teaching in Schools and Colleges*, London: Council for Educational Technology.
Department of Education and Science (1978) *Mixed Ability Work in Comprehensive Schools*, London: HMSO.
Harris, N.D.C., Bell, C.D. and Carter, J.E.H. (1981) *Signposts for Evaluating: a Resource Pack*, London: Council for Educational Technology and Schools Council.
Howe, A. (1981) *International Yearbook of Educational and Instructional Technology 1980/1981*, London; Kogan Page.
Irving, A. and Snape, W.H. (1979) *Educating Library Users in Secondary Schools* (British Library Research and Development Report 5467), London: British Library.
Lewis, R. (1981a) *How to Tutor in an Open-Learning System* (Self-Study Version), London: Council for Educational Technology.
Lewis, R. (1981b) *How to Tutor in an Open-Learning System* (Group Study Version), London: Council for Educational Technology.
Lewis, R. (1981c) *Guidelines 10: How to Write Self-Study Materials*, London: Council for Educational Technology.
Raddon, R. (1979) *Annotated Bibliography on Educational Resource Organization and Related Topics*, London: Council for Educational Technology.
Taylor, L.C. (1972) *Resources for Learning*, London: Penguin.
Thomas, J.B. (1980) *The Self in Education*, Slough: National Foundation for Educational Research.
Thornbury, R., Gillespie, J. and Wilkinson, G. (1979) *Working Paper 16: Resource Organization in Secondary Schools: Report of an Investigation*, London: Council for Educational Technology.

Waterhouse, P.S. (1983a) *Managing the Learning Process*, London: McGraw Hill.
Waterhouse, P.S. (1983b) *Working Paper 24: Supported Self-Study in Secondary Education*, London: Council for Educational Technology.
Waterhouse, P.S. (1983c) *Supported Self-Study: A Handbook for Teachers*, London: Council for Educational Technology.

SECTION 4

HOW CAN WE IMPROVE STUDENT ASSESSMENT?

INTRODUCTION
Malcolm Skilbeck

One of the commonest findings in research on teachers' perceptions of curriculum change is that widely used systems of student assessment are among the first two or three named obstacles to curriculum reform. It is the external examination in secondary education, just as in the past it was the levels or grades of examination in the elementary school and the 11+ examination in the primary school, that is singled out as the major structural inhibitor of desirable change. The philosopher and mathematician, Alfred North Whitehead, long ago identified the school's control over its own curriculum and modes of assessment as the keystone of educational reform:

> Each school should have its own leaving certificates, based on its own curriculum. The standards of these schools should be sampled and corrected. But the first requisite for educational reform is the school as a unit with its approved curriculum based on its own needs, and evolved by its own staff.
> (Whitehead, A.N. (1932) *The Aims of Education and other essays*, London: Benn.)

In the world of secondary school examinations there are few, today, who will speak up as cogently as this about the direction reform needs to take. But one who does is examinations board (Certificate of Secondary Education) secretary, Henry Macintosh. The first obstacle, he notes, to an educative assessment of students is the external examination. After decades of criticism, damaging research findings and proposals for reform (mainly by the Schools Council) which governments have ignored or rejected, we are now in a position to effect significant reform since it is widely agreed that at least at the 16+ stage the system is unacceptable. The devices that Henry Macintosh, among others, find most hopeful in this respect are student profiles. Whatever limitations critics have discovered, profiles do have the merit of firmly linking teaching with assessment, and putting emphasis on diagnostic or forward-looking assessment through which students might themselves learn to improve their own performance. There are, as Henry Macintosh acknowledges, difficulties about profiling, not least, as several research studies have shown, the lack of teacher expertise in the techniques and procedures of profiling. It is thus towards staff development with strong local education authority backing that energies need to be directed.

The link between profiling and school-based curriculum development is much closer than that between the widely canvassed reform of secondary examinations through graded tests, externally devised and administered through examination boards. The role of the boards is itself a major factor in any consideration of school assessment since it is the boards that are decisive in validating awards, they guarantee a standard which has public credibility. But need the boards do this in the conventional manner of approving examination syllabuses and setting and marking externally devised examination scripts? Despite the evident popularity and practicality of this procedure, significant variations are possible and some secondary schools, albeit a small minority, have explored the existing opportunities for schools to set their own syllabuses. John Stephenson would like to see this taken much further. Using the example of the North East London Polytechnic scheme of independent study, he argues for a shift in secondary school assessment towards internal course construction and assessment, locally validated. His proposals are undoubtedly practical but the machinery to implement them does not exist and could be created only if examination boards were prepared to play rather different roles from their present ones. This, in turn, would require backing from the Schools Examinations Council and the Secretary of State for Education and Science. The chief tasks in far-reaching examination reform with schools centrally involved as internal assessing agencies seem, therefore, to be: developing the readiness and ability of teachers to provide valid assessment of student learnings; creating the local, regional and national machinery to administer and validate internal assessments; reducing public suspicions about teacher and school-based assessments; convincing higher and further education bodies and employers of the value of the changes. These constitute a formidable challenge but not an insuperable one, and it must be taken up if school-based curriculum making is to become a significant reality beyond the middle years of secondary schooling.

CHAPTER 20

ASSESSING AND EXAMINING: POLICIES, PRACTICES AND ALTERNATIVES
Henry G. Macintosh

The impact both direct and indirect of the present system of public examining – in particular the GCE and CSE – upon the secondary school curriculum in the United Kingdom is now too well chronicled to warrant further justification. Amongst the latest and most telling accounts is that provided by Her Majesty's Inspectorate in their secondary survey *Aspects of Secondary Education in England* (DES 1979). Those features of the present system which have a direct and potentially negative impact may be summarized as follows:

(a) It is single subject in its orientation, thus making for difficulties in dealing with integrated curricula.
(b) It is too concerned with content and in consequence places too little emphasis upon the assessment of skills and concepts.
(c) It assesses the individual and not the group.
(d) It is largely academic in its orientation and is thus not appropriate for substantial numbers of those who actually take the examinations.
(e) It is rigid in its timing and lacks in consequence any notion of readiness for assessment. It thus creates difficulties for those who wish to undertake mixed-ability teaching.
(f) It is norm referenced (that is to say its processes are designed to facilitate comparisons between individuals). As such it presents information about performance in ways which are unhelpful for diagnostic or evaluative purposes.
(g) It has developed in ways which prevent the practical emergence of assessment for all. (The General Certificate of Education at the

Ordinary Level – GCE O level – is, for example, designed for the 20% of the 16-year population in ability terms whilst the Certificate of Secondary Education – CSE – is designed for the next 40%.)
(h) It is closed in its operational format with a very low level of risk taking and a minimum involvement of those who actually teach the students being assessed.

Indirectly its most significant impact has been upon the style and practice of classroom assessment. This tends to be largely end-of-course (terminal) rather than continuous in nature, largely written, largely formal and largely concerned with cognitive outcomes and with generating marks and grades for the purposes of comparing students. Moreover, the long backwards shadow cast by an examination system theoretically confined to the fourth and fifth years of an 11–16 curriculum makes it extremely difficult for schools to develop cohesive assessment programmes for the full period of compulsory secondary education.

It would be unfair to suggest, as the last two paragraphs have done, that the impact of public examinations has been wholly undesirable. Public examinations have for many teachers and many students provided direction and relevance to courses, teaching and learning. They have promoted and sustained curriculum innovation at both local and national level notably through Mode 3 and the arrangements made for examining national curriculum projects. They have also provided substantial in-service training in assessment for many teachers. All these very real benefits have, however, been second-hand in the sense that their prime motivation has been to facilitate the work of the examining boards rather than to promote curriculum development and to improve classroom practice. The teacher's role has thus been that of a hired hand rather than an equal let alone a senior partner.

Moreover the climate of the 1950s and 1960s when the present GCE and CSE examination system was created was very different from that of today and there is little evidence to suggest that the present system can reform itself sufficiently to meet the curriculum needs of schools over the next fifteen or twenty years. Growing emphasis upon accountability arising out of political and community concern about the effectiveness of the school system; the emergence at long last of a serious debate about the kind of curriculum which would best enable a comprehensive school to serve all its pupils and the community of which it forms a part; growing and probably permanent youth unemployment – to name but three factors – have all underlined the need for schools and local education authorities to develop comprehensive assessment programmes for all their students. Such programmes will need to direct their attention to such issues as the progressive measurement of skills and the communication of information informatively about student performance. Requirements such as these merely serve to underline still further the inadequacy of the present public examination system and to emphasize the need to look at its reform in a rather more thoroughgoing fashion than is currently the case. It is arguable indeed that the present reforms, based as they are upon age-related normative notions in which traditional academic models at 16+ and 18+ under the control of existing GCE and CSE boards are being developed alongside a more radical 'pre-vocational' 17+ under the control of further education examining bodies like the City and Guilds of London Institute (CGLI) and the Business and Technician Education Council (BTEC), can only lead to greater division and confusion.

The kind of analysis contained in the previous paragraphs, particularly in a period of severely strained resources, is of little practical use to teachers faced with the development of assessment programmes within the day-to-day context of the classroom. What is wanted is not more analysis and talk but suggestions for implementation which are both practicable and based upon sound general principles. The starting point for any workable school assessment programme must be a commitment by all concerned to the centrality of the relationship between teaching and assessment. These two must be seen as two sides of the same coin and not as being in conflict with one another as is so often the case today. Any lasting reappraisal of the role of the teacher as assessor must, therefore, start with changes in attitude. Ironically the present confused state of examination reform taken in conjunction with the economic situation can contribute significantly to promoting such changes and indeed is already beginning to do so. Faced with a buyers' market it is possible for employers to do one of two things: either raise the paper qualifications for entry or acceptability (i.e. higher GCE or CSE grades) or ask for supplementary information. There is evidence of both these practices at the present time. The bodies responsible for recruiting nurses for example have raised their grade requirements for entry in recent years quite significantly. On the other hand many employers, particularly those who recruit locally rather than nationally (still a majority incidentally), are starting to ask for information about general characteristics often of a personal nature. For some this information is not merely supplementary but is beginning to replace examination grades. The present uncertain economic climate has also placed greater emphasis upon the development of transferable skills, that is to say skills which are not geared to a specific job or post but which if mastered are likely to make an individual more employable. Not only is this kind of information not available through current examination certification but it may well not be generated adequately through the kind of single-subject curriculum which these same examinations tend to reinforce. Most schools moreover, despite long experience with student reports, are not geared to produce the kind of information required in an orderly and systematic fashion both for their own internal use and for individuals outside the school who might wish to use it.

The name currently used to describe the provision of information of the kind suggested in the previous paragraph is profiling. What exactly is a profile?

The term 'profile' in relation to educational measurement is used to describe multidimensional methods of presenting information, usually about individuals and their achievements, attributes or performances. A profile is thus not a method of assessment, but an approach to presentation and it is in consequence only as full and as varied as the information it seeks to present. Profiles differ from one another therefore in two major ways: in the 'content' of what is being presented and in the ways in which that presentation takes place. Whatever its outward form, however, a profile ought to contain three basic elements:

(a) A list of items, such as subjects, skills, personal qualities, course descriptions.
(b) A means of indicating the level and/or nature of performance in respect of each chosen item. The descriptors used can include such things as marks, grades, verbal reports, percentages, histograms or graphs – the list is endless, but they all make use of some combination of letters or numbers.
(c) Some indication of the kind of evidence that has been used to arrive at the descriptions provided.

Many profiles in current use incidentally neglect the last of these to their disadvantage.

Enough work has now been undertaken upon the development and use of profiles to permit an appraisal of their potential, of the basic principles upon which they might be based and of the practical problems that need to be overcome if this potential is to be realized. As far as their potential is concerned, Geoff Stanton (in *Profiles and Profile Reporting* 1982) lists some eight possible functions for profiles which range from acting as a structured reference through to the provision of feedback to learners and quality control of courses. Profiles and profiling thus constitute a powerful tool for promoting and facilitating the constructive use of information derived from assessment in a wide variety of ways and for the benefit of individuals, courses and institutions.

So much for potential. As far as principles are concerned, the following six should constitute an adequate basis upon which to build a satisfactory system of profiling for use in schools and other educational institutions: first, that of negotiation between student and tutor/teacher, which implies the existence of specific and agreed contracts; secondly, the need to involve a wider range of people, including peer groups, in contributing to the profile than simply 'the teacher and the student'; thirdly, that character interpretations and personal characteristics should not form part of the recording system – information in these areas will in practice emerge profitably and extensively from the nature of the negotiation and from the ways in which agreed tasks are carried out, but that does not justify their forming part of the recording system itself; fourthly, that profiles should remain wherever possible in the possession of those to whom they refer and should be completely 'open' documents; fifthly, that the across-the-board emphasis on profiles should be upon validity and not upon reliability although this does not mean that the recording system where it relates to particular tasks or specific activities will, of itself, be unreliable, nor that reliability in relation to recording is an insignificant activity. Finally, that there is a need to stress the ongoing nature of profiles as a recording system – in marked contrast to the terminal nature of almost all current reporting practices, one of the results of which is to give the certificates which usually constitute the formal record of what has occurred a life of their own. Records, unlike reports, ought to be much more easily related to the period of time with which they are directly concerned and come in consequence to have their own in-built self-destruct mechanism which makes them disappear as other records become available.

The principle obstacles to the future development of profiles would seem to be two in number. The first relates to the question of whether a single profile can be made to serve a number of major needs at once, and in particular whether it can face both inwards and outwards and satisfy both learner and user. This is the record/report formative/summative issue. On the evidence available to date this problem has yet to be satisfactorily resolved. Part of the problem lies in the retention within so many profiles of norm-referencing and a desire to compare students with one another, rather than criterion-referencing where the basis for comparison is stated levels of performance or mastery. Another part of the problem lies in our inadequate knowledge of how young people think and hence learn, and in particular how they acquire and use skills.

The second major problem is a practical one and shows itself in two ways. The first of these is the question of handling profiles as an organizational problem. The second relates to assessment.

The implementation of profiles which meet the demands likely to be placed on them in the future requires an understanding of a range of assessment techniques beyond those used by most teachers on a regular basis. It also requires assessment methods to be matched to course goals, an exercise which is all too rarely carried out in either classroom or school and is, moreover, one which many teachers find extremely difficult. The implications of the very real practical problems created for schools by the introduction of profiles are highlighted in two recent Schools Council Reports by Balogh (1982) and Goacher (1983). The answer must therefore lie in staff development and in-service training both for individuals and for institutions.

We thus have a situation in which there is for the first time real pressure upon schools to provide information about all their pupils; information which has in the past been largely provided for a proportion of them by the public examination system. These pressures are likely to continue and indeed intensify regardless of the outcome of the proposed examination reforms, and there is a real possibility that the impact of that system upon the school curriculum will begin to lessen. It will not, however, do so unless the additional information provided by schools is seen by the community to be worth while and to be the product of care and thought. It is absolutely essential therefore that the teaching profession resolves its current ambivalence about its role as an assessor and that the necessary staff development, both pre- and in-service, takes place. Such staff development will need to place its major emphasis upon understanding the uses of assessment rather than upon a capacity to construct tests of varying kinds as has been the case hitherto.

The achievement of these ends requires the education service to address itself to and to find solutions for two complementary curriculum and assessment problems: first, the implementation of a curriculum which is not solely dependent upon single subjects and secondly, the development of assessment programmes which start from the bottom up and not the top downwards and concern themselves with the measurement of progression in relation to a wide range of skills and concepts. The key to the solution of these problems and to the development of profiles adequate to describe pupil achievement in relation to such a curriculum are the local education authorities. Why the LEAs? For a number of very good reasons. They have statutory responsibility in respect of the curriculum and ought in consequence to be concerned to provide ongoing programmes of evaluation; they ought to have the capacity and the wish to mediate between national requirements and local needs; they have the means if the will is there to promote staff development without which lasting change is impossible; they have the standing to make locally based programmes credible; and finally they have the contacts with the local community and local industry whose support is vital if change is to come about.

The pay-offs from the successful implementation of such a programme in terms of enhanced feedback for student, teacher, parent and employer and its positive impact upon professional development are enormous. Such a programme also represents the only real possibility of freeing the curriculum from the impact of a public examinations system which is unlikely in the future ever to meet the needs of all students. It is surely, therefore, worth a major and concerted effort by all concerned at the present time.

References

Balogh, J. (1982) *Profile Reports for School Leavers*, Schools Council Programme 5, London: Longman for Schools Council.

Black, H. and Broadfoot, P. (1982) *Keeping Track of Teaching: Assessment in the Modern Classroom*, London: Routledge and Kegan Paul.

Burgess, T. and Adams, E. (eds) (1980) *Outcomes of Education*, London: Macmillan Education.

Department of Education and Science (1979) *Aspects of Secondary Education in England*, London: HMSO.

Further Education Curriculum Review and Development Unit (1982) *Profiles: A review of issues and practices in the use and development of student profiles*, London: DES.

Goacher, B. (1983) *Recording Achievement at 16+*, Schools Council Programme 5, London: Longman for Schools Council.

Harrison, A. (1982) *Review of Grades Tests*, Schools Council Examinations Bulletin 41, London: Methuen Educational.

Harrison, A. (1983) *Profile Reporting of Examination Results*, Schools Council Examinations Bulletin 43, London: Methuen Education.

Nuttall, D. (ed.) (1982) Assessing educational achievement, *Educational Analysis*, vol. 4, no. 3.

Stanton, G. *Profiles and Profile Reporting*, Coombe Lodge Report, vol. 14, no. 13, Blagdon, 1982.
Schools for the Next Generation, Centre for the Study of Comprehensive Schools, Report of Second Annual Conference, University of York, July 1982.

CHAPTER 21

PUBLIC EXAMINATION OR VALIDATED SCHOOL ASSESSMENT?
John Stephenson

There is no doubt that the sector of the education system most in need of major innovation is that which serves our adolescent youngsters of 13 to 16. Nowhere are the evils of the present system better chronicled than in James Hemming's aptly named book on secondary education *Betrayal of Youth* (1980). (See also Ch. 27 below). The resistance to change, however, is stronger than the drive to change because of the widely held belief that public confidence in the public examination system must be preserved at all costs. In spite of general scepticism about the value of external examinations, it is assumed there is no alternative so they must be preserved or, at best, rearranged to minimize their worst features. It is this resiliance of the assessment system which frustrates the creativity and educational aspirations of many schools and teachers, or which channels interesting innovations into fringe schools or the less able groups of pupils. This chapter examines this problem, reports on a well-established break-through in higher education, and considers whether some of its features might be used to advantage by those wishing to overcome the stranglehold of GCE and CSE examinations in schools.

It is worth being reminded of the current views of the world of work and of the wider educational establishment on the present situation. Len Murray, General Secretary of the TUC, wrote in 1981:

> Many – probably most – young people still leave school ill-equipped for adult life. (Murray 1981)

The Confederation of British Industry was able to persuade the Select Committee on Higher Education to report to Parliament that, though qualifications were important, personal qualities such as motivation, ability for original thought and ability to get at and solve real problems should be given the greatest priority. (House of Commons Select Committee on Higher Education 1981).

The Educational Establishment joined in with its Manifesto for Change. Thirty leading educationalists, including John Tomlinson, Chairman of the Schools Council, put the blame squarely on the school curriculum which

> gives insufficient time and attention to the preparation for life as persons, workers, parents, and citizens (Tomlinson et al. 1981)

and in particular they criticised the kind of teaching methods encouraged by public examinations:

> Many skills essential to effective living, sensitivity about others, commitment to common tasks, making choices, facility in communication, getting along with others, social awareness, an appreciation of moral values, and the rest, cannot be effectively taught by pedagogical methods. (ibid.)

The commercial and industrial community came together under the aegis of the Royal Society of Arts in 1980 to publish its Education for Capability Scheme, in support of which they argued:

> Individual satisfaction stems from doing a job well through the exercise of personal capability. Acquisition of this capability is inhibited by the present system of education which stresses the importance of analysis, criticism and the organisation of knowledge and generally neglects the formulation and solution of problems, doing, making and organising: in fact, constructive and creative activity of all sorts. (Royal Society of Arts 1980)

In summary, both the educators and the employers would prefer something different and better. Employers continue to use the system for selection because that's the way education chooses to describe its leavers, while schools use it in the belief that employers prefer public examinations as a major selection tool. Neither side has the confidence to go beyond their statements about the inadequacies to argue for major changes, because it is assumed that it is not possible both to release the creativity of pupils and teachers and, at the same time, protect public confidence in something called educational standards.

The examination system is unsuited to the development of the personal skills and qualities for 'life' because it is geared to the production of rank orders of pupil performance so that they can be graded, passed, or failed. Standards are preserved by ensuring that roughly the same proportion of an age group passes each year. As a result, emphasis is put on devising the fairest system of measuring comparability rather than on facilitating the development of the educational experiences required. The exam boards therefore publish or negotiate syllabuses so that pupils can be assessed on the same material. Credit is given for simple recall or the analysis of data because these are easiest to mark objectively, thus ensuring the statisticians' dream of a standard distribution curve of candidates' performance, so that cut-off marks between pass and fail can be determined in accordance with traditional pass/fail rates. This in turn encourages didactic teaching to predetermined syllabuses or, at best, ingenious attempts by talented teachers to do the same thing in palatable, stimulating ways. The educational experience for most pupils is therefore of a kind least likely to develop the qualities referred to earlier.

Both teachers and pupils conspire to operate the system because of the lure of 'decent' jobs or places in higher education. Now that less than half of school leavers can expect any sort of job, and places in higher education are being squeezed, this particular discipline is fast receding. Instead, more youngsters, with the passive condolence of their teachers, are opting out of school either physically or emotionally. In this context, the time is ripe for attempting something better.

At the School for Independent Study (SIS) of North East London Polytechnic (NELP), we have tried to tackle this problem head on. We were concerned to devise ways in which the conventional interest of our own external award bearing body, The Council for National Academic Awards (CNAA) could be safeguarded whilst, at the same time, providing a course for students based on the development of their own individual competence and independence. The opportunity for this arose when the James Report (Lord James of Rusholme 1972) first raised the idea that there should be a new qualification of general education, Dip HE, for intending teachers. The Government White Paper *Education: A Framework for Expansion* (1972) set in motion a NELP initiative aimed at the general education of a wide variety of post-18 year olds.

The aims of the course are as follows:

> Our purpose is to provide students with an educational experience that enables them to become generally competent and independent. By this we mean that they should be capable of coping with a wide variety of different situations, many of them unfamiliar, both as individuals and as members of a community, without needing to be dependent upon the direction of others. (Stephenson 1982)

The challenge was to achieve these purposes within the context of a Government-sponsored award to be assessed by the CNAA.

This was to be particularly difficult because of our belief that the best way to develop personal skills and qualities is to provide opportunities for them to be practised in real situations. The logic of this was that students would best learn how to cope with whatever difficult or unfamiliar situation they found themselves in, without dependence on others to show the way, by giving them the problem of coping with their own higher education. This in turn meant asking the students to set out the terms of their own educational problems, their proposed areas of study, how they would organize their own work, and finally how they would demonstrate they had achieved their purpose to the satisfaction of the CNAA. The Polytechnic's role would be to provide support and access to specialist advice and tuition and to enable the CNAA to inspect students' work. The key element of this proposal was that we were proposing to remove from the CNAA the control of the syllabus and give it to the student. This would therefore remove all possibility of rank ordering of student marks because each would be based on a distinctive set of work on an individually negotiated syllabus.

The problem of public acceptance of student-planned learning was the crucial one to be tackled. The answer was to build a different system of safeguards aimed at the validation of what is being proposed by the student rather than the preparation of common syllabuses for ease of assessment, whilst at the same time giving the external examination board the role of certifying what each student has done. In brief, it works like this. Each student must secure for her/his plans the approval of the Polytechnic to ensure that resources will be available, and the support of appropriate academic specialists that the proposal has coherence and credibility in terms of the award being sought. Finally and crucially, the Polytechnic submits samples of the judgements on students' proposals to the searching scrutiny of an external validation board established for that purpose.

The validation board is the main safeguard and has the confidence of the CNAA, whilst at the same time being independent of it. It currently consists of individuals outside the Polytechnic who carry personal credibility through their history of success in their own fields, and not because they are experienced in the traditions of public examinations. They are a retired top civil servant, a business consultant, an architect, former inspectors of schools, and a business executive in a large corporation.

To enable the board to judge on these matters, full and detailed student propositions (called Statements) must be submitted. Preparation of statements for validation is a formidable task for the student. The board has the status of an examinations board and is therefore taken seriously. Failure to achieve validation means there is no course of study and therefore no final award. This means that the students have to be explicit to themselves, to their tutors and to the board about what they wish to do, why it is appropriate that they should do it in terms of their existing skills and experience and their intended future, how they propose to do it, and finally the criteria by which they wish to have their work judged. It is this very process of planning, persuading, and negotiating which develops the personal qualities and skills referred to earlier. The great bonus, of course, is that once the validation board has validated a statement, the student's self-confidence and motivation are raised substantially and the commitment to the completion of the course is sufficient to encourage high performance.

Over the last nine years over one thousand students have been through this process. To give some idea of the freedom which this gives to students, here is a brief selection of the work recently submitted for assessment:

- A study of the education and training of ESN(s) school leavers in transition to adult training centres.
- The role of the European Court of Justice and its part as an integrative mechanism of community law.
- Electronic soundscape poetry realization.
- Poetry from 16th Century to end of 19th Century in a sociological and historical context.
- Handbook for would-be fish farmer on the setting up of a fish farm.
- Inspection and maintenance of submerged offshore structures.
- Batik – portfolio containing 'reference material' sketch books design and drawing books. Thesis on Batik, 5–8,000 words. Examples of image making, essays and Batik painting.
- The biology and conservation of commercially important cetacean species.
- 'Let them speak' – communication skills for the hearing impaired.
- The distribution and ecology of sparganiaceae.
- Air and water pollution and its effects on human physiology.
- Tenant participation in council housing management.

Inevitably, and properly, each topic represents the distinctive experience, interest, and intentions of each student. The topics are presented here as titles only and each represents a very wide range of related study and skills. A detailed example of one student's individual programme can be found in *Outcomes of Education* (Burgess and Adams 1980).

Assessment of this work is done under the same general regulations as apply to more conventional subject-based courses. There is an assessment board on which sit external examiners approved by the CNAA. Each case is considered by the full board together with the assessments of performance by at least two specialist tutors, one of whom will not have worked with the student. External examiners have access to all these reports and can interview both staff and students. The big difference is that the board is constrained by the content and criteria previously and separately validated, and the only questions it can ask are: 'Has this student achieved what is in the Statement?' and 'Has it been done to a level appropriate for the award?'

The advantages of this arrangement are considerable in terms of the release of student creative energy, the development of appropriate personal qualities and skills, and the giving of self-confidence. There is also a slight danger that a new orthodoxy might arise to subvert these benefits. A major research project (Adams et al. 1981) revealed different ways in which opportunities for student initiative and creativity might be distorted. In most cases this was unintentional. When first being asked to approve the scheme, the CNAA's natural wariness almost led it to impose on the Polytechnic safeguards which would have had the effect of reestablishing the grip of the external examiners on what was considered to be valid study. The external examiners, through their annual reports, were unintentionally suggesting greater conformity by drawing attention either to the difficulty of assessing affective skills or to the importance of the 'general' intellectual skills associated with all academic work at this level. The Polytechnic's resource management system is dependent upon the preplanning of educational activity by course control teams, while the accountant is not geared to dealing with requests for money from students. With good will all these difficulties are kept to the minimum, but more serious is the pressure to conform to patterns of work or types of proposals which experience shows are easier to operate or assess. Once pointed out this is easily corrected but the natural desire of tutors to make their own lives easier needs constant vigilance to preserve the full openness that was intended. One important function of the external validation board has been to identify such trends as they have occurred.

An important post-script to this brief description of the work of the School for Independent Study – more fully described elsewhere (Boud 1981) – is that in May 1982 after a full two days' scrutiny of students, their work, the Polytechnic, and the tutors, the CNAA declared that the scheme had been a major success and they had the confidence to grant continuing approval for the course to run under its original conditions.

The separation of the control of validation from the control of assessment is the main breakthrough which has enabled this innovation to succeed and to maintain its public credibility. Schools may not wish to follow the exact path of the SIS, but they may well be interested in exploring whether a similar separation of powers might encourage the achievement of the kinds of educational experience envisaged by the Manifesto and RSA groups quoted earlier. Would this lesson survive the journey from higher to secondary education?

It is important to recognize the ways in which the two sectors are similar and different. Taking the differences first, one obvious difference is age. NELP students by definition are over 18 and many are a good deal older. Schools have to contend with 13–16 year olds. Teachers often claim that adolescence creates particular personal problems which require them to be treated differently from adults. Yet adults can be just as emotionally 'mixed up' if not more so whilst primary school children are clearly capable of using initiative and accepting responsibility for some aspects of their own learning (Davies 1980). Are 13–16 year olds the only people on earth who cannot be helped to develop their own self-responsibility? The other question frequently put by teachers – 'How can we expect teenagers to know what's good for them?' – can be met by another – 'How are they ever going to learn to do it for themselves?'

A second difference is that education for 13–16 year olds is compulsory but only voluntary for the 18+. This is a very significant point but one which is containable. First, in many city secondary schools, teachers already conspire with their pupils that they should not attend if they are not interested in examination work. Absenteeism is tolerated to such an extent that the term 'voluntary attendance' isn't totally inappropriate. Secondly, the NELP experience shows that improved student motivation is a great bonus. Increased pupil motivation would also be a major asset in schools.

These differences are relatively minor hurdles to cross if the benefits include the opportunity to develop in school leavers personal competence and independence. The considerable similarities between the two sectors should give encouragement. Both sectors are in the control of local authorities; have subject departments and tutors who identify themselves as much by their subject labels as by anything else; have externally appointed boards managed by the country's educational establishment responsible for the awards given to their leavers; and each has an interest in maintaining its public credibility.

It is for individual teachers to decide for themselves whether there is sufficient overlap for something to be tried. In their book *Outcomes of Education* (1980), Tyrrell Burgess and Betty Adams set out some ideas on how schools might attempt to establish local validation boards. Already a number of schools are discussing initiatives with their own examination boards. Briefly, Burgess and Adams suggest that use may be made of the governors' existing legal responsibility to oversee the curriculum by appointing, perhaps as a subcommittee, an external validation board consisting of locally acceptable figures in whose judgement there would be confidence. Pupils, parents and teachers could usefully discuss ways in which the last two years might be most constructively used, the validation board could scrutinize the proposals, and the examination board would receive and assess the outcomes of that work for assessment. Pupils would therefore be in a position to leave school with a full statement of their last two years' work which would have been validated by the local community and its quality testified by an existing established examination board. By having to devise and negotiate the programme of work each pupil would have had the kind of educational experience most likely to lead to the personal skills and qualities associated with the needs of modern life.

Such a scheme would not have the effect of diminishing the role of the external examining boards. On the contrary, they will have the important task of establishing and preserving public confidence, but they will do it more constructively by describing what has been done (and at what level) rather than by prescribing what should be learned. Whether it is successfully developed in schools will depend largely on the extent to which the teachers themselves are willing to relinquish their traditional role of custodians of the examination syllabus, and therefore controllers of what is learnt, by whom and how, in exchange for constructive negotiations with pupils and parents. Our experience at NELP suggests that teacher autonomy is the biggest obstacle but once this is overcome the many logistic and educational problems are fairly readily solvable.

References

Adams, E., Robbins, D. and Stephens, J. (1981) *Validity and Validation in Higher Education*, London: North East London Polytechnic.
Boud, D. (ed.) (1981) *Independent Study in Tertiary Education*, London: Routledge and Kegan Paul.
Burgess, T. and Adams, E. (1980) *Outcomes of Education*, London: Macmillan.
Cmnd. 5174 (1972) *Education: A framework for expansion*, London: HMSO.
Davies, E. (1980) Primary school records, *in* Burgess, T. and Adams, E. (1980).

Hemming, J. (1980) *The Betrayal of Youth*, London: Marion Boyars.
House of Commons Select Committee on Higher Education (1980) Report to Parliament, Hansard.
Lord James of Rusholme (Chairman) (1972) *Teacher Education and Training* (James Report), London: HMSO.
Murray, L. (1981) Shift the curriculum, *The Times Educational Supplement*, 6th February.
Royal Society of Arts (1980) *Education for Capability Recognition Scheme*, London: Royal Society of Arts.
Stephenson, J. (1982) *Diploma of Higher Education*, North East London Polytechnic.
Tomlinson, J. et al. (1981) Manifesto for change, *The Times Educational Supplement*, 30th January.

SECTION 5

THE SCHOOL AS A CENTRE FOR CURRICULUM RESEARCH AND PROFESSIONAL DEVELOPMENT

INTRODUCTION
Malcolm Skilbeck

Piecemeal, small-scale and short-term change has characterized much school-based curriculum development. It is as if school-based curriculum development has been seen as a marginal activity in two respects: marginal to the main concerns of the school as an organization, and marginal to the main thrust of curriculum development through large-scale, funded public projects or publishers' ventures. Neither the concepts of school-based curriculum development nor the procedures and resources necessary for its execution have been built into the design of schooling, save for those exceptional cases where a new school has been built expressly to develop a curriculum philosophy or energetic and creative individuals have seized opportunities as they have emerged. Generally speaking, the old model of the school as a transmitting and processing agency has prevailed even where individual teachers and sometimes whole school staffs have expressed attitudes favourable to in-school curriculum making and have undertaken small-scale projects. The curriculum is thus largely a given: it exists independently of the school and the central task of the school is to transmit the given curriculum, perhaps modifying or varying details but not seeing itself as the agency that reconstructs the given and helps to construct the future by designing, implementing, evaluating and developing its own curriculum. Very few schools are equipped, resourced or organized to undertake this wider role although, as we have seen throughout this volume, increasing numbers are participating in small-scale review, evaluation and specific projects.

For the school to become a major centre for curriculum research and professional development, a number of conditions must be met. Interestingly, realization of what these conditions are has grown partly as a result of the large-scale curriculum development movement. That movement has contributed to building a system of ideas, a language of curriculum and, by its very shortcomings, has highlighted school roles. It was one of the early large-scale Schools Council projects, the Humanities Curriculum Project (HCP), that led Lawrence Stenhouse into his well-known advocacy of the teacher as researcher and of case-study and other qualitative methods of curriculum research which might come naturally to the teacher working in the classroom setting. Jean Rudduck thus appropriately starts this section of the readings by discussing Stenhouse's preoccupations with the art of teaching and the curriculum not as given but as problematic. The HCP ultimately was offered to schools as a set of propositions about student learning which they were invited to test. This placed the school into the role model of a small-scale research and development agency, and turned teaching away from transmissions of the given, to the construction and reconstruction of knowledge and understanding through engagement with issues and evidence (action research).

But HCP, while it identified a new role for teachers as curriculum researchers, did not address the full range of difficulties arising for teachers. Jean Rudduck takes the story further by discussing examples of teacher-as-researcher in practice. One of the greatest difficulties about this view of teaching and learning is the school itself: unless the school is a social institution organized – and resourced – to act as a kind of research and development centre, we may expect only a very limited growth of the teacher-as-researcher/developer movement.

A vital element in the teacher-as-researcher movement, from the perspective of school-based curriculum development, is the teacher's role in evaluation. The primary consideration in curriculum evaluation is improvement: improvement in the quality of student learning and improvement in the programmes, structures, resources and strategies that are provided as a means of enhancing student learning. It is this that most clearly differentiates evaluation from research although, in the practice of evaluation, research goals, values and methods have a place. The recent history of the teacher-as-researcher movement, inspired in part by the project evaluations of the early curriculum projects and partly by the philosophy of school-based curriculum development, provides us with an understanding of the range and variety of tasks facing the school as itself an evaluation agency. Neil Russell, a leading figure in the Australian teachers-as-evaluators project, outlines the history of the movement, pin-points the major functions of evaluation, and defines the levels, within the school, at which evaluation needs to be conducted. His emphasis is on evaluation for curriculum improvement, at the whole-school and programme levels. Notwithstanding the pressure towards evaluation for accountability and the external direction of school curriculum processes, Neil Russell shows how teachers can effectively plan and implement evaluations involving large areas of the curriculum and the whole school staff. His chapter strengthens the belief underlying many of the case-studies reported in Section 3, that the school can work towards a strong research and development role, with curriculum evaluation as a key factor (Skilbeck, M. (ed.) (1984) *Evaluating the Curriculum in the Eighties*, London: Hodder and Stoughton).

In his chapter, Glen Evans confronts this challenge. Drawing upon a wide array of Australian research data, he argues that it is in the processes of schooling and not from outside sources – of whatever kind – that the teacher is most likely to find the motivation for and the means of professional development. This is an interesting and important point since it links three key development processes which, often treated independently of one another, can in union provide a powerful framework for school-level action: curriculum development, teacher development and school organization development. Glen Evans' argument enables us to see how, through carefully designed school-level projects, we can energize the whole system, drawing upon powerful motivations for change. The key process in all of this is active problem solving, by small in-school teams and focused on specific issues in the school as a teaching–learning institution. Taking this process as central, relating it to the three forms of development and treating outside resources as potentially supportive of school-focused problem solving, we have a way of thinking about school-based curriculum development which overcomes many of the shortcomings of the past.

CHAPTER 22

CURRICULUM DEVELOPMENT AND TEACHER RESEARCH
Jean Rudduck*

One way – in my view the most exciting and productive way – of making a connection between school-based curriculum development and teacher research is through Lawrence Stenhouse's notions of 'the art of teaching' and of 'the curriculum as problematic'.

The curriculum development movement and the idea of the curriculum as problematic

The extensive and energetic wave of nationally funded curriculum development projects that swept into and over schools and classrooms in the late 1960s and early 1970s has ebbed and people have begun to examine what remains in its wake. Some ask why there are not more visible patterns of effect across a larger number of schools. Behind such a question lie certain assumptions about what would count as evidence of 'impact': the questioner might look, for instance, at titles on school timetables finding out how often 'Man: a Course of Study' appears, or 'Keele Integrated Studies' or 'Geography for the Young School Leaver'. But the most important residue of the curriculum movement is what has lodged not just in the timetables of schools but in the minds of practitioners, policy-makers and researchers: fragments of experience that combine to yield a better understanding of the conditions and processes of curriculum development.

---

* I should like to thank Fred Walton, Val Dagley, Rita Preston and Ray Tarleton, whose work I discuss in this chapter. A full account of my work with Fred Walton is given in Rudduck (1983).

One of the most important things that I learned as a member of a national curriculum development team was how damaging the authority and supposed integrity (i.e. wholeness) of a curriculum 'product' could be to the professional autonomy of the teacher. Curriculum packages, as they came to be called, were made intellectually tidy and resource-sufficient by the central development team and then they were mass-produced for schools on an ill-founded faith that the similarities among schools were more important than their differences and that what worked in one field setting might be expected to work in any other (an assumption challenged by Parker and Rubin 1966). If the new course failed in practice to lead pupils and teachers to the promised land, then teachers might respond by rejecting themselves – they were not up to the demands of the course – or by rejecting the course – it made unrealistic demands on pupils and resources. The right to adapt, rather than the obligation to adopt, was a liberating notion, and although it entered the curriculum campaign in the 60s, was not taken seriously until fairly late in its history. And yet adaptation could have been the key to the effective dissemination of curriculum projects provided that it implied something more than a cautious or casual remoulding of whatever was intellectually jagged or practically awkward to make the 'new' course fit the established pattern of teaching and learning, and support the established framework of values. What adaptation *can* mean is thoughtful adjustment of a course and of the way it is handled in the classroom in the light of critical reflection on the experience of using it in a particular context. The right to adapt a curriculum course underlines the importance of the teacher's professional judgement; the obligation to adopt undermines it.

A curriculum course is, after all, no more than a way of expressing ideas in a form that allows those ideas to be tested in practice. In emphasizing the possibility of viewing curriculum in this way, I am echoing Lawrence Stenhouse (1981a), who said 'that [its] first and most important legacy . . . is the possibility of regarding all curricula as problematic and hence as hypothetical'. There are no curricula which are good or right. There are, instead, curricula which are interesting and engaging and which are worth working with to see what professional insight they can yield. So, no matter whether new curriculum courses are centrally developed or school based, the important point is that they can claim to offer an intelligent thought through educational theory which teachers can test in the laboratories of their own classrooms. A clear-cut example and one that is reasonably widely known is 'Man: a Course of Study' which embodies Bruner's theory of learning. Teachers might find Bruner's *books* difficult to use but when his ideas are articulated in a *course of study*, then teachers working with that course of study are both extended by access to the ideas and empowered by having a platform of experience from which to criticize them.

In curriculum development, 'the error', says Stenhouse (ibid.) 'is not one of location of initiative (i.e. central development versus grass roots development); the error is in adopting the conception of curriculum development as something distinct from curriculum research.' What research does is to ensure that the teacher holds the curriculum problematic: he or she is able, therefore, constantly to learn from teaching it.

The art of teaching

At this point we need to pick up another strand in Stenhouse's argument: the idea of the art of teaching:

> To say that teaching is an art does not imply that teachers are born, not made. On the contrary, artists learn and work extraordinarily hard at it. But they learn through the critical practice of their art . . . if my words are inadequate, look at the sketch books of a good artist, a play in rehearsal, a jazz quartet working together. That, I am arguing, is what good teaching is like. (1980)

Stenhouse develops this theme, using the analogy of the school as a repertory theatre:

> What plays are for actors and directors – media through which to learn by their everyday activity about the nature of life and their art – curricula are for students and teachers. (Stenhouse and Torrance 1980)
> . . . note that a good repertory company is . . . concerned with the development of its actors as artists . . . And the medium of this development is the very same medium as that which entertains – motivates – and educates its audience. It is the curriculum of the theatre: the plays. The good company chooses plays on several grounds. They must, overall, appeal to an audience . . . They ought to be justifiable and worthwhile . . . Importantly, however, they should also develop the actors. 'We chose Antony and Cleopatra rather than Othello because Larry and Viv were just at the point where those parts would contribute to their development. And, you know, the audience profits enormously from the development of our art. It is not done at their expense.' (ibid.)

In these passages is the nub of the argument: Stenhouse implies that the curriculum is both the means of learning for the pupils and the means of professional development for the teacher. One justification for curriculum development, for trying something which is new and difficult, is that it helps teachers to refine their art, extend their repertoire of skills and maintain excitement in their work:

My response is positive to the teacher of A level French who says: 'The main problem of the financial stringency is that I have to keep teaching the same set books year after year. I need the challenge of changing them.' Like all arts, teaching develops by setting itself new problems. (Stenhouse 1981a)

A characteristic of artists – dancers, actors, musicians, painters, sculptors – is that improvement can only come through performance and the constant monitoring of performance. It is important, therefore, that teachers actively seek opportunities, through curriculum development, for professional development. The notion of the curriculum as problematic is, then, the key to the improvement of the art of teaching through research. And improvement is a process that has no term:

> Teachers must be educated to develop their art, not to master it, for the claim to mastery merely signals the abandoning of aspiration. Teaching is not to be regarded as a static accomplishment like riding a bicycle or keeping a ledger; it is, like all arts of high ambition, a strategy in the face of an impossible task. (Stenhouse 1983)

The position I have outlined might well be attacked for seeming to put the development of the teacher as a higher priority than the selection of appropriate content for children's learning; if the curriculum is hypothetical and teaching is experimental, are not the children guinea-pigs – mere pawns in the self-interested pursuit of teacher professionalism? McPherson (1983) reviewing the work of Holt (1981) comments: '. . . education as the performance of teachers is incomplete; the appropriate metaphor must also encompass learning and pupils.' Stenhouse has, of course, anticipated such criticisms. He suggests that the learning of the teachers need not and should not conflict with the welfare of pupils (1980): teachers develop their art not as an end in itself but to benefit pupils, and the art is not, therefore, being 'adequately practised unless that benefit is there'. Pupils may well learn better, and more, if they are taught by teachers whose minds are curious and alert about aspects of their everyday practice.

Are Stenhouse's notions dreams or a contribution to practice? Let us see what a research stance can do for teachers in two different contexts: first, in the context of curriculum change and then in the context of curriculum unease. The first situation is one where a teacher has a clear curriculum aspiration and embarks on a programme of change; the second situation is one where a teacher senses that something may be wrong but needs to be more informed before taking action.

Teacher research in practice: some examples

Fred is head of humanities in a semirural high school. He planned to introduce a new inquiry-based approach to history with one group of 12-year-old pupils. Fred had been inducted into teacher research by the Ford Teaching Project (Elliott and Adelman 1978) and had subsequently tried to involve other teachers in his own school (see Rudduck 1982). He sought support from myself and a colleague, knowing that we would be interested in what he was trying to do.

The pupils who were to be involved in the new history course were a mixed-ability group – 'some borderline grammar school pupils . . . and at the other end, ESN'. Fred knew what he wanted to achieve: to change pupils' conceptions of history by giving them some experience of the historical method. Preliminary interviews with small groups of pupils confirmed that their view of history was narrow: 'Old stuff what happened years ago'; 'Kings and famous people. Things they've done'; 'Victorian times and Vikings'. For them, history was just a subject on the timetable, and when asked how history differed from other subjects, the responses showed a curious logic: 'The people that are famous are usually in history so if you've got a famous person it must be in history'; 'You have to look in books more in history'; 'Teacher's always talking away and you're not doing anything'.

With our help, Fred planned a one-day event away from school which would give the pupils a sustained experience of the new approach and help him understand the problems they would encounter as they moved from an instructional, recall-of-facts approach, to the more self-reliant evidence-based approach of inquiry learning as he defined it. A key activity of the day was a 'writing history' task. Pupils were divided into small groups, given copies of historical documents relating to an episode that took place in 1864 concerning the stealing of some hens' eggs, and asked to write a history of the event. There were sufficient ambiguities across the documents to generate considerable questioning of their status as evidence. The small-group discussions were tape-recorded.

It was apparent from the recordings that pupils had a strong task completion ethic: finishing the work set was more important to them than struggling with meaning. For example, faced with a dilemma, pupils tended to take a quick and easy way out rather than to interrogate their theory with additional evidence:

> 'Why should he [the man accused of stealing the eggs]
> be going to look after the horses with eggs in his hand?'
> 'Perhaps because – I don't know.'
> 'Perhaps he was going to have them for his dinner.'

And again:

> 'What's a turnpike?'
> 'Look [reads from document]: "Near a roadway which runs from a turnpike into Mr Paine's farm." '
> 'It wouldn't be a river, would it?'
> 'Yes, a river or something like that.'
> 'Yes, a stream.'
> 'Come on.'

This readiness to seek closure on a problem was interpreted as reflecting both a habit of mind – pupils are not used to checking out the logic of their conclusions, and a habit of pace – they are used to working in short spans of time and to finishing the work set within the time available. Indeed, there were many references to time and to task completion:

> 'What time do we get finished?'
> 'A quarter to.'
> 'Do we get marked?'
> 'Come on. Get on with it or we're not going to get done.'

The pupils carried over another habit that was dysfunctional given the aims of the new course. This was their tendency to work on texts one by one and to summarize each in turn rather than to analyse evidence across documents and then attempt a synthesis: the discrepancies in the evidence tended, therefore, to elude them. Other problems included the pupils' lack of experience of collaborative working and in particular the difficulty they had in improving the work of the group through critical response to what group members contributed.

So, the recordings of the day's work (only one activity has been discussed here and one in which the teacher did not figure) showed where the overhang of the conventional teaching/learning style was impeding transition to a new learning style. Fred saw what to concentrate on, back at school, to help his pupils and himself accomplish that transition. After two months, we helped Fred check out the effects of the new course, comparing the pupils' comments on their present course with those they had made four months earlier about history as they knew it then.

The interviews suggested that pupils had developed richer perceptions of history: it was no longer just 'about the past' or about 'Kings and Queens and Romans'. Conceptualizations were more subtle: 'History's about ordinary people'; 'History is discussing things and discussing people. It's about individual people, how they behave . . . what sort of background they come from'. They had also shifted their perception of historical method: no longer was history about copying from books or writing down what the teacher said. Now pupils were using words such as 'investigate', 'evidence' and 'proof'. And history was no longer classified as one of the school subjects that dealt in right/wrong answers. There were also indications of a readiness to take risks in the classroom and this was clearly a new experience for these pupils:

'I think you can sort of make your own decision better – it aint necessary to be right or wrong.'
'Well, some history doesn't agree. There's not actually an answer.'
'If I was putting my hand up to say something I wouldn't be worried.'
'You're not just doing things out of the book. You're discussing things before you actually write them down, so you understand them.'

The interviews also revealed that the back-at-school tasks compared unfavourably with those that pupils had tackled on their one-day introduction to the course: the latter, taking on, no doubt, a certain lustre from the excitement of the day's outing, had a memorable intensity, whereas the classroom tasks, which spanned several lessons, tended to lose impact, and the pupils, failing to see the logic of the task, showed a slackening of commitment over time. What Fred needed was tasks that had immediacy of appeal and a coherence that pupils could grasp quickly and that would survive the waiting time to the next history lesson and the intrusion of other lessons conducted in a different teaching style. Research had enabled Fred to understand the particular problems that his pupils, as a result of the history of their learning in that school, were experiencing, to judge what action he might take to improve the structure of the situation in which they were working, and (although this short account has not focused on Fred as a teacher) to refine the criteria by which he was judging his own performance as a classroom facilitator of inquiry learning. (For a more detailed discussion of this attempt at curriculum change, see Rudduck 1983.)

Fred had used research as a tool to help him launch, adapt and sustain a curriculum course that represented a sharp break with the familiar past, but classroom research can also offer teachers the kind of insight that enables them to make small-scale adjustments to their teaching.

Three teachers, all from the same secondary school, tried to get a grip on some aspect of the courses they taught that they suspected might be capable of improvement. To be fair, it was not the impulse towards the improvement of their art as teachers that motivated them to take action: it was a pervading sense of professional staleness:

> 'I wanted to do something different – something with a bit of a challenge.'
> 'I'd got to the stage where I wanted to think a bit more about what was going on in the classroom. I have been teaching now for three years and sort of felt I needed something to interest myself in.'

The tone of these comments suggests a desire to stand back from the monotonous regularities of everyday teaching and claim a right to professional excitement: the teachers needed a professional pick-me-up. It seems from their accounts of their work (see Hull et al. 1984) that classroom research can save teachers from the rut of boredom and give them insight into aspects of curriculum practice that have become dulled by habit and made obscure by their very familiarity (see Greene 1973). Once they had accepted the possibility that research might be the means of recommitting themselves to their teaching, then they were able to locate those areas of their practice that they thought it might be worthwhile to focus on.

Val, a geography teacher, suspected that children's grasp of mapping conventions was less sure than might appear from their work products. She asked children in different classes to draw maps and she was able to compare the responses of younger with older children, of less academically able with more academically able children. She made copies of a selection of maps and invited pupils to evaluate them in small groups, recording their discussions. She had, therefore, the evidence of the maps themselves (where the criteria the pupils were working to had to be inferred) and the evidence of the recordings (where the criteria were explicit). It was clear that some pupils had a conception of a map that was different from the teacher's, and that work which she was inclined to mark as wrong *was* sometimes following a set of conventions – but the conventions, for example, of maps that appear at the front of children's books and that chart the territory in which the narrative is to unfold rather than the conventions of ordnance survey maps! The evidence forced Val to think about and modify many aspects of her teaching; she commented: 'What I have been able to do has been of great help to me as a teacher and I hope it may provide a starting point for others.'

Val's colleague, Ray, an English teacher, was curious about the criteria pupils use to distinguish poetry from prose and to judge quality in poetry. He first gathered some written responses to a set of open questions about the nature and character of poetry and then offered the pupils, in small groups, a poem rewritten as prose, asking them to 'put it in a way that would make it easier to understand'. The discussions were tape-recorded. He then invited them to compare their version with the original, and also asked groups not so far involved to respond critically to both versions. Again, the discussions were recorded. Ray concluded: 'The study made accessible to me the ways in which 11- and 12-year-old pupils thought about poetry and the criteria they were using for making judgements about quality, particularly in relation to form. What I found – especially the preoccupation with rhyme and punctuation – helped me to reconsider the way we "do" poetry at school.'

Rita, the biology teacher, was interested, like Val, in seeing whether the formal work products that she demanded of her classes accurately reflected the quality of their understanding. One of the most successful – and the simplest – of the research exercises that she designed to inform herself was a comparison of pupils' written descriptions of biological specimens with their sketches of biological specimens. She found that there was a much greater range of intellectual competence within the groups than could be inferred from the drawings alone. For instance, one first-form child, while producing a fairly competent sketch of a geranium leaf, had not in fact mastered the way of thinking of a biologist (as the teacher defines it) nor the language of biology, and her impulse was to put a red ring round the last five lines of the description, indicating that it was unacceptable.

> The Geraneum leave is very hairy and soft. The stem is more hairy than the leave itself, and the colour of them is white, underneath the leaf looks as if it is dying, because you can see the vains very clearly. They look as though they have got bones, and their bones are taking over.

This small study helped Rita to face some important issues in her teaching: for example, the possibility of finding ways of valuing what a pupil offers by trying to understand the pupil's construction of the task and sense of what counts as an appropriate response, and seeing how that differs from the teacher's construction of the task and her judgement of what counts as an appropriate response.

Now, perhaps, we can begin to see more clearly the advantages of teacher-initiated curriculum development compared with the adoption-oriented centre–periphery model that dominated the curriculum movement. If – to go back to Lawrence Stenhouse's analogy – theatre were nationalized, and if local theatres across the country had to accept a centrally determined programme of plays – a theatrical common curriculum – however carefully the programme was selected, graded, balanced and sequenced, it would not allow individual companies to choose plays that offered the very challenge that would help the actors improve those aspects of their art which most needed strengthening: for example, the handling of verse, whether in Shakespeare or Eliot; managing the stylized body movements that sustain the elegance of restoration comedy; maintaining the unflagging speed of good farce; holding the knife-edge of credibility that prevents some period tragedy from becoming absurd. The curriculum development movement – which did not of course 'require' all schools, or indeed any schools, to incorporate the new curriculum courses it generated (here my analogy breaks down) – responded to broad, topical concerns with, often, highly intelligent propositions, many of them so innovative that if teachers had been able to regard themselves as partners in a curriculum experiment, rather than as customers, then their art as teachers would certainly have advanced. (And, of course, this happened to some teachers whose professional training gave them confidence to view centrally developed curricula and themselves in this way.) But even had the curriculum movement succeeded in these terms there would still be a place for local initiatives in curriculum development which reflect the concerns and aspirations of individual teachers or teams of teachers in particular schools.

The advancement of teacher research

The idea of teacher research has not had an easy passage. In particular, teachers have found it difficult to manage the transformation that the role requires. Aronowitz's condemnation (1973) of teacher trainers' preoccupation with discipline, though overstated, has an element of truth: he regrets 'the generations of . . . school teachers whose main skill has been maintaining control over the class rather than understanding . . . the process of learning'. Preoccupation with finding a survival kit of teaching tips can also displace concern to lay a proper foundation for career-long professionalism – which, for me, means the capacity of the teacher to continue to develop his or her art as a teacher. Giroux (1981, p.155) suggests that teacher training programmes have 'simply not given teachers the conceptual tools they need to view knowledge as problematic' – and, I would add, 'to view curriculum, therefore, as problematic'.

The providers of in-service courses for teachers have, not surprisingly, been able to support teacher research more robustly and the movement is now gaining ground rapidly. A recent landmark was a conference organized in January 1983 by Jenny Nias at the Cambridge Institute of Education called 'Teaching research-based courses'. Fifty-four people from thirty-six institutions – from Glasgow to Plymouth, from Northern Ireland to the North Sea – were brought together by their common concern about structuring, resourcing, teaching and ensuring standards in courses in which classroom research by teachers was the main focus. By this time, numerous courses had been set up, and validated by universities and by the CNAA, which have research at their core. (Some of these courses are in initial training.) The issue of validation is important, as Stenhouse pointed out at the 1980 SITE conference:

> What is required of the universities is that they . . . recognize forms of research alternative to the still dominant tradition of scientific positivism with its emphasis on experimental and survey procedures conducted on samples in field settings and giving rise to 'results'. Among these alternative forms are experimental or descriptive case studies which may be based upon the teacher's access either to the classroom as a laboratory or to the school or classroom as a setting for participant observation. In Britain standards for these research paradigms are now in process of being worked out at masters and doctoral level, both through discussion at conferences and in the consultations between internal and external examiners. This alliance with universities is important for the teachers because it provides access to a pattern of part-time study, right up to the level of doctorate, which turns one towards one's professional work rather than away from it, and offers a systematic training in the appropriate research skills as well as a grasp of the theoretical issues applicable to . . . practitioner research. (Stenhouse 1984)

Clearly, the acquisition of appropriate research skills is vitally important if teacher research is to be accepted as a medium for the improvement of the art of teaching.

Obstacles to the advancement of teacher research do not lie solely in the caution of academics; they are also to be found within the teaching profession itself among those teachers who openly acknowledge their scepticism towards anything which is called 'research'. Burgess puts the case in a paper on 'teacher-based research' (1980):

> They (teachers) consider that much educational research has little relevance for the work they do in schools and classrooms. Second, they consider that research reports are relatively inaccessible given their content and style of presentation. Third, they feel that many researchers exploit schools for their own purposes but provide little evidence that will influence classroom practice.

These criticisms are probably just and are probably voiced by many teachers – including Barbara, a primary teacher, who was about to set out on her maiden teacher-as-researcher voyage:

> I've done a lot of studying in the past, reading research reports . . . the actual research is meaningless and irrelevant to any working teacher. I don't think the teacher in the classroom is really taken seriously enough. . . . If teachers have largely contributed to it (research) then it's going to be more relevant to other teachers than if it's just 'academic researchers' work . . . 'Cause that's what happens with so much research, doesn't it? It's done in an artificial environment . . . and it hasn't really got any connection with the teeming world of education they're supposedly trying to influence. (Quoted by May and Rudduck 1983)

Experience of the process of teacher research, or of the insights and language of teacher research (see Nixon 1979; Nixon et al. 1979; Rowlandson 1983) may serve to dispel the negative attitudes towards research in general that linger within the profession and thereby pave the way for a more wholehearted endorsement of the claim that teacher research is worth trying.

References

Aronowitz, S. (1973) *False Promises*, New York: McGraw Hill.
Burgess, R.G. (1980) Some field work problems in teacher based research, *British Educational Research Journal*, vol. 6, no. 2, pp. 165–173.
Elliott, J. and Adelman C. (1978) Reflecting where the action is: the design of the Ford Teaching Project, *Education for Teaching*, November.
Giroux, H. (1981) *Ideology, Culture and the Process of Schooling*, Brighton: The Falmer Press.
Greene, M. (1973) *Teacher as Stranger*, Wadsworth Publishing Company.
Holt, M. (1981) *Evaluating the Evaluators*, London: Hodder and Stoughton.
Hull, C., Rudduck, J. and Sigsworth, A. (1984) *A Room Full of Children Thinking*, London: Longman for the Schools Council.
May, N. and Rudduck, J. (1983) *Sex-Stereotyping and the Early Years of Schooling* Norwich: School of Education, University of East Anglia.
McPherson, A. (1983) Accountability and the Know-Nothing Movement, *Journal of Curriculum Studies*, vol. 15, no. 2, pp. 215–223.
Nixon, J. (ed.) (1979) *A Teacher's Guide to Action Research*, London: Open Books.
Nixon, J., Magee, F. and Sheard, D. (1979) *Teachers in Research*, a conference report, London: Schools Council Publications.
Parker, J.C. and Rubin, L.J. (1966) *Process as Content: Curriculum Design and the Application of Knowledge*, Chicago: Rand McNally.
Rowlandson, S. (ed.) (1983) *Teachers Studying Children's Thinking*, a publication of the Leicestershire Classroom Research IN-Service Education Scheme.
Rudduck, J. (1982) School-based study groups, *in* Rudduck, J. (ed.) *Teachers in*

Partnership, London: Longman for the Schools Council, pp. 11–26.

Rudduck, J. (1983) In-service courses for pupils as a basis for implementing curriculum change, *British Journal of In-service Education*, vol. 10, no. 1, Autumn 1983, pp. 32–42.

Stenhouse, L. (1980) Curriculum research and the art of the teacher, *Curriculum*, vol. 1, no. 1, pp. 40–44.

Stenhouse, L. (1981) Applying research to education: one experience, *Northern Ireland Committee for Educational Research Information Bulletin*, no. 15, pp. 1–4.

Stenhouse, L. (1981a); Curriculum Research and Educational Process, mimeo, Centre for Applied Research in Education, University of East Anglia.

Stenhouse, L. (1983) Research as a basis for teaching (inaugural lecture given at the University of East Anglia, 1979), *in* Stenhouse, L. *Authority, Education and Emancipation*, London: Heinemann Educational.

Stenhouse, L. (1983a) The legacy of the curriculum movement (paper given at the annual conference of the Association for the Study of the Curriculum, 1982), *in* Galton, M. and Moon, B. (eds) *Changing Schools, Changing Curriculum*, London: Harper and Row, pp. 346–355.

Stenhouse, L. (1984) The teacher as focus of research and development (paper given at the SITE conference, Simon Fraser University, 1980), *in* Hopkins, D. and Wideen, M. (eds) *Alternative Perspectives on School Improvement*, Brighton: Falmer Press.

Stenhouse, L. and Torrance, H. (1980) Curriculum Knowledge and Action: a Dialogue (paper given at the American Educational Research Association conference), mimeo, Centre for Applied Research in Education, University of East Anglia.

CHAPTER 23

TEACHERS AS CURRICULUM EVALUATORS
Neil Russell

'Teachers as curriculum evaluators': the phrase arouses an immediate response from many concerned with education. Reactions such as 'trendy', 'simplistic', 'sloganistic', 'contemporary' and 'professional' have been heard.

This chapter seeks to describe and analyse the evolution of the contemporary concept of teachers as curriculum evaluators, by tracing the developments in the curriculum evaluation field over the last twenty years, and reviewing the policy and practice of teachers as they take up new roles and responsibilities in this area.

Problems associated with the concept of teachers as curriculum evaluators will be canvassed and suggestions made for improving teaching and learning through more systematic evaluation initiatives at the school level.

The antecedents to the concept

Before the mid-60s teachers viewed evaluation as the assessment of their students' performance (typically in the cognitive area only and using a term or end-of-year exam as the measuring instrument). Alternatively it was seen as the assessment of teaching performance by inspectors for the purpose of a teacher's promotion (Hughes et al. 1981). Several writers have pointed out that this tradition of evaluation was influenced greatly by researchers such as Tyler and those involved with the psychometric tradition (Davis 1981).

It is interesting to note that there were only two curriculum evaluation texts published in the 1960s and the term itself was not used as a descriptor for information retrieval until 1967 (Fraser 1982). Not only was curriculum evaluation poorly represented in the literature but as far as teachers were concerned curriculum evaluation was a remote activity.

In the mid-60s national curriculum development projects abounded. The Schools Council in the UK, various bodies in the USA, and the Australian Science Education Project (as a forerunner of the national Curriculum Development Centre in Australia) created material production projects including expert, full-time, professional evaluators. These evaluators used methods appropriate to large-scale projects and reported findings in extensive reports and professional journals.

This practice had as one of its unintended effects the mystifying of evaluation for the classroom practitioner. For teachers evaluation appeared to be something that somebody else did (Harlen 1978).

In the late 1970s we witnessed a number of trends which counteracted these influences:

- More emphasis was placed on school-based decision making in the curriculum development area, as opposed to central office decisions and national development projects. (Evans 1981; see also ch. 24 below)
- In a number of countries the role of school inspector was abolished or significantly altered, creating a situation where it was far more advisory and less mandatory than previously.
- The number of major curriculum development projects initiated in the UK, USA, Australia and New Zealand was dramatically reduced, with greater emphasis being placed on school-based curriculum initiatives.
- Accountability issues became clearer with increased pressure being placed on schools to account for the programmes they had devised. (Elliott 1980)
- We witnessed a dramatic increase in the published material available in the curriculum evaluation area, with 27 books and many articles published from 1975 onwards. (Fraser 1982)
- Growing numbers of tertiary institutions offered broader-based courses in curriculum evaluation at the undergraduate and postgraduate levels as opposed to fewer, more restricted courses in educational measurement emphasizing statistics.

In summary, these trends have led to dramatic changes in the purpose of curriculum evaluation at the school level and made many rethink the roles that teachers play in the evaluation initiatives in the 1980s. As a result of these changes we have quite different working definitions of the terms 'evaluation' and curriculum evaluation in the 1980s.

In its simplest form evaluation means 'to place a value on'; curriculum evaluation in the 1980s refers to the process of placing a value on the curriculum that is taught. Many teachers mistakenly believe that the collection of information is sufficient to complete the evaluation process. The process must also involve the examination of criteria, goals, objectives or aspirations, the means by which these are created, the manner in which they are implemented together with the intended and unintended effects of attempting to obtain them.

Definitions, such as that by Terry Tenbrink (1974) 'Evaluation is the process of obtaining information and using it to form judgements which in turn are used for decision making', may appeal to some; however, the concept of the 'process of placing a value on' has more direct appeal to teachers as a definition.

What purpose should teachers consider in curriculum evaluation activities?

The debate on curriculum evaluation in countries with similar cultures, such as Australia, Canada, the United Kingdom and the United States, exhibits common features. Three types of purposes seem to occur commonly in public debate:

(a) using formal assessment in education for student placement or selection (e.g. external examinations for certification and tertiary entry);
(b) informing various audiences in appropriate fashion concerning the programmes of schools;
(c) developing procedures to improve teaching and learning and the relevance of programmes in schools and systems.

Each of these purposes raises the use of curriculum evaluation in a particular sense:

1. for vocational or educational placement;
2. for accountability;
3. for curriculum improvement.

The teachers' curriculum evaluation role in a particular school will be determined by the relative emphasis or priority placed on the three key purposes of improvement, accountability and placement.

In describing what the teacher is doing when conducting curriculum evaluation activities we need to consider the level of the task (whole-school level, programme level or individual-teacher level), the purpose of the task and the support available inside and outside the school to carry out the task.

Describing the teacher's curriculum evaluation role

Level of the activity

Teachers may operate at three different levels in curriculum evaluation:

1. whole-school level;
2. programme, department or issue level;
3. individual-teacher level.

Whole-school level

At the whole-school level many larger schools charging substantial fees use a set of guidelines or a manual for evaluation based on the New England (USA) approach (Herbert 1981). Teachers using this method are involved in a process which seeks to obtain information on a wide range of programmes and administrative aspects of the entire school and uses an external committee to validate its findings (Russell 1982).

The process involves teachers' collecting information over a period of one to two school terms and determining whether important criteria identified in the evaluation manual and by teachers have been met. An external committee reviews both the processes of the teachers and their findings and reports on the veracity of the process to the school council.

In a number of states in Australia, a form of whole-school evaluation where teachers have a significant role is in operation. Teachers are provided with a manual of evaluation processes prepared by the education department and conduct an evaluation of the school against published school objectives. When this has been completed a review board of community members, teachers and inspectors (or advisers) reviews the evaluation processes of the teachers. Whilst these approaches have the potential to provide improvement in teaching and learning, it can be argued that the whole-school-evaluation approach is more concerned with accountability and there is the requirement that these whole-school evaluations be conducted at prescribed intervals of time – every five to seven years in the case of Victoria high schools – (Ford 1980).

Indeed many reports of these exercises give only passing attention to important areas of the curriculum such as music, art, drama and physical education, and often concentrate on aspects such as the size and furnishing of buildings, together with the need for more equipment, rather than on the teaching and learning going on in class. The public nature of reports generated at the 'whole-school' level appears to militate against a detailed process of valuing the curriculum and places more emphasis on administrative arrangements, listing of courses and school records.

What can be achieved in this exercise is that a school may identify specific areas which need closer examination. For example, enough evidence may be collected to suggest that the pastoral care system being used in the school may need to be reviewed internally by the school. The driver education programme may be achieving quite unexpected results suggesting that an evaluation be planned to determine the extent to which the interests and needs of the students are reflected in the course design.

Whole-school evaluation has the potential to change the curriculum to meet important goals of the community; however, the scope and nature of the exercise often results in: 'Well that is over for another seven years, let's get back to the classroom.'

The method used to train teachers for this role in evaluation is now well established. Workshops are conducted using a simulation or case-study approach in conjunction with the evaluation manual.

Programme level

The role of teachers participating in school-initiated curriculum evaluations at the subject or programme level (e.g. a primary school reading programme) or at the issue level (e.g. reporting to parents) is different in both scope and emphasis from whole-school evaluation. Education systems encourage teachers to be involved in evaluation at this level (Hughes et al. 1981). This includes choosing the issue or area to be evaluated, identifying questions to ask, planning, reporting and implementing the evaluation findings (Hughes et al. 1979).

Experience in many school settings in Australia and the South Pacific suggests that teachers do not need structured guidance for programme-level evaluation activities to ensure that there is improvement in teaching and learning following an evaluation. The structured questions included in the following section indicate an approach that has been found to be most successful.

The Teachers as Evaluators project in Australia has provided over 6000 guidelines to teachers and conducted training workshops attended by over

4000 teachers at the early childhood, primary, secondary and technical school levels. Experience suggests that teachers *can* plan evaluations effectively with well-trialled guidelines that are reasonably jargon-free, decision or action orientated and produced in the form of a series of questions.

The following questions can be used to develop an evaluation plan at the school level. Teachers may set out their curriculum evaluation plans using the suggested subheadings (such as purpose, motivation, evaluators . . .) and answering the questions outlined in each section.

Questions to ask when planning an evaluation – an evaluations planner

1. Purposes
   What are the purposes of the evaluation?
   Are they expressed in specific terms, for example improving school morale?
   Are criteria available to make judgements, for example programme objectives?
   Are the purposes understood by and acceptable to all those concerned?
   Who is likely to oppose the evaluation?

2. Motivations
   Why is the evaluation being undertaken now?
   Will the evaluation meet a felt need of those involved with the school?
   Who wants to be involved in the evaluation?
   Who should be involved:
   – principal?
   – senior staff?
   – teachers?
   – those with a vested interest, for example parents, students, members of school board, Department of Education?
   – others?

3. Evaluators
   Who will carry out the evaluation:
   – principal and/or senior staff?
   – classroom teachers?
   – pupils?
   – parents?

- representatives of an outside body, for example consultant, adviser, school board members, principal or teachers from another school?
- a combination of the above, for example a group consisting of teachers, a parent and a consultant?

What will be the nature of the involvement of various participants?
Will there be a representative planning team or steering committee?
Is the evaluation likely to be seen as threatening to any of the participants?
How can any perceived threat be minimized?

4. *Evaluation roles*

There are a number of possible roles (not necessarily separate people):
- evaluator (one involved in information collection and judgement)
- facilitator (one involved in assisting an evaluation but not in judgement)
- consultant (a person called on for special contributions to one or more aspects, for example assisting with interviewing only).

To what extent are such roles used in the evaluation?
Is the evaluation organized in a realistic fashion for the people involved, particularly with respect to:
- time (to obtain valid results, to maintain interest, time for organization)
- personnel (is the central figure organizing or coordinating the evaluation being given time-release for the activity?)
- finance?

What is the time-span of the evaluation?

5. *Intended audiences*

Are those who are to receive the evaluation clearly defined?
What access to information will the various people have?

6. *Collection of information*

Available methods include:
- observation – structured or unstructured
- interviews – structured or unstructured
- questionnaires (rating scale type, open choice, closed choice)
- documentary analysis of reports, records, minutes, etc.
- content analysis of curriculum materials
- reports of informal discussions and conversations

- achievement tests – criterion and norm-referenced
- standardized tests
- diaries and self-reports
- audio and video tape-recordings

Are there appropriate safeguards to ensure that the information is valid and reliable?

7. *Feasibility of methods used to collect information*
   In terms of:
   - time available
   - availability of personnel with the necessary expertise
   - acceptability to those whose views and activities will be documented.

8. *Analysis of information*
   What are the procedures for the analysis of information?
   How will the information be categorized?
   Are there appropriate safeguards to validate the information?

9. *Release of information*
   Who will have control over what is collected and reported?
   What procedures will govern the collection and release of this information?
   Who will have the right to reply to, correct and validate reports of the views and activities of individuals and groups?
   Will all, or only part, of the information be released?

10. *Reports*
    Is the evaluation going to be reported in a form (content, style and format) which is readily available to those for whom it is designed?
    Will negative aspects of the school be reported, and to whom?
    Has the release date for reporting been identified?
    Are different reports for different groups necessary, for example parents, school staff, Education Departments?

11. *Timeline for your evaluation*
    Consider the amount of time you have available for evaluation and the main issues and activities which emerge in your answers to 'Questions to ask when planning an evaluation'. Attempt to plot these on a timeline (and timetable them if you can at this stage), allocating people to

activities, noting resources you will require.

This approach has the advantage of enabling teachers to focus on important areas for curriculum evaluation and to manage resources, particularly those of time and personnel, so that effective systematic evaluations may take place. Whilst the rationale for evaluation at this level is improvement, the fact that teachers are involved with the process means that they are able to give an account of their programme.

In summary: programme evaluation at the school level To establish a curriculum evaluation of a school programme the following desiderata are recommended:

(a) Obtain the support of the principal and school executive for the evaluation process.
(b) Invite all those who will be involved in implementing evaluation findings. If the area is Physical Education in the High School then obviously all Physical Education staff should be participants.
(c) Determine what it is that is being evaluated and why (see 'Questions to ask').
(d) Establish an evaluation team with clear roles for those involved with the evaluation. In particular if there are outsiders in the evaluation team (that is people not teachers, parents or students at the school) ensure that roles are clear particularly in the area of who 'owns' the information and who releases information and judgements.
(e) Follow an evaluation plan (such as 'Questions to ask') which allows people to see all of the steps in the process from the outset.
(f) Make a point of trying to give time to evaluation participants by reducing commitments in other areas where possible.

Individual-teacher level

Evaluation at the level of the individual teacher in his/her own classroom has been the focus of a number of studies. The self-monitoring-teacher concept has been promoted by writers such as Harlen (1978) and Elliott (1980) and education authorities such as the Lancashire Education Authority. In Australia Grundy and Kemmis (1981) have been conducting training workshops and producing materials for teachers involved in 'action research' which is in fact an evaluation process at the individual-classroom level.

In action research initiatives, the teacher identifies an issue or problem in her/his classroom and invites a 'critical friend' (another teacher or tutor at a tertiary institution) to assist in clarifying the issue, collecting information and coming to conclusions for action (Grundy and Kemmis 1981).

Information-gathering techniques used by teachers in curriculum evaluation

The main technique used by teachers to gain information is undoubtedly the questionnaire method. Even when the method is inappropriate for the information that is required teachers seem to rush headlong into survey techniques. Other techniques of gathering information such as interview, folio methods, content analysis, diary methods, observation and standardized test results are used far less frequently.

This presents obvious problems that some information collected will not be either as reliable or as valid as it could be if other more appropriate methods were used. Overcoming this problem will not be an easy task in the short term. Those who prepare undergraduates and graduates for teaching may have to assign students to experienced teacher-evaluators so that a range of evaluation techniques can be used and observed in field situations. In addition, far more attention will have to be given to *planning* an evaluation (using techniques such as 'Questions to ask').

When an evaluation has been completed comes the tricky exercise of making changes to improve teaching and learning. If the evaluation has the support of the school executive and has involved all of those centrally involved in implementing the evaluation results, then experience suggests that many changes will be made before the evaluation is even completed. In any case those involved with the evaluation may need to publish results on large sheets of paper in the staff room, in the school newsletter, in meetings, as a prelude to changes in policy and practice.

It should be kept in mind that teachers tend not to read discussion papers, bibliographies or commentaries on evaluation methods (Hughes et al. 1981). Rather, they are prepared to use well-trialled guidelines and copies of instruments and plans developed by other teachers, or to view realistic evaluation video case-studies (McConachy 1980). Training teachers to use a variety of techniques will require more materials of the preferred type to be developed, in conjunction with in-service training workshops (Skilbeck 1977, 1984).

Resources available to assist teachers in their role

Shaping the teacher's role in curriculum evaluation to allow improvements in teaching and learning will require more than skill in collecting and analysing information and a carefully prepared evaluation plan. Research evidence from teachers indicates that time and support need to be made available to complete evaluation tasks successfully.

Time can be provided to teachers using pupil-free days, teacher time release, teachers from other schools and consultants or advisers in classroom situations.

Advisers, consultants or facilitators may be able to assist a group of teachers to work through evaluation guidelines (such as 'Questions to ask') and provide examples of tests, observation methods, sampling techniques or interview schedules if these are appropriate. The important attribute for advisers from outside the school as far as teachers are concerned is that they should be experienced in school-level evaluation and in touch with resources available to assist the school (Hughes et al. 1981b).

Finally principals and senior administrators in a school need to actively encourage, support and resource curriculum evaluation at the school level. Teachers' enthusiasm for improvement of the curriculum using evaluation processes needs to be sustained and fostered by support at the top of the school both during the evaluation and at the stage of implementing findings.

Summary

In the short space of time of twenty years, evaluation in education has experienced something of a revolution. From a situation where teachers' formal evaluative role was concerned with assessing students' performance, we have moved to a far more complex and professional role for teachers who are placing judgements of worth on programmes following a structured evaluation process.

At a conference involving teachers and evaluation specialists in the mid-70s, a number of the evaluation specialists asserted that teachers could not operate in the school evaluation area without expert assistance. This assertion has been shown to be quite false. Given carefully trialled materials, and the availability of in-service training, teachers have clearly demonstrated both a willingness and skill to place a value on the curriculum at their school. A return to the days of an inspector parachuting into a class to evaluate the curriculum could be over. If we are genuinely concerned to improve teaching and learning in our schools we will be looking at ways of encouraging teachers to systematically, objectively and skilfully evaluate the work of the school.

References

Davis, E. (1981) *Teachers as Curriculum Evaluators*, Sydney: George Allen and Unwin.
Elliott, G. (1980) *Self Evaluation and the Teacher* part 2, Hull: University of Hull.
Evans, G. (1981) *Classroom Activities of Teachers at Lower Secondary Level* (Research Report to the Educational Research and Development Committee), Brisbane: University of Queensland.
Ford, T.J. (1980) School Review, memorandum, Melbourne: Education Department of Victoria.
Fraser, B.J. (1982) *Annotated Bibliography of Curriculum Evaluation Literature* Sydney: Macquarie University School of Education.
Grundy, S. and Kemmis, S. (1981) Educational Action Research, The State of the Art, paper presented at Australian Association for Research in Education Conference, Adelaide.
Harlen, W. (ed.) (1978) *Evaluation and the Teacher's Role*, London: Macmillan.
Herbert, J. (ed.) (1981) *Manual of School Evaluation*, Melbourne: Independent Headmasters Conference of Australia.
Hughes, P.W., Russell, N.A. and McConachy, D. (1979) *Teachers as Evaluators Project: A Guide to Evaluation*, Canberra: Curriculum Development Centre.
Hughes, P.W., Russell, N.A. and McConachy, D. (1981) *Curriculum Evaluation: How it can be done*, Teachers as Evaluators Project, Canberra: Curriculum Development Centre.
Hughes, P.W., Russell, N.A. and McConachy, D. (1981a) Accounting for our schools: problems and possibilities, *Australian Administrator*, vol. 2, no. 3, June.
Hughes, P.W., Russell, N.A. and McConachy, D. (1981b) Perspective on school-level curriculum evaluation in Australia, *Curriculum Perspectives*, vol. 1, no. 2 May.
Kemmis, S., Cole, P. and Suggett, D. (1983) *Towards the Socially-Critical School*, Melbourne: Victorian Institute of Secondary Education.
McConachy, D. (1980) *School Level Evaluation*, a videotape (25 min.), Canberra: Curriculum Development Centre.
McConachy, D. (1980a) Improvement: 'School Level Evaluation', *Newsletter* no. 1, Queensland Catholic Education Office.
Russell, N.A. (ed.) (1982) *Readings on Curriculum Evaluation*, Canberra: Curriculum Development Centre.
Skilbeck, M. (1977) Curriculum Evaluation in Australia, paper presented to the 1977 Annual Conference of the Australian Association for Research in Education.
Skilbeck, M. (ed.) (1984) *Evaluating the Curriculum in the Eighties*, London: Hodder and Stoughton.
Tenbrink, T. (1974) *Evaluation: A Practical Guide for Teachers*, New York: McGraw Hill.

CHAPTER 24

THE SCHOOL AS A CENTRE OF PROFESSIONAL DEVELOPMENT
Glen Evans

In this chapter, it is proposed that one of the most salient aspects of the teacher's role is that of the need to solve problems. Using evidence mainly from Australian studies, it traces some of the problems faced and the responses of teachers to the task of solving problems at the school level. The relationships between teachers' innovations, support within the school, and support from external in-service education provisions are critically examined, and some suggestions made for improving the links between in-service education and school-based development activities. It is argued that solving curriculum problems at the school level is a potent form of in-service education.

Fox (1980), in reviewing national case-studies undertaken for the OECD/CERI project on teacher education, distinguished three broad purposes for in-service education of teachers (INSET) – stimulating professional development, improving school practice, implementing social policy.

The in-service education of teachers might well be expected to help them address issues of community expectations, school function and organization, and shortfalls in the practices of schooling. There is some evidence, however, that traditional sources of in-service education do not, at least directly, influence teachers' practices. Teachers appear to draw most on their own ideas and skills, and to some extent on significant school personnel, in addressing problems. What contributes to these ideas and skills is unclear. Formal award-bearing courses as well as out-of-school in-service courses apparently contribute. At the same time teachers modify their views of reality as system and school constraints come to be seen as the natural condition.

It can be argued that the traditional direction of in-service education, from teacher development to school improvement, might well, in many cases, be reversed. That is, in-service education of teachers might focus initially on tackling school-level problems, utilizing the more powerful school-related influences. This chapter is concerned with exploring this contention.

The teacher in school

Recent studies, such as those of Collins and Hughes (1979) and Campbell and Robinson (1979), suggest that community expectations of schooling are increasingly concerned with constructive skills such as how to discover new knowledge or how to assemble facts, pose questions, and arrive at tentative answers. They are also concerned with contents such as career education, social awareness, personal development, and practical skills and knowledge appropriate in a particular community. By their nature, such contents are difficult to classify strongly into traditional kinds of school subjects. These kinds of expectations imply that much curriculum problem solving will take place at school level; they imply some differentiation of goals and content according to the particular school clientele and community; and they seem to imply a level of community involvement in curriculum planning.

While the organizational structures for school-level planning are increasingly available, the evidence so far is that, in most schools, the rhetoric of community involvement and school-based development is ahead of the practice (Brady and Pope 1980; Campbell and Robinson 1979; Meade 1981). In order to understand this gap, which continues to pose an essential problem for teacher education and organizational development, it is useful to examine the activities which teachers actually undertake in schools.

One set of data for such an examination is available from a study by Evans (1981) who surveyed an Australian sample of 772 teachers of secondary students in grades 7 to 10 from 97 schools. This survey indicated that while teachers regard a wide variety of teaching activities as very desirable, there appear to be constraints within the school context that reduce the extent to which some, although not all, of their goals are achieved. Providing for student access to the teacher, for example, is both highly regarded and frequently practised by most teachers; so too is providing encouragement or approval and praise. On the other hand, there were a number of activities seen as very desirable but relatively less frequently used – for example, helping students become more aware of their own values and abilities or providing students with marks or comments about their performance almost immediately. These differences point to unfulfilled goals in curriculum planning, school organization, or teacher education.

Again, other activities were judged by only some teachers as important to practise, and were rejected by others. Chief among these controversial activities were various types of teaching procedures aimed at enhancing student choice and autonomy, e.g. some choice by students of content, free student access to resources, use of small groups undertaking different tasks, and providing students with the opportunity to gather information, form and test hypotheses, produce arguments, cooperate in groups on projects, and the like. Apart from differences among teachers in their perceptions of how desirable these activities might be, they were practised much less frequently than teachers on the average considered ideal, again suggesting constraints in the school and/or needs in teacher education.

The project was also concerned with the nature of the influences on teachers' activities. Outstandingly the most frequently mentioned constraints, or discouragers, were seen as class size, time available to cover the work, and school resources, and the most frequent encouragers of desirable activities were the teacher's own knowledge, own teaching skill and the particular students taught. The particular subject taught also seems to generate its own influences. Of lesser importance, but still apparently strong encouragers of some teaching activities, were educational publications, the opportunity for discussion with other teachers, and the subject master or head of department. Other influences seen as constraints were external and school syllabuses, the availability of textbooks, the school timetable, and local examination or moderation systems.

Although often thought to be important influences on teachers, out-of-school sources such as inspectors, advisory teachers, in-service education, and subject and professional associations were hardly ever chosen as either encouragers or discouragers for teaching activities of any kind. Community resources were not seen as strong influences, while parents, like principals, were only mentioned as influences in encouraging teachers to use incentives and to assess by marks rather than by comments and discussion. These findings illustrate the conclusions reached in much research, that it is in the processes of the school itself that teachers are most likely to find the motivation for, and means of, genuine professional development: the closer the process to the teacher's daily work, the greater the influence (Perrott 1979; Cohen and Harrison 1982). For example, in Evans' (1981) study, subject masters or department heads were seen as the most important positive or encouraging influence apart from the teacher's own knowledge and skill and students. Principals were seen as important at whole-school level, subject heads and staff groups at the level of innovation in teaching.

These various results make several strong points. Teachers vary in the particular pattern of activities they use in their teaching, but there are some broad similarities across classrooms. Some of the main variation is concerned with the dimension of student choice and the clearest group differences are related to the particular subject being taught. In general, the influences which bear on teachers' choices of style are closely related to their own knowledge and skills, to gross frame factors such as class size, class time, and resources, and to those in the school setting with whom they have most contact. Professional development activities, if they are to be effective, must presumably help teachers cope better with the matrix of constraints and narrow the gap between ideal and actual use of particular teaching activities.

Supporting the teacher as developer and learner

It is not hard to find support for the efficacy of in-school participation as in-service education. Batten (1979), for example, quotes strong evidence in her review of evaluations of the Australian Schools Commission's Development Program. She writes:

> The Commission, development committees, teachers, administrators, parents, consultants, teachers centre personnel – all these people have expressed strong support for the idea and reality of school centred development work . . . The school centred element . . . favours active participant involvement and in-service continuity; it presents an opportunity to benefit from peer group interaction and influence; and it provides an answer to the perpetual cry from teachers that in-service work should be directly relevant to their work in the classroom. (pp. 287, 288)

The 1979–81 triennial report of the Schools Commission made a similar commitment to school-based development. Similarly, Logan and Dore (1976), after interviewing groups of teachers and administrators in order to establish hierarchies of in-service needs, concluded, first, that the school should be the focus and venue of in-service education and, secondly, that guided self-analysis and seeking of solutions to problems should be the basic mode.

There is also theoretical support for using school-based decision making as a form and focus of INSET. Concrete experience occasions reflection and generalization, which may be used to improve practice. Freire (1974) argues for the learning programme as a series of problems to be unveiled. From the problems dealt with, themes may be developed which help the learner both codify experiences and reflect critically on them. Such action changes the relationship between teacher and learner and role definitions blur.

Apparently the *de facto* role of *external* INSET provision is to provide teachers with a wider repertory of ideas and to broaden horizons. In fact, this is often seen as the main virtue. As Skilbeck et al. (1977) put it;

> A focus on school situations and tasks can be a means of bringing to bear upon concrete, practical problems a very wide range of understanding and skills. However, in a total INSET program, this focus should be complemented by the provision of learning situations for teachers which take them completely away from the school environment, to residential centres, schools other than their own, tertiary institutions, factories, offices, and so on. (p. 165)

The evidence points to school-based activities being most highly regarded as a means of carrying out INSET, but to external award and nonaward courses as contributing highly to professional development (Batten 1979, pp. 69, 95). When it comes to school decision making and action, it is the teacher's own knowledge and skill (Evans 1979), the teaching skill and knowledge of team members (1978), and 'self-motivation' (Batten 1979, p. 76) which are most important. It is, conversely, almost a truism that very frequently teachers are fired with enthusiasm at the end of an in-service activity but return to their schools to find they can do little by way of implementing the new ideas in the face of old constraints of time, school organization, and the like.

There are at least three possible approaches to in-service teacher education: (1) *external focus* which seeks to help teachers develop new orientations, knowledge, and skills without particular consideration of their own school setting; (2) *school-focused*, with an essentially transmission model involving the learning of externally developed skills in the school setting; and (3) *school origin*, with a basic problem-solving model, involving groups of teachers in the identification and resolution of school problems and calling on external expertise as needed. The 'external focus' approach is traditional, and includes formal award-bearing courses as well as shorter in-service courses. An interesting example of the second, school-focused, approach is reported by Smyth (1981), who uses clinical supervision as a means of helping teachers incorporate potentially useful findings from research on teaching into their own instructional repertoires. In the 'school origin' approach, by contrast, the problem and, in fact, the solution, originates in the school itself. There is still the need for much research to suggest what might be viable mixes of these three approaches, the resources and changes to school organization needed, and their relative effectiveness. Certainly, the first approach, taken alone, does not appear to be directly effective. Ingvarson (1982) asked teachers in Victoria about the sources of actual changes in their teaching. Of the 474 (out of 619) teachers who reported changes, many more mentioned self-motivation, experience, better understanding of children, dissatisfaction with existing methods, and the like, than in-service activities. Discussion with, and observation of, other teachers were also very frequently mentioned. Other research also emphasizes the teacher's own knowledge and skill and the teaching skill and knowledge of team members (Cohen and Harrison 1978). Ingvarson's data, however, also show that teachers readily attribute influence in their *professional development* not only to in-service education courses, but also to formal study, professional reading, original teacher training, and meetings in the school to discuss educational topics.

These results suggest possible mechanisms for both professional development and school improvement. It seems that teachers are often impressed with what they learn from formal coursework, publications and in-service offerings, but that they are also often unable to apply these learnings directly in their own school setting. On the other hand, problem situations are dealt with in school by individual teachers and groups of teachers. The question is to what extent a teacher's performance in these problem settings is enhanced by his or her general background knowledge. Can this approach of using indirect derived knowledge in specific situations be systematically improved? Is it better to focus in-service education much more closely on specific skills to be practised in the classroom under supervision? Or should in-service education be perceived as support for in-school problem solving?

Support within the school

There are some problems in the nature and organization of such support. For example, who is the leader of attempts at school improvement and teacher development? Perrott's (1979) study suggests that, in many primary schools, the principal's influence on how the curriculum is operationalized may be minimal. Even though their role is potentially very significant, principals may well be too engaged in system maintenance to be effective curriculum leaders and professional supports. The same situation applies to the secondary school where most real curriculum decisions seem to be taken within the subject departments. Studies by Evans (1979), Cohen and Harrison (1978), Evans and Cotterell (1976), and Bartlett and Ogilvie (1980) all report similarly on the prepotence of the subject department and subject master. It largely falls to the subject heads to introduce resource materials into the school and to develop a cooperative approach within their departments. The subject department thus provides an outstanding opportunity for group decision making and learning. But on the negative side, it may reduce the openness of the school to examining problems which cut across subject organization, for example meeting the needs of each student as a totality, cooperating with parents and community on a whole-school basis, obtaining curriculum balance, core curriculum, and pastoral care. At the same time, as Grassie argues from his findings (1978), principals run the risk of seeing their main task as running the school efficiently and of losing the role of educational leader.

Advisory personnel who visit schools are seen as having little effect on teachers' actions or decision making. One reason for this may be that the actual time contribution of such visitors to the work of the school is a very small component of school staffing – according to Evans' (1979) study, it is equivalent to about one-fifth of a full-time staff member in a school size of 56 teachers. Another reason may be, as Perrott (1979) shows, that visitors who are not sufficiently familiar with the particular context and conditions of a particular school are not much use in helping with the solution of particular problems. The role of the principal as consultant and teacher educator could thus be all the more significant.

From Evans' (1979) survey, some of the main sources of change in schools were innovative staff members, staff members working informally in groups, and appointed groups of staff. As promotional opportunities in school systems become more limited, it may well be that the expression of professional growth will be increasing participation of teachers in less formal staff groupings and as individuals. This raises the possibility of supporting teachers in school problem solving and professional development outside of strict hierarchical structures. One possibility is through the appointment of one or two staff members in schools to a position not concerned with official administration but with staff development. Such a person could, for example, be responsible for coordinating professional studies courses, ensure that all information on in-service education opportunities reaches the staff members involved, plan for accommodating staff absences from school for INSET purposes, help staff make contact with consultants and resource literature, coordinate the flow of information into the school, and help with the overall planning of curriculum or evaluation projects. Bolam (1980) gives a description of a role rather similar to this which has been tried in many UK local authorities under the name of a professional tutor, and Bolam, Baker and McMahon (1979) have also evaluated some aspects of this pilot scheme with positive results. The success of subject masters has no doubt been because they have combined many of their administrative functions with just these support services, and done so in a way which consolidates teaching specialties.

Award and nonaward in-service activities as out-of-school support

According to the National Inquiry into Teacher Education in Australia (1980), in 1977–78, about thirteen percent of teachers were enrolled in courses leading to a formal award, while a large majority of teachers attended some form of nonaward in-service activity. As has already been suggested, the most common effect of such activities on the work of the school might be indirect. Some of the courses have specific purposes to assist teachers to cope with a particular curriculum change, but generally they provide a backdrop of ideas and viewpoints which teachers must then utilize, if at all, in problem situations. The actual provisions of all of these programmes have been extensively reviewed (National Inquiry into Teacher Education 1980; Evans 1980; Schools Commission 1979) and evaluated (Batten 1979; Ingvarson 1982). The concern here is with how they might more successfully link with the processes of teacher deliberation, decision making, and action in school.

One important problem is the relationship between pre-service courses, induction programmes, and other in-service activities. If genuine understanding of curriculum planning and design, evaluation, action research, or group processes rests on reflection on practical experience, there may well be a point of diminishing returns in what is offered as educational studies in pre-service courses. There is a strong argument for increasing all pre-service courses for both primary and secondary teachers to a minimum of four years in order to allow the inclusion of a reasonable liberal studies component, as part of the teacher's general academic education, but not for increased professional studies. Campbell et al. (1979) offer some empirical evidence for this view, and the 1978 Review of Teacher Education in Queensland (Bassett 1978) suggested a mandatory one year (or equivalent) of formal course work to be taken in-service early in the teacher's career, the essential argument being that some formal study is both necessary and only able to be utilized by the teacher with some experience.

The main strategic problem concerns the linkages. Evans (1982) has suggested that links are likely to be strongest when teachers actively engaged in development within the school have interests and involvement in common with the providers of in-service education outside of the school. Subject associations, for example, have the ability to forge this kind of linkage since they involve teachers, tertiary staff members, and curriculum specialists in a number of joint enterprises, such as working on central syllabus committees. Some national and state-level projects also forge such links, for example The School and Community Project (1977–1980), which has linked schools with each other and with a national development team and also provided an important dissemination project.

Many *award*-bearing courses are concerned with practical procedures in curriculum, administration, counselling, special education, and the like. Others are concerned with principles, validated in a variety of ways and sometimes borrowed from feeder disciplines. One way of improving their links with school-based development is through helping the teacher-students to examine practices in their own setting through the filters provided by their formal studies. This can be done in a general fashion. It could also be undertaken in a very particular way through either individual projects undertaken in the school as part of course requirements or through school-based projects. There is an increasing number of examples of courses at bachelors, masters and graduate diploma levels which make this kind of reference. It would be useful now to undertake case-studies which describe the actual tasks and procedures and which attempt to trace the effect of linking award courses to school-based projects.

Nonaward activites and the use of resource and teacher centres should readily lend themselves to the kind of linkage envisaged, and, because of this, they deserve even closer scrutiny. A number of criteria might be suggested by which to judge their worth. For example, to what extent do in-service activities impel teachers to define and work on problems in their own teaching? Do they take into account the conditions in the particular school? To what extent are school administrators made familiar with the aims and procedures of the course? To what extent are the teachers involved in formulating the procedures and arrangements for the activity? What resources are made available for the activity? What support is there for follow up? What opportunities are there for continual evaluation and reappraisal? What arrangements are made for networks of teachers to be set up, possibly from several schools? Teachers' subject associations have been an example of groups which meet many of these criteria. They involve teachers at all levels, are supported and controlled by teachers, often attract strong allegiance and commitment from their members, foster exchange of ideas and offer continued support.

Any move to link in-service education more closely with school development has important consequences for the work roles of both teachers and in-service educators. First, it raises the important question of the extent that teachers can participate in school-based development, formative evaluation, and the like. What is suggested is to commit the teacher more fully to inquiry about teaching not as an extra but as an integral part of his or her planning. A second, more difficult question, perhaps, is the role of the in-service providers, many more of whom, under what is proposed here, would be working beside teachers as colleagues in the school. Apart from lessening the deep-rooted suspicion that teachers have of those who are not practitioners, such involvement would seem necessary to a proper analysis of problems and a proper grounding of theory. This kind of involvement would entail fairly major changes, in many cases, in the administrative arrangements and the perceptions of roles of tertiary personnel and the staff of educational authorities. (See ch. 10 above)

A third consequence is the need for materials which embody procedures that can assist teachers in the developmental task, which are easily assimilated, and which are sufficiently robust in application to be usable in a variety of settings. Fortunately, such materials are beginning to appear. One example is *The Action Research Planner* by Kemmis et al. (1981) who write: 'The Action Research Planner is a procedural guide for teachers and administrators interested in improvement and change in the school. It provides a way of thinking systematically about what happens in the school and the classroom, implementing action where improvements are thought to be possible, and monitoring and evaluating the effects of the action with a view to continuing the improvement.'

Action research is thus seen as a means of inproving practice, of liberating the participants through reflection, and evaluating both the steps in the process and the outcomes. In a profound way, the cyclical processes of data getting, reflection, design, implementation, and evaluation are the essence of research, but they are also, arguably, the essence of experience and professional development, particularly when combined with appropriate consultative support.

A second example of materials relates to the evaluation component of the developmental cycle. One systematic survey of school-level evaluations was that in the Teachers as Evaluators Project (Hughes et al. 1980), which is discussed more fully by Russell in this volume. The research component here was a detailed study of the school-level reports which resulted in published guidelines (Hughes et al. 1979), that have in turn contributed to teacher development by offering such down-to-earth advice as 'facilitate the problem identification so that the one chosen is of the greatest concern to the greatest number of participants'.

Conclusion

The thrust of the argument advanced in this paper is that active problem solving by teams of teachers, or even individual teachers, in the school is itself a form of in-service education, particularly for the development of professional knowledge and skills, and that it should be seen as the focus of in-service activities. In many cases, it is the schools that have necessarily led the way in important innovations, or at least in converting policy changes into day-to-day operations. One notable Australian example of this process arises from the replacement of external examinations and examination syllabuses in some systems by school-level assessment and school-level interpretations of broad syllabus guidelines. Another is the development of transition education programmes for students of 15+. It would be fair to say that, in these innovations, it has been left largely to the schools to solve the problems with the framing of aims and course objectives, the design of courses, and the assessment of students. Assessment by schools of their own programmes and consequent school-based programmes of curriculum and organizational improvement, a system sometimes known as 'cooperative school evaluation', has also depended on teachers' mastering many new skills. The most profound expertise in these innovatory areas now lies with teachers in schools that have weathered the initial problems involved in what were potentially drastic changes.

That in perhaps too many cases simply handing the problems to the schools to solve has not been effective indicates that, without adequate support from in-service providers, neither school-based curriculum development nor the by-product of teacher development may eventuate. Without support, the process may be too variable in its outcomes, with many failures as well as successes. On the other hand in-service education of teachers without authentic opportunities for them to change practice may be even more prone to failure.

Theory, experience, or procedures in curriculum evaluation and development, instructional design, group processes, community–school interaction, catering for individual differences, and other activities, have now developed to a useful level in many projects, but some of the best practices are not available for general use in schools and some have not been codified into course work. In many cases there are indications that, presented as courses, much of this information might not be readily assimilated. The most intensive motivation and learning arises from the solution of school-based problems. This again means that more effective means must be found to link school-based development and external INSET provisions. A number of such linkages have been suggested – including the use of professional tutors and a more comprehensive reliance on school-based problem solving as data for award and nonaward coursework. The deeper implication is a change in role for many teacher educators, involving much more direct work in schools. While there is now a trend towards such involvement, the administrative and promotional arrangements for universities, colleges, and in-service branches of education departments will need to be altered to allow for active school involvement and to encourage a more action-oriented approach to research.

Finally, at both the school level and among people involved in INSET outside of the school, any proposals of this kind are likely to entail an extra time commitment. At a time when resources are being withdrawn, it is too hopeful to wish for more funding, teacher release, and the like. The solution will have to be that two or more tasks are performed simultaneously.

Teachers frequently see school-based curriculum planning and development as involving a vast increase in time in an already burdensome programme. The extra burden can be absorbed in several ways. First, the tasks can be made to be seen to be worth while in that they provide materials and methods, as a result of team efforts and resource networks, which help solve teaching problems and improve job satisfaction. This needs to be the recognizable aim of a school's efforts in curriculum planning and development. Active participation in school-based development needs to be recognized in terms of career advancement and teachers need to achieve a sense of autonomy and competence in the process of school-based decision making.

Secondly, there can be a rationalization of some aspects of teachers' time. Tasks of programme planning, lesson preparation, in-service study, and, for some, student-teacher supervision, are related activities each of which can benefit from the other. Some promising approaches to school-based pre-service teacher education have the advantage that they combine and coordinate these tasks.

The involvement of tertiary staff may provide opportunities for similar rationalization of time demands, particularly where pre-service and in-service development can be promoted together in the same school. Another approach to combining two tasks in one job is to undertake research in conjunction with school-level problem solving, such as participation in action research. The school-based approach in general provides an excellent opportunity for tertiary staff to combine teaching, research and development. It also suggests a way out of the dilemma experienced by many teacher educators that they are engaged in teaching teachers without themselves having a continuing link with the practice of teaching in schools.

References

Bartlett, L. and Ogilvie, D. (1980) The subject coordinator: significance of the role, *Australian Journal of Education*, vol. 24, pp. 186–193.

Bassett, G.W. (1978) *1978 Review of Teacher Education in Queensland* (G.W. Bassett, Chairman), Brisbane: Board of Advanced Education and Board of Teacher Education.

Batten, Margaret (1979) *Report of a National Evaluation of the Development Programme*, Canberra: Schools Commission.

Bolam, R. (1980) In-service education and training, in Hoyle, E. and Meggary, J. (eds) *World Yearbook of Education 1980: Professional Development of Teachers*, London: Kogan Page.

Bolam, R., Baker, K. and McMahon, A. (1979) *Teacher Induction Pilot Schemes: Final National Evaluation Report*, Bristol: School of Education, University of Bristol.

Brady, P. and Pope, B. (eds) (1980) *School-Based Decision Making*, Report of the Second National Conference, Lorne, Victoria, 1979, Canberra: Canberra College of Advanced Education.

Campbell, W.J. and Robinson, N.M. (1979) *What Australian Society Expects of Its Schools, Teachers and Teaching*, Brisbane: University of Queensland, Department of Education.

Campbell, W.J., Evans, G.T., Philp, H.W.S. and Levis, D.S. (1979) A study of the pre-service and initial in-service development of primary school teachers, in Hewitson, M. (ed.) *Research into Teacher Education: The Practical Teaching Skills*, Canberra: Education Research and Development Committee.

Cohen, D. and Harrison, M. (1978) *Curriculum Decision Making in Australian Secondary Schools*, Paper presented at the Annual Conference of the Australian Association for Research in Education, Perth.

Cohen, D. and Harrison, M. (1982) *Curriculum Action Project*, Report to the Education Research and Development Committee, Macquarie University.

Collins, C.W. and Hughes, P.W. (1979) Expectations of secondary schools: a study of the views of teachers, *in* Williams, B.R. *Education, Training and Employment*, Report of the Committee of Enquiry into Education and Training, vol. 2, Canberra: Australian Government Publishing Service.

Evans, G.T. (1979) *The Main Classroom Activities of Junior Secondary Teachers: Ideal, Actual, and Influences*, Paper presented at the Conference of the Australian Association for Research in Education, Melbourne.

Evans, G.T. (1980) The role of Australian colleges and universities, *in* Hoyle, E. and Megarry, J. (eds) *World Yearbook of Education 1980: The Professional Development of Teachers*, London: Kogan Page.

Evans, G.T. (1981) *Classroom Activities of Teachers at Lower Secondary Level*, Report to the Education Research and Development Committee, Canberra.

Evans, G.T. (1982) Teacher participation: learning on the job, *in* Hewitson, M. (ed.) *Recurrent Education and the Teaching Role*, Canberra: Education Research and Development Committee.

Evans, G.T. and Cotterell, J.L. (1976) Curriculum development and curriculum practices, *in* Campbell, W.J. et al. *Some Consequences of the Radford Scheme for Schools, Teachers and Students in Queensland*. AACRDE Report No. 7, Canberra: Australian Government Publishing Service.

Fox, G.T. (1980) *In-Service Education and Training of Teachers: Towards New Policies. Reflecting Upon Evaluation*, Synthesis Report, CERI-OECD: Paris.

Freire, P. (1974) Education: domestication or liberation? *in* Lister, I. (ed.) *Deschooling*, Cambridge: Cambridge University Press.

Grassie, M. (1978) *Australian Government Schools 1972–1977*, Principals' Report on Change, Brisbane: University of Queensland, Faculty of Education.

Hughes, P.W., Russell, N.A. and McConachy, D., (1980) Discussion Paper No. 2. *Curriculum Evaluation in the 1980's: A Review of Current School Level Evaluation Initiatives*, Teachers as Evaluators Project, Canberra: Canberra CAE.

Hughes, P., Russell, N., McConachy, D. and Harlen, W. (1979) *A Guide to Evaluation* (Teachers as Evaluators Project Workshops), Canberra: Curriculum Development Centre.

Ingvarson, L. (1982) Some effects of the teacher development program in Victoria, *Australian Journal of Education*, vol. 26, pp. 86–98.

Kemmis, S., Fitzpatrick, M., Henry, C., Hook, C., McTaggart, R., Dawkins, S. and Kelly, M. (1981) *The Action Research Planner*, Geelong: Deakin University.

Logan, L.D. and Dore, C.K. (1976) *The Perceived and Real In-Service Needs of Primary School Teachers in Queensland – Some Findings and Programs*, Paper presented at the Conference of the South Pacific Association for Teacher Education, Brisbane.

Meade, P. (1981) *The Education Experiences of Sydney High School Students. Report No. 2*, Canberra: Australian Government Publishing Service.

National Inquiry into Teacher Education – J.J. Auchmuty, Chairman (1980) *Report*, Canberra: Australian Government Publishing Service.

Perrott, C. (1979) *The Context of the Operational Curriculum in the Primary School and Its Impingements*, Master of Education Thesis, Centre of Curriculum Studies in Education, University of New England.

School and Community Project (1977–1980) *School and Community News*, vols. 1–4, Canberra: Canberra College of Advanced Education, School of Education.

Schools Commission (1979) *Issues in Teacher Education: A Discussion Paper*, Canberra: Schools Commission.

Skilbeck, M., Evans, G. and Harvey, J. (1977) *In-Service Education and Training*, Canberra: Curriculum Development Centre.

Smyth, J. (1981) *Two for the price of one: Staff development through the utilization of findings from research on teaching*, Paper to the Annual Meeting of the American Educational Research Association.

SECTION 6

CURRICULUM FUTURES

INTRODUCTION
Malcolm Skilbeck

In this, the final section of the book, we consider what is at one and the same time the most basic and yet the most neglected curriculum question facing the school: what is to be the future shape, structure and content of the whole curriculum? A great deal of attention, in the school-based curriculum development movement, has been given to so-called 'process versus product' issues. That is to say, processes conceived as different types or ways of planning, designing, implementing and evaluating the curriculum have taken precedence over aims, values, objectives, outcomes and whole-curriculum designs. The inspiration for this process emphasis is understandable: resistance to early curriculum projects which, especially in the USA, were dominated by subject content concerns at the expense of practical problems of teaching and learning; and rejection of the rationalistic excesses of models of the curriculum dominated by behavioural objectives and prespecified learning outcomes. Progressive pedagogy seemed to demand a concentration on the realities of everyday classroom life, on relationships between teachers and taught, on the kaleidoscopic interests of students, on the value of communication and participation. Combined with sociological and political critiques of intellectual and cultural imperialism and affirmations of the relativity of all knowledge structures and of cultural modes and preexisting political, economic and social relations, these trends had mixed results. There has been a disinclination to view the whole curriculum as other than either an arbitrary (if inevitable) assemblage of distinct subject-cultures or the territory of distinct interest groups – for example subject departments or special interest groups within or outside the school. When, in Britain, the Department of Education and Science began to reaffirm an interest in the overall design and content of the curriculum, the initial reaction in the teaching profession was hostile. The curriculum, it was said, belonged to the teachers and, in any case, there were no adequate grounds for any national body to argue for a whole-curriculum philosophy from an affirmation of national needs. Meanwhile, within the education profession itself, a number of writers had been urging the need for schooling to give thought to new designs for whole, common or core curriculum but, at least until the late 1970s, these were isolated voices which seemed to be speaking against the tenor of the times.

The key curriculum problem schools face in curriculum development is this: how can we construct, justify and implement an overall programme of studies? Schools being established and functioning institutions, working in a concrete social world, the answer must lie in a complex of arguments to do with the needs of students, what has been customarily taught, the capabilities, skills and resources of the teachers, the expectations of the wider community, the various constraints and requirements through laws, funding and so on, and the educational philosophies which are current or can be invoked. Other factors operate but what is crucial is the complexity and variety of issues and the need for schools to make and implement choices about the totality of students' learning experiences.

It is in the context of the need for schools to take decisions about the composition of the whole curriculum and not only about how to teach or organize learning with respect to preestablished parts that this final section of readings has been assembled. Denis Lawton, one of the most prolific and persuasive advocates of a common curriculum, pin-points the inevitability of schools' confronting abstract and difficult concepts of culture. How can schools handle these abstractions and difficulties without merely adopting customary practices? Denis Lawton develops the idea of the 'cultural map', by showing how, in an anthropological approach, any society can be seen to operate through a number of distinct but interrelated socio-cultural systems. In essence, what Denis Lawton attempts is the critical application of those well-known systems to the curriculum content and organization of schools. He generates, thereby, a set of criteria for schools to use in their own activity of review, evaluation and development. Such criteria are needed and they need to be constructed with reference to a general view of the curriculum. By contrast, most of the guideline statements issued by public bodies focus on why and how to review, not on the substantive educational ideas against which the results of review must be assessed.

Typically, our assessments have been structured by assumptions and values that are familiar through past experience. Our curriculum orientation has been backward looking. Yet education constantly claims the right to have its procedures and results judged on a long time-scale, stretching years or even decades into the future. There are some paradoxes here, yet to be resolved but, as Richard Slaughter points out, unless we are prepared to find ways of relating curriculum review, evaluation and development to the future, our curriculum making will always be condemned to a fundamental irrelevance. This is not merely a matter of the well-known phenomenon of social lag: our social institutions and processes lagging behind our systematic knowledge, our present and emerging values and the driving force for change in our society. The real difficulty is attitudinal and intellectual: unwillingness or, perhaps in a quite profound sense, inability to project forward, developing curriculum on the uncertain platform of images of the future or alternative futures, instead of on the apparent (but perhaps illusory) certainties of the past.

However, for this 'obscured dimension' to claim attention in curriculum making, we need not only a generalized account of the field of futures studies and a disposing of some of the cruder criticisms of futurism – which Richard Slaughter gives. We also need some indication of what schools might actually do and, if possible, evidence of innovations and experiments. Although, in Britain and in most other countries as well, futurism in the curriculum is still unfamiliar, Richard Slaughter does take up the challenge, giving examples of recent curriculum experiments, providing practical advice on how to build the notion of alternative or possible futures into the curriculum, and suggesting needed developments in teacher education and educational policy.

As our final contribution, we return to where we started the volume: curriculum focused on the learner, the student in the school. School-based curriculum development is not, ultimately, a process wherein teachers and their actions are central but one in which student learning is ministered to in the school setting, with teachers among the primary agents but always in a supporting, guiding, structuring role. James Hemming, for many years one of Britain's most prominent and active proponents of child-centred education, picks up the central question in learning: why should a student become engaged with the curriculum at all? Putting this differently, if the curriculum does not succeed in engaging the student, and if the student does not learn through the curriculum, the energies of design, construction, implementation and evaluation are wasted. The main educative role of the curriculum, as James Hemming affirms, is to sustain cycles of learning in the service of personal growth. Children, he argues, have energy and disposition for self-improvement, and our task in the school is to provide curricula that tap these qualities. What we must avoid, however, is the temptation to reduce the curriculum – a phenomenon of the social and cultural worlds and a primary interest of the whole society – to episodes centring on transitory, expressed student interests. A general framework is needed to convey these wider concerns, and principles must be enunciated to express them, in addition to the psychological principles relating to personal growth and motivation. So far from finding an opposition between these two broad orientations, James Hemming draws them together. He then points up the role of school curriculum review, evaluation and development in bringing into a single arena the diverse but not irreconcilable interests of culture and personality.

CHAPTER 25

CURRICULUM AND CULTURE
Denis Lawton

Curriculum studies is often discussed in a way which makes it seem very remote from classroom practices. To some extent, this is difficult to avoid since curriculum involves difficult abstract concepts such as 'culture', and 'social change' which need careful explanation. This chapter does not wholly escape this tendency, but it may be worth while trying to point out, at the beginning, the practical implications of this view of curriculum. One of the problems every teacher has in the curriculum planning process is how to *select* 'high-priority' content and processes leaving less relevant material as a lower priority. By what criteria does a teacher do this? How can a teacher justify his selection to potential critics (including parents and pupils)? What follows is one way of looking at the problem of curriculum planning in a manner which may help to provide teachers with useful arguments, if not with complete answers.

It has been suggested (Williams 1976) that the word 'culture' is one of the most difficult in the English language; other writers have also pointed out the many ambiguities surrounding the word 'curriculum'. In this paper, I want to define culture not in terms of 'high culture', but to cover those aspects of our environment – social and physical – which are the product of human experience. Definitions at this stage sometimes cease to be helpful, but I have found the following quotation useful because it focuses attention upon ideas and thought processes rather than artefacts:

> believing that man is an animal suspended in webs of significance he himself has spun, I take culture to be those webs and the analysis of it to be, therefore, not an experimental science in search of law, but an interpretative one in search of meaning (Geertz 1975).

Curriculum may be thought of as a selection from the culture of a society. For each generation decisions have to be made about priorities in the cultural transmission process. Schools cannot be expected to be responsible for transmitting the whole of culture, so choices have to be made in terms of what is considered to be particularly valuable and of what the school is most appropriately equipped to transmit. All societies have the problem of passing on to the next generation certain kinds of knowledge, skills, beliefs and values: in some societies, school will be used as one of the agencies for transmission of culture, but societies will differ in what responsibilities will be given to schools as compared with the family, the church or other religious agencies, perhaps in modern societies, the mass media.

One of the dangers for a school system within a changing society is that the curriculum will nearly always tend to adjust very slowly to the process of change. Schools are, to some extent, inevitably traditional and conservative in their outlook, so that 'cultural lag' and 'curriculum inertia' are frequent complaints about them.

One response to such accusations or complaints is for the educational system to undertake a programme of curriculum development. But curriculum development may be patchy or even completely misguided, reacting to the 'wrong' kinds of change. Schools may then be open to another kind of charge – that of being too trendy or embracing change for its own sake.

Such was the general picture of curriculum development in England for the last twenty to twenty-five years. In 1960, the Conservative Minister of Education, Sir David Eccles, proposed a Curriculum Study Group (CSG); his motive was that schools were generally not succeeding in the task of regenerating the curriculum. The indirect result of the Minister's desire to improve curriculum planning was the creation, in 1964, of the Schools Council. Throughout its existence (1964–1983) the Schools Council was constantly criticized both for the kind of innovation it wished to initiate and, paradoxically, for failing to implement such changes at school level.

In order to avoid completely haphazard programmes of curriculum development, a more systematic approach has sometimes been advocated. The attempt to match curriculum with a changing society in a more systematic way is sometimes referred to as 'cultural analysis'. Essentially cultural analysis rests upon asking few fundamental but extremely difficult questions:

1. What kind of society already exists?
2. In what ways is the society developing?

3. How do the members of the society appear to want it to develop or change?
4. What kinds of values and principles will be involved in deciding on the kinds of change?
5. What kinds of change should schools (a) encourage, (b) resist, (c) ignore?

This view of cultural analysis and curriculum planning immediately launches us into the area of values because in order to make judgements about (4) and (5) above, we inevitably move out of 'neutral' description into prescription based on value preferences. Some would, of course, deny that descriptions as in (1) and (2) above would be possible in a value-free way. I would tend to agree that the distinction between description and prescription is, to some extent, artificial. But even so, the change from the relatively neutral description in (1) and (2) to the value-laden areas of (3), (4) and (5) does represent a clear involvement in decisions based on values. Perhaps the only way out of this difficulty is for any curriculum prescriber or planner, at any level, to make his or her own values as clear as possible.

Apart from the problems of values in a pluralistic society referred to above, there are other reasons why the process of matching curriculum to culture is very difficult in practice. A major problem is the gap between macro and micro planning. Some writers tend to move from the grand concept of cultural analysis to specific and detailed prescriptions in the curriculum without further justification. Where this is the case, the term cultural analysis is no more than a way of concealing the curriculum planner's own idiosyncratic preferences. Sometimes another 'justificatory concept' is introduced – cultural mapping or seeing the curriculum as a map of the culture. All metaphors in education are potentially dangerous, but the idea of a cultural map is a useful one if not pushed too far or 'overworked'. A map of a country is not, of course, the same as the country itself; it is a symbolic representation of certain features. The features chosen in a map of Europe, for example, might show the boundaries between countries (sometimes referred to as a political map), or physical features or the railways. A map can be used to emphasize any single feature from population density to the location of coal mines. To some extent, any juxtaposition of features is arbitrary, but it may also depend on certain concepts and ideas which have been accepted by the geographers involved.

If curriculum is to be regarded as an exercise in cultural mapping, then we must first agree on the categorizing concepts which are likely to be most useful. I would suggest the following lists of categories or cultural systems derived from anthropological studies:

1. socio-political system
2. economic system
3. communication system
4. rationality system
5. technology system
6. morality system
7. belief system
8. aesthetic system

I would suggest that these eight systems are not completely arbitrary, but include those features of any society without which it would be impossible to regard a group of people living together as having something worthy of the title 'society'. It might indeed be possible to find a group of people who lacked one or more of those eight features, but that would be the result of a society having broken down in some way. The definition of a society in terms of the eight cultural systems is, therefore, partly a circular definition and partly an empirical one. Anthropologists everywhere have found societies to resemble each other in this way. But the value judgement implicit in the circular definition is that human beings living without the benefit of certain universal human features would be living life which is not fully human.

It may be helpful at this stage to describe very briefly the eight systems, without making any attempt to apply them to any one society. It may also be useful to revive the idea of the cultural map at this stage. The eight cultural systems should be thought of as distinct but overlapping and interrelated categories – when applied to any particular country it would sometimes be useful to have eight separate maps, but sometimes even more useful to superimpose one map on top of another. Rather than a list of eight cultural systems it may be more useful to think of eight overlapping and interrelated circles. This may be one way of stressing that the whole process of cultural analysis is a dynamic rather than a static one.

1. The socio-political system

By definition any society will have some kind of social structure and social system. No society exists where there are no rules about human interaction, and where certain distinctions are not made between individuals on the basis of age, sex or possibly rank. The family is central to social structure although the range of relationships which constitute 'family' varies considerably from one society to another. As societies become larger and more complex they tend to develop political as well as social structures – some form of internal government which may be justified in terms of the common good. Much of the discussion of early political theorists, such as Rousseau's idea of the social contract, was centred on the question of the relation between the individual (and possibly the individual's rights) and the needs of the society as a whole. But this kind of speculation is usually a sign of an 'advanced' self-conscious society, whereas in simpler societies the socio-political structure will normally be taken for granted rather than examined in any analytic way. Within the socio-political system there are many classificatory distinctions useful for comparing one society with another, or for describing one society in cultural-mapping terms. For example, it may be useful to contrast feudal and capitalist societies; rural, urban, autocratic, democratic systems and so on; although each of those terms will need careful definition. One problem for modern industrial societies is that few individuals understand the whole of the socio-political structure. But all societies have the problem of passing on knowledge and skills of the socio-political system to the next generation, and whereas in simpler societies this is a relatively easy process, in a complex, urban, industrial society it is extremely difficult.

2. *The economic system*

Every society has some means of dealing with the problem of distribution of scarce resources. In very simple societies there may not even be a need for any kind of 'exchange' process, but with the development of specialization and the division of labour, some mechanism for exchange such as barter may be necessary, and sometimes the idea – and the actuality – of a 'market' eventually appears. One of the problems of modern capitalist societies is that the machinery of exchange involving banks, stock exchanges and multinational companies becomes so complex that few individuals really understand the system, either in principle or in practice. The contrast between simple societies where work is not only meaningful but often personally satisfying, and bureaucratic industrial societies where work is a burden rather than a fulfilment, is very clear.

3. *The communication system*

One of the major differences between human beings and other animals is the existence of language and the complexity of human communication systems. Animals such as bees do have communication systems, but they are instinctive rather than learned and they lack the flexibility and open-endedness of the human communication system which depends so largely on language. Part of the cultural mediation process for any human society is to pass on language and other aspects of the communication system to the young. One of the remarkable facts of human learning is that the young child can learn very complex patterns of linguistic structure without any or much teaching. So remarkable is this achievement that some linguistic theorists such as Noam Chomsky postulate the existence of genetic linguistic structures. Societies vary enormously in the complexity of their communication systems although socio-linguists frequently remind us that there is no such thing as a 'simple language'. The invention of writing, and later of print, make enormous differences to the communication system of a society and indirectly to the socio-political system. Writing has many advantages over the spoken word, especially its potential for keeping permanent records, but it has to be taught rather than acquired by simple imitation; similarly the development of printing can make knowledge widely available and open up the written word to a much wider range of readers. But the existence of writing as a skill and the existence of printed books as a learning resource are also potentially divisive in a society: in most societies when writing first develops it is an esoteric skill confined to an élite group; similarly, in any society where printed books are available the society begins to be divided into those who are highly skilled at 'reading' and those with more modest skills, or perhaps even completely lacking in 'literacy'. Access to knowledge thus becomes a social divider.

Human beings also have to master other forms of communication as well as language. For example, the American Indians use hand signs and smoke signals which have to be taught to the young; and in modern industrial societies, all sorts of signs have a great importance – for example, traffic signals which have to be learned in order to gain a driving licence.

The linguist, de Saussure, suggested that language should be thought of as only part of the science of 'signs'. The scientific study of sign systems known as semiology or semiotics has developed out of de Saussure's structuralist approach to language and communication systems. The communication system in any society is likely to be complex, but in modern industrial societies it is extremely difficult for the young to get to grips with all features of the communication system and it is clear that many of the necessary skills and understandings are neglected by most formal schooling systems.

4. The rationality system

All societies are rational in the sense of using language and thought to explain reality; cause and effect relationships are explored and patterns of consistency developed. What is accepted as a 'reasonable' explanation will, of course, differ from place to place and from time to time, but nowhere is there a 'rational vacuum'.

Some groups will explain disease, for example, in terms of 'humours', others will invoke Freudian theory, or talk of germs and bacteria, some may use belief in magic or witchcraft as explanations. Human groups will fall into traps of irrational behaviour from time to time, and superstition will be used where, to an outside observer, a more open attitude would be 'superior'. No society is completely rational or completely irrational. A rationality system is usually a complex mosaic of the rational and irrational, but human beings in all societies display the same pattern of development of the capacity for rational thinking, sufficient to convince Piaget and others that rationality has genetic roots, common to all normal human beings, and develops largely by maturational processes though dependent on suitable social environments.

Once again, however, there are important differences between societies. In Western European countries, for example, the dominant form of rationality is often said to be the scientific. This has some advantages, but philosophers such as Marcuse have pointed out the dangers of a society's thinking being dominated by an incomplete view of rationality. The danger of 'one dimensional man' is that the scientific way of thinking will obliterate other forms of thought and thus impoverish the individual's life; part of the cultural analysis process will therefore be to identify all forms of reasoning in any society rather than be satisfied with the concentration on the dominant form.

5. The technology system

Another common anthropological way of describing human beings which is used to distinguish them from other animals is to refer to the human race as tool-making and tool-using animals. Other animals, for example chimpanzees, have been observed to make occasional use of 'tools', but human beings in all societies have developed tools as a way of gaining extensive control over the environment. The history of technology may be traced from flint axes, weapons for hunting, early agricultural implements, to the microcomputer technology of the 1980s. In all cases, a society has the task of transmitting technological knowledge and skills to the next generation. In very simple societies, the task is not difficult because it will be possible for every adult to acquire mastery over most, if not the whole of, the available technology. In such societies, children acquire technological knowledge and skills by observing, imitating adults and practising the skills. As technology develops, however, some division of labour necessarily takes place and a few individuals will become semispecialists, but the whole of technology is nevertheless still accessible to all members. A major difference arises in a society where no one person could possibly master or even understand the whole of the technology system. Specialization is essential, but at what stage should it begin? A tension begins to exist between the need to give as many people as possible a general understanding of technology and the necessity for society to have specialists. Another kind of tension exists – namely, the relation between technological knowledge and the socio-political system. 'Knowledge is power' is too simple a formula, but it is not completely wrong. One of the problems for cultural analysis will be to identify the kind of technological knowledge and skills which all should possess, and those which can be left to specialists; another is how to allow specialists to be trained and educated without the rest of the population becoming deskilled and ignorant of the technological system.

6. *The morality system*

No society exists without a system of rules about right and wrong behaviour. The details of morality will, clearly, differ from one society to another but a deep-rooted concern for good and evil is always present. Just as Piaget has traced the development of 'rational' structures in the maturing child, so too has he traced the development of moral concepts; Laurence Kohlberg (1964) has made extensive cross-cultural studies to show that this kind of 'moral development' is more or less uniform in all cultures, despite important social differences.

It might be suggested that there are social groups such as the Ik (Turnbull 1973) who appear to lack anything which might be described as a moral code or a moral system. The existence of one or two groups such as the Ik does not, however, refute the hypothesis that all societies must have a morality system. The point about the Ik is precisely that due to the various kinds of social change, the tribal society was destroyed so that the remaining groups of Ik people have lost important aspects of their traditional culture, including their morality system. The anthropological explanation of this kind of loss of traditional culture will include the fact that the Ik are hunting people who had been forced out of their hunting grounds and encouraged to practise 'agriculture' without adequate equipment, land or training. The description of the Ik, therefore, is not an example of a society lacking one or more cultural systems, but of a group of people whose culture has been so inadequately transmitted or so badly damaged as to make their existence virtually subhuman.

Important distinctions exist between simple societies and the more complex. In some societies the moral code is unitary and taken for granted; in other more complex societies, value pluralism exists and the problem of educating the young by passing on values is much more difficult because total agreement is lacking. Yet some kind of morality system needs to be mapped out and transmitted to the next generation. In mapping out this system it may assist curriculum planners to think in terms of cultural variables such as religious or secular morality systems, and of identifying those values which are common to all groups and subgroups in a society.

7. The belief system

All societies have some kind of belief system or systems. Societies can be categorized in various ways according to the beliefs and structure of the belief system. In some societies, beliefs will be of a religious kind or associated with creation myths of various kinds. In such societies the basic belief system will permeate the other cultural systems so that, for example, a creation myth may also explain aspects of technology and the moral code; similarly a religious belief may justify the socio-political system ('the rich man in his castle . . . ') and explain rationality as a gift of the God.

A major change occurs in any society when one belief system ceases to be accepted as an all-embracing explanation for the whole culture. For example, within medieval Christendom there was no rival or alternative belief system. Alternative views were classified either as heretical or infidel. A major change came about with the Renaissance and Reformation, coinciding with the transition from the feudal to the capitalist socio-political system: one church split into countless denominations and sects; one unified belief system gave way to a plural system. Not only did the Reformation pluralize religious beliefs, it also stimulated rival explanations such as science and eventually rival philosophies to the theology-dominated world view of the Church.

It might be argued that some modern industrial societies such as Soviet Russia still possess a unified belief and value system in the form of Marxist-Leninist political philosophy which dominates all other cultural systems, but what is more characteristic of highly industrialized societies is the existence of plural belief systems. Such belief systems are plural in two senses: first, there is no one set of beliefs most of which all members of a society hold; second, any beliefs which might be regarded as 'common' are derived from a variety of sources rather than a single (religious) source. Thus, in the UK and in many other Western 'democracies' the common belief system is a complex mixture of religious vestiges (including a belief in God or at least some superhuman 'Providence'), some scientific dogma (rather than scientific understanding), and some ideals from political philosophy such as freedom, social justice and a need for law and order, all of which are probably held as a haphazard collection rather than a coordinated set of beliefs. It has been suggested that a society without a genuine concept of 'the sacred' will create its own spurious sacred symbols such as pop stars, sporting heroes or the Royal Family.

8. *The aesthetic system*

Nowhere is there a society, however near to subsistence level, where pots are made without decoration or where there is no attempt made to decorate the person or the environment. No society exists without some kind of art and music. The idea of beauty is always present, as is the urge to 'create'. This aesthetic aspect of human nature is just as important as 'human beings as rational animals', or 'human beings as language users'; in any society, the aesthetic system – the rules and criteria concerning art and craft, music and drama, oratory and story-telling – is always very important although it may be more difficult to analyse than other systems. In simple societies the arts and crafts and other aspects of the aesthetic system tend to be easily transmitted to the next generation; in modern complex society not only are the rules and criteria increasingly obscure to practitioners as well as the general public, but also many members of a society have become 'spectators' rather than participants in the aesthetic field. This is in itself a danger, and perhaps one of the tasks for cultural analysis is not simply to describe the current state of society, but to look back to see what traditional arts and crafts have been lost.

The cultural network as a whole

Two points about the eight cultural systems should be made at this point in order to avoid misunderstanding. The first is that although the cultural systems have been listed separately as eight systems, beyond a certain stage in the analysis this may be misleading, and it will be necessary to look at overlaps and interrelations: ultimately it is necessary to think of culture as a complex network (reference has already been made to Geertz) rather than to eight watertight categories. The second point is that a list of eight is potentially misleading in another way: any order given may, mistakenly, be seen as an implication either of a ranking priority or a determining order – that is, that if socio-political, for example, is placed first this might be taken to imply that the socio-political system is logically prior to the others and determines, or influences, the economic system which in turn determines the mode of communication and so on. Neither kind of ranking is intended. I would not accept the vulgar Marxist notion of economic base determining cultural superstructure, but would be more in sympathy with the revisionists such as Althusser, Habermas, Raymond Williams and others, who postulate a much more complex pattern of interaction. My proposed set of eight cultural systems is similar in as much as I would regard all the systems as quasiautonomous: I would suspect that some would have less determining power than others, but that the pattern is certainly not reducible to base and superstructure.

Another cautionary note may also be helpful at this point. Attempting to analyse culture in this way might be misinterpreted as a static view both of culture and of curriculum planning. Such is not the intention. In fact, by postulating eight interacting cultural systems it is easier to describe, if not to explain, social and cultural change.

Cultural analysis applied: the cultural map of one society

Turning now to the task of analysing the culture of a specific society – England – I will make use of the same eight categories. Given more space it would have been preferable first to analyse society, and then to prescribe an appropriate curriculum. As a short cut to this end, however, it will be necessary to attempt both tasks – however incompletely – at the same time. A full cultural analysis will not, therefore, be attempted but only a few examples given to illustrate the inadequacies of the typical curriculum in an English school by use of the terms 'gaps', 'mismatches' and 'contradictions'.

System 1 – socio-political

Any exercise in the cultural mapping of the socio-political system in England would have to focus on the fact that England is a highly industrialized society, urbanized, with a high population and a high density of population. These social categories are important for the education system, but perhaps even more important is the political claim that England is a democratic society. This brings us to the first of our cultural contradictions. Many educationists and writers have pointed out that the ideal of democracy and equality of opportunity in England is belied by the actual practices of schools. Leaving aside the tremendous problem of the independent sector of schooling which exerts an influence far above the numbers of pupils it caters for, even within the state system the dominant ethos is one of competition which generates failure. In a society which is attempting to be democratic it would be more appropriate for schools to concentrate on common culture, a common curriculum rather than a divisive one, and an organization which would respect all children and accord them some degree of success.

England is also a society with a highly complex political and social structure; but most young people leave school very ignorant of that structure. This is an example of a gap in the curriculum, related to the basic contradiction referred to above.

Finally, to give an example of a 'mismatch' between society and curriculum, many schools would claim to provide young people with 'political education', but in practice this would be found to be what the Americans refer to as 'Mickey Mouse politics': more attention being paid to 'the duties of Black Rod' and 'how a Bill becomes an Act' than to 'real' politics such as pressure groups, trade unions, the differences between political ideologies and so on.

System 2 – economic

A cultural map of England would include the development of an industrial society, its decline and the present problem of a country failing to earn its living in economic terms.

Once again, the curriculum of most schools is curiously deficient in meeting the needs of a modern industrial society – and that does not mean simply providing the labour market with the kind of trained workers it needs. The basic problem is that most young people leave school with very little understanding of the economic system. Economics may be taught in schools, but it tends to be an option for the 14–16 age group rather than part of the common curriculum. The majority of young people leave school with almost no attempt having been made to provide them with economic understanding of their own society. Another important example of a serious gap in the curriculum provision.

System 3 – communication

English is the common language for the UK, but the fact that there are linguistic minorities is often ignored. Cultural mapping in the form of linguistic mapping has, in fact, been carried out by the Linguistic Minorities Project at the University of London Institute of Education, but this only shows the deficiencies of the schooling provision rather than being used as a means of remedying the problem.

Even for native speakers of English the curriculum is inadequate. Oral language still tends to be neglected, according to HMI primary and secondary surveys, and most schools have yet to develop a policy for language across the curriculum.

System 4 – rationality

The kind of rationality which would usually be claimed to dominate English culture is that of science. But the typical science curriculum fails to 'match' the needs of the majority of pupils: most young people 'learn' science without acquiring real scientific understanding or being able to apply scientific methodology. Perhaps even more important is the fact that schools fail to distinguish between this kind of scientific rationality, and other kinds of rationality which would enable young people to gain deeper insights into the nature of their society and their own existence in it – aesthetic and spiritual values, for example.

System 5 – technology

This is another serious gap. England is a highly industrialized society with complex technology, yet the typical school curriculum does not enable young people to acquire a basic understanding of twentieth-century technology. For example, the history of technology tends to stop somewhere in the eighteenth century; the curriculum tends to stress pure science rather than an understanding of applied science and technology. Very few schools attempt to incorporate technological understanding as part of the common curriculum, rather than an option for a few.

System 6 – morality

Here is another kind of mismatch: England is no longer a Christian society, its values are increasingly secular, but schools are required to persist with compulsory religious instruction and a compulsory daily act of worship.

The corresponding gap in the curriculum is the fact that most schools have not even attempted to teach elementary ethics which would enable young people to work out a moral code in a secular society. Another problem in England is that it is now a multicultural, multiethnic society which makes reliance on Christian doctrine as a basis for ethical understanding even more untenable.

System 7 – belief

It is sometimes asserted that a characteristic of modern England is that there is no belief system. But various attempts at cultural mapping have been made and it is quite clear that there are a number of beliefs which are shared by the vast majority of the population. What is lacking is not so much a belief system as a coherent pattern of beliefs. One of the dangers of schools in a modern technicist society is that this very important aspect of growing up is very badly neglected by the school system. Schools have a responsibility for mapping out the conceptual territory and related experiences and then working out how they could be covered within the existing subject areas; gaps will be identified in the course of this process, and someone should be given responsibility in every school for planning the development of the belief system within the curriculum. It is not, of course, suggested that 'belief system' or any such title should appear on the timetable; merely that in this case, as in many of the other systems described, greater attention needs to be paid to the overall planning of the whole curriculum.

System 8 – aesthetic

At a time of rapid social change, the standards, forms and media in the arts tend to outpace the school curriculum. The existence of cultural confusion is not surprising since critics and practitioners of the arts are themselves unsure of what criteria and standards they are working to. Although this is an extremely difficult area, it must be the responsibility of some teachers within the school to pass on criteria and standards; schools should also offer a much wider range of aesthetic experiences. These two aspects of aesthetic education should go hand in hand and produce children who are more able to spend their time enjoyably and, at the same time, have a greater awareness of their own aesthetic environment.

Summary

I have attempted to identify in this chapter a number of deficiencies within the existing school curriculum as well as a means of planning a better one. A major message which emerges from any kind of cultural mapping exercise is that in modern Western society any tendency to revert to a basics or 'three Rs' curriculum would be a cultural disaster. Cultural analysis shows quite clearly that all societies have the task of mediating a whole range of knowledge, skills and values to the next generation, and that it is not simply the function of schools to service the labour market. Another important result is that in any democratic society, one of the major functions of the school is to provide some kind of social cohesion. One of the strange inconsistencies or contradictions of modern English society is that lip-service is paid to democracy and equality, whereas the reality is gross inequality and cultural divisiveness. A third conclusion would be that Western society generally, and England in particular, is in danger of being dominated by a technicist, bureaucratic kind of rationality which, although it brings many material benefits, is also an incomplete way of looking at the world or belief system. Part of the function of schools must be to balance this tendency in society by reaffirming the part that schools must play in aesthetic, political and moral education.

Exactly how schools might set about planning a curriculum along these lines would take more space than I have available here. For a number of practical suggestions see Lawton (1983).

References

Geertz, C. (1975) *The Interpretation of Culture*, London: Hutchinson.
Kohlberg, L. (1964) Development of moral character and moral ideology, *in* Hoffman, M.L. and L.W. (eds)*Review of Child Development Research*, Sage.
Lawton, D. (1975) *Class, Culture and the Curriculum*, London: Routledge and Kegan Paul.
Lawton, D. (1983) *Curriculum Studies and Educational Planning*, London: Hodder and Stoughton.
Turnbull, C. (1973) *The Mountain People*, London: Picador.
Williams, R. (1976) *Keywords*, London: Fontana.

CHAPTER 26

FUTURES STUDY IN THE CURRICULUM
Richard A. Slaughter

Introduction

Most people involved in education would probably admit to a generalized concern about 'the future'. Yet, curiously, the past retains much greater weight and reality in the profession. In spite of a series of social, technical, economic and cultural transformations which have entirely altered our individual and collective prospects, futures study has remained an empty category, a missing dimension, in British education. While curriculum initiatives in futures-related areas can be identified, the centrality of futures research, futures thinking, to educational tasks has yet to be explored in depth. The reasons for this omission are complex but may include factors such as the relative youth of the futures field, the existence of misconceptions about futures, the continuing dominance of conservative, subject-oriented, academic traditions and the practical difficulties of innovation within an embattled education system.

In the following pages we touch on such issues and attempt to show why future-focused developments are practicable and necessary. We first consider an outline rationale, examine several conceptual building blocks and advance a number of propositions which may serve to focus further debate. The latter part of the chapter discusses aspects of an innovation strategy and refers to four different initiatives which have already taken place in Britain. The chapter concludes with a view of curriculum which has wide applicability in the context of present debates about educational change. Above all, the view taken here is that futures study and research are not merely new areas or categories of curriculum activity, though they may be treated as such. Rather, they are aspects of the forward-looking counterpart to history and, as such, represent a fundamental dimension of education at all levels.

Why futures perspectives are essential

It has become a truism that 'change' in the wider world has become rapid and pervasive: new technologies seem to demand new skills, far-reaching social and economic shifts occur, new conflicts arise, the world moves on to an era of fragile interdependence and uncertainty. Schools are seldom exposed directly to these forces. But they do experience a range of conflicting pressures to compensate for social problems, make room for new subjects, accommodate political demands and so on. Furthermore, while the rhetoric of schooling may suggest a concern to prepare pupils for future living, schools are, in fact, heavily constrained by the instrumental requirements of an obsolescent examination system. The conflicts created by these cross-cutting pressures within a context of pluralism, lack of consensus and economic decline help to explain why the system has become so resistant to change and why teachers' energies are commonly taken up in 'system maintenance', rather than innovation and adaptation. Yet this is symptomatic of a more profound difficulty. Curriculum innovation appears to be a slow, uncertain, and difficult process. No truly systematic method of inducing educational change has yet been found, nor, perhaps, could it be. Yet life outside the schools is not subject to these constraints. It moves ahead much more rapidly. Hence, one may detect growing discontinuities between school curricula which hark back to the past for the greater part of their content and inspiration, and the wider, dynamically evolving environment in which teachers and pupils actually live. In such conditions curricula rapidly become dated, their rigid constellation of subjects and 'basic skills' reflecting a safer, simpler and more complacent world.

In this view, schools become involved in preserving a form of society which has passed, or is passing, away rather than contributing actively to building the future. They appear to be caught in a web of meanings and purposes which, in some respects, no longer ring true. As Taylor has noted, 'the structures of this civilisation, interdependent work, bargaining, mutual adjustment of individual ends, are beginning to change their meaning for many, and are beginning to be felt . . . as hateful and empty'.[1] These and many other aspects of industrial era culture – values, ideologies, symbols, belief systems – are also under stress. Thus teachers find themselves in the unenviable position of mediating or sponsoring cultural forms and meanings which may have lost many of their former structural supports. In relation to 'work', Woods suggests that teachers 'are in the curious position of sponsoring an ideology they neither follow themselves nor is any longer appropriate for the structural situation of their charges'. He adds, 'it persists because it is associated with the self perpetuating practices and beliefs that have been mastered by the teacher in his defence against the exigencies of the job . . .'[2]

With this in mind, we can suggest that many of the underlying difficulties now being experienced by teachers and others stem not merely from fairly obvious causes such as falling rolls, material constraints and political interventions but, more fundamentally, from the tensions and strains attending the decline of an industrialized society and the transition from one cultural era to another. The resulting dilemma for teachers was described more than a decade ago by Donald Schon. He wrote:

> a social system does not move smoothly from one state of its culture to another . . . Something old must come apart in order for something new to come together. But for individuals within the system, there is no clear grasp of the next stable state – only a clear picture of the one to be lost. Hence, the coming apart carries uncertainty and anguish for the members of the system since it puts at risk the basis for self-identity that the system had provided.[3]

Schon discusses two types of strategies that can be adopted to manage the contradictions and pressures arising from the conflict between strongly felt imperatives arising from the past and the demands of uncertain and dimly perceived futures. One is that of *dynamic conservatism* in which perceived threats are defused by selective inattention, containment, isolation, least-change responses and the like. Perhaps the 'back to basics' movement may be partly explained in these terms. In any event, strategies of this type are extremely common but they exert a heavy toll upon individuals and organizations who may become dissociated, inward looking and set against adaptive change. Of far greater value are strategies that are *projective or anticipatory* in nature. Broadly speaking, these recognize that individual well-being, organizational development and cultural continuity are best achieved not by a damaging withdrawal to the here and now, or to obsolescent routines which served in the past, but through a *broadening* of horizons, conscious adaptation and continuous renewal. In the present context this involves developing long-term, global perspectives from which a future-focused pedagogy may be derived, identifying a range of forward-looking images and tasks, exploring with pupils the significance of the futures dimension. The relevance of these issues to educational policies and practices at all levels should not be underestimated. The word pedagogy itself, with part of its root in the Greek 'to lead', implies that teaching has an inherent concern for the future. Yet forward-looking work which exhibits both depth and coherence is notably absent from the theory and practice of curriculum. In order to redress this overemphasis on the past we need to look more closely at the meaning and significance of the future.

The idea of studying the future may, at first sight, appear paradoxical. How, one may ask, can one study that which has no material existence? Similarly, futures study is falsely equated with a crude notion of prediction. In fact, neither of these stereotypes bears close examination. Those who are engaged in prospective study are generally much more interested in trends, choices and the implications of forecasts than in prediction *per se*. The former are ubiquitously involved in our perceptions of the present while the latter strictly apply only to closed systems or to the use of extra-rational powers. Again, to view the future merely as an abstraction is to adopt a most unsatisfactory caricature. It can be viewed much more productively as *a dynamic field of choice, opportunity and action* which impinges upon our lives on many levels and in countless ways. Limitations of space preclude a full discussion so we restrict ourselves here to a few brief observations.

First we may note that the term 'future' is somewhat misleading since there is no singular condition or state that we are constrained to accept. The existence of choices, alternatives, indeterminate and unpredictable outcomes underlines the value of referring where possible to futures in the plural. Second, it is worth recognizing that we are already involved in futures and they in us. That is to say, aspects of futures exist within and around us in both material and nonmaterial forms. They are inherent in *structures* of various kinds which exhibit continuity and thereby provide frameworks upon which many of our understandings, expectations and purposes rest. Some are physical (landforms, buildings, cities) while others are not (languages, values, laws). However, all are affected by *processes of change*. Consequently we all accept, and act upon, the principles embodied in such traditional maxims as 'a stitch in time saves nine', 'look before you leap' and 'forewarned' is forearmed'. In other words, we routinely observe the interaction of structures and processes in the course of everyday life and *necessarily* construct forecasts, projections and scenarios in order to guide our behaviour in the present.[4]

It follows from the above that our future scanning capacities in no way depend upon special training or expertise (though, like any innate ability, they may be enhanced and developed by training). Rather, they appear to be *constitutive of consciousness*. Were this otherwise, it is doubtful if we could perform simple tasks, much less plan a trip or a curriculum, for we would be locked into an attenuated and unchangeable present which would deprive us of the ability to choose or act. Clearly we cannot exist without drawing upon frames of reference, maps of culture and the wider world, practical understandings which embody aspects of past, present and future. If this is true for individuals, then the futures dimension takes on major significance for school curricula through which meanings and traditions are mediated to future generations. Hence futures study is not merely relevant to curriculum planning, but to the whole educational enterprise.

Several brief propositions may now be drawn from the foregoing:

1. Past, present and future are deeply interrelated. The latter is not simply an empty space but a dynamic field of potentials which is accessible to exploration even by the very young, and perhaps especially by them.[5]
2. The scope, pace and weight of change processes now at work in the world make linear views of futures untenable. Thus past experience becomes a decreasingly reliable guide to action and foresight becomes more important.
3. In an unstable, fast-changing environment individuals and organizations require strategies of adaptation drawing on global, long-term perspectives and conveying a sense of stability in change.
4. By thinking ahead more systematically students can develop a rich network of linkages between their own life structures and the wider dimensions of continuity and change which underly, or threaten, them.
5. If teachers and curricula occupy a pivotal position in the culture, a crucial point of interchange between past and future, the former need to come to grips with the futures dimension, interpret what they find and integrate this into every aspect of their work.

With these propositions in mind we may now turn to some of the conceptual building blocks of future-focused curricula.

Conceptual building blocks

Curriculum proposals should be as concrete as possible and provide foci for developments in theory and practice. Here we draw on four concepts or themes from the field of futures study. By commenting briefly on their relevance to the thesis set out above we may seek to open out an area of discourse which may inform curriculum making generally and contribute to school-based innovation. The four are as follows: the concept of alternative futures; images of futures; commonalities between the study of past and future; and, finally, notions of the present. These by no means exhaust the list, but they are central to what follows.

Alternative futures

This is widely regarded as the master concept of the futures field. It can be applied holistically in developing broad views of complex phenomena (e.g. scenarios of world futures), or in more specific, concrete situations (e.g. marketing strategies, organizational development, career options etc.). In a classroom context the distinctions between possible, probable and preferable futures can form the basis of an entire curriculum offering. That is to say, a sense of possible futures in any context grows out of assessments of existing trends. This involves a search for relevant data and the use of elementary techniques of extrapolation and forecasting. Once trends have been identified and projected into the future, probabilities can be assigned. There are many ways this can be achieved, but, in general, intuitive assessments have proved successful with younger pupils. With increasing age, intuition can be supplemented by hard data and more sophisticated reasoning. The final stage involves deciding what is preferable. Clearly it raises questions of values, priorities, purposes and focuses attention on social decision-making procedures. This progressive narrowing down of options represents one way that individuals can begin to come to grips with their own immersion in social processes. Furthermore, a strategy of this kind can reveal many interesting discrepancies between dominant trends and individual views of preferable futures. Such insights appear likely to encourage active involvement in community, and national, affairs.

Images of futures

Images of futures are much more important than is commonly realized. They powerfully affect what people believe, and do, in the present, and are continuously being negotiated at all levels of society.[6] Large and powerful organizations have long realized this and have assimilated aspects of planning and forecasting into their public relations activities. Thus some forms of futures research have become associated with the interests of such groups with the result that partial, or biased, views of futures are sometimes presented as if they were natural or inevitable extensions of the present. Teachers and others will find it useful to bear in mind that whenever this occurs, whenever images of futures are presented as nonnegotiable or finished, they are likely to conceal an attempt to persuade by stealth and to secure one set of interests at the expense of others. This process of mystification becomes visible in some educational debates when a preferred form of society is accorded uncritical prominence. Such strategies implicitly cast individuals in the role of helpless bystanders: observers of, rather than participants in, the historical process. But teachers do not need to accept a passive role for themselves or their pupils. They can begin to explore and analyse images of futures, identify the interests they represent, develop their own vision and explore commonalities with others. In these and other ways they may promote active, responsible notions of citizenship which encourage people to participate in creating the future they want rather than the ones which flow from remote and impersonal forces.

Commonalities in the study of past and future

The retrospective bias of school curricula seems increasingly anomalous when we consider that historians and futurists have much in common.[7] Both require comparable frameworks of theory and interpretation and must regard their work as open to revision by succeeding observers and generations. In both fields certainty and objectivity are elusive, and information quality deteriorates the further one moves away from the present. There are, of course, important differences: the past cannot be altered (though our understanding of it changes continuously) and, strictly speaking, there are no future facts. But there is enormous value in regarding history and futures as *complementary partners in the constitution of the present*. Without a sense of history we would have no basis for considering futures; without the goals, opportunities and dangers embodied in the latter our past experience would be of little value. Both are vital to our well-being. They draw on similar human needs and permit us to live fully within the richness of the present.

Notions of the present

To a physicist the present may appear so short as to defy human perception. To an impatient driver it may seem interminable. There is clearly a world of difference between attempting to measure time objectively and experiencing it in the course of living. But where do schools stand in the broad stream of history and to what time frame should curricula refer? We recall that the present necessarily embraces aspects of past and future. It is a distinct period of time, that part of an endless continuum to which we refer in order to make meaning. We therefore have the freedom to *choose* where, when or even whether to draw boundaries. Thus, in functional terms, the present can begin with the fleeting moment of immediate experience, but we may choose to extend it at will. The historical present may span many years. From a broad cultural viewpoint our roots are very ancient and the consequences of our actions undoubtedly stretch far into the future. It follows that the cultural field within which we exist embraces a very broad span of space/time. But from a curriculum viewpoint such a notion may be overpowering. We require something which is more manageable, falling between these extremes.

Elise Boulding's concept of a 200-year present is about right.

> It is our space, one that we can move around in directly in our lives, and indirectly by touching the lives of the linkage people, young and old, around us. . . . Familiarity with the events over this span will give us a sense of social process . . . and enable us to identify possible contours of the social landscape of the next hundred year half of our present with more equanimity.[8]

This concept is extremely valuable in the context of school-based curriculum innovation. It is neither too long nor too short. It emphasizes the way that our reality grows out of past history and, in turn, helps to shape the reality of others. In this view, the present does not vanish into the alienating moment which cuts us off from past and future. Instead it becomes part of the wider scene, a moving fulcrum upon which both past and future depend. It links us explicitly with the wider, common, world which we share with the living, with past generations and with those yet to come. This sense of being related through a shared culture in time is analogous to, and complementary with, the notion of a global sensibility. Together, these provide a frame of reference in space and time which is entirely appropriate for education in a changing, interdependent world. (See Ch. 7 above)

Aspects of an innovation strategy

We have suggested above that curricula which focus primarily upon the past cannot, in principle, provide an adequate basis for future living. Of greater value is a notion of curriculum which *balances* past, present and future, and represents these to pupils in meaningful and accessible ways. Elements of such an approach already exist in proposals for core curricula which utilize maps of contemporary culture, in projects which focus on aspects of cultural change and in the form of small-scale innovations such as those discussed below. To draw work of this kind together in a sustained and coordinated manner will require developments at a number of levels. Here we confine ourselves to a brief discussion of three: policy and planning, teacher training and support, and school-based innovation.

Some major developments can be envisaged at the level of policy and planning as the need for forward-looking approaches becomes more widely appreciated. Even at the level of planning for changes in employment patterns it is obvious that assumptions about future conditions are highly relevant to policy decisions in the present. To take a further step and regard the young not merely as passive inheritors of culture but as interpreters and creators of it is to go a long way towards accepting that the futures dimension is a primary focus of attention. It, not the past, is the repository of all our hopes, purposes, plans, goals and intentions. Many consequences flow from this insight. If schools are to adapt to changing conditions, futures issues, concepts and techniques must be brought to bear on the theory and practice of curriculum at the highest levels. For example, the world futures debate can be regarded as an appropriate backdrop or context for educational theorizing, teacher training, research and practice. To systematically locate educational concerns in this wider framework of global and long-term issues is to help teaching to avoid the intellectual and cultural insularity into which it so readily descends. It also serves to focus attention upon the needs, life chances and prospects of pupils, and raises the possibility of bridging the gulf between the inward-looking culture of schools and the wider world.

Expressed in such general terms, these ideas remain problematic. It is a task for research to explore their implications, concretize them and assist in the innovation process. To these ends, institutions of higher education, teacher organizations, LEAs, and so on, can initiate basic research, carry out surveys of relevant work and participate in the production of suitable materials. These need not rely solely on print technologies but may also exploit the potential of computers and video, thus encouraging new interactive forms of learning. Equipped with these tools pupils can learn to model the future as readily as the past, to study and monitor processes of continuity and change and, in so doing, to 'take the pulse of the planet'.[9]

Other tasks at the policy and planning level include the evolution of specific programmes and proposals, the coordination of support for innovators and the organization of symposia, conferences and meetings. Above all there is a need to establish a firm and defensible foundation in theory for teaching futures.[10] As this process proceeds, so forward-looking conceptions of curriculum will acquire greater credibility and meaning.

Work at the foregoing level merges into teacher training and support where, at present, some of the contradictions of educating for uncertain futures out of past-oriented academic traditions are most clearly revealed. Teachers face an uphill struggle when their initial training lacks many of the concepts and understandings which would permit a more creative cultural role. It is also extremely difficult to keep abreast of wider changes when in-service training remains available to the select few, and even then only on an irregular basis. However, as forward-looking conceptions of teaching and learning become more common the nature of the whole enterprise may change: it can become *future responsive*, drawing fully on the symbolic, intellectual and methodological resources of the futures field to equip teachers and pupils alike to participate in defining and creating convivial and sustainable futures.[11] Foundation courses in education now draw heavily on historical and comparative sources, but there is no reason why they cannot also include prospective elements. The decline of work, the nature of postindustrial society, the communications revolution, global trends are surely at least as important to the theory and practice of education as the potted histories of how our schools came to be as they are! In time, more specialized options can be developed which bring educational concerns together with a wide range of future issues and methodologies. Eventually it is likely that futures study will come to be seen as indispensable in many existing curriculum areas and a core component of education itself.

School-based innovations will be assisted by such developments but, in the present context, it is important to note that they are by no means dependent upon them. A great deal of innovative work has already been carried out, and this provides some useful insights. First, the growth of futures education in numerous Western countries (and some non-Western ones) suggests that such initiatives meet widely felt needs. While such work requires evaluation and testing (a major research task in its own right), there is no need to 'reinvent the wheel' as it were. Second, close study reveals that many teachers and schools in the UK are already engaged in developing one or more of a growing 'family' of futures-related activities, and, further, these draw on concerns which are neither faddish nor transient.[12] Finally, it is evident that most innovations in this area are primarily the work of highly motivated individuals. Hence, for those already at work in the system, questions of vision, attitude and purpose may be more central than those relating to formal training and the provision of resources.

Four examples of British innovations in futures

Perhaps the earliest taught course in Britain was entitled 'Possible Futures'. It was designed as a term course within the framework of sixth-form general studies at Pocklington School in Yorkshire and begun in 1976. The principal purpose behind the course was 'to encourage our sixth formers to think constructively about the future of our society and to see how they might be able to influence it when . . . they will be in a position to do so'.[13] To this end, aspects of the present (including cities, energy resources and medicine) were examined for their importance in the future. A strength of the course was the way that contrasting views of futures were introduced through a variety of speakers and materials. Lectures, talks and films were interspersed with group discussions, short essays and simulation exercises. Abstracts and short papers were made available each week to facilitate preparation for the following week's work. The course was judged a success and one pupil wrote that it was 'not only worthwhile, but an education'.[14] Among the conclusions were that 'choices . . . and viable alternatives do exist'; these 'will affect the direction in which society develops'; 'the choice of a technology implies a concomitant social structure'; and finally that students' preferences were 'tied up with . . . views on the nature of man'.[15]

The Community Participation by Children in Futures Project differs from the Pocklington work in a number of ways. It has involved children of various ages in several countries, including the UK. It is supported by the Open University under the direction of Simon Nicholson. Its central concerns are to overcome the preoccupation of schools with the past by placing various communications media in the hands of children and promoting community-based approaches to education. The view is taken that

> most of learning, especially learning in school, is concerned with the past, and that children are taught to drive into the future through a rear-view mirror. As a consequence, children have a distorted view of culture, society and politics. [Furthermore] adults take it in turn to be at the controls and children are not permitted to 'clear the windscreen' or 'do the driving'.[16]

In an attempt to overcome this 'communication backlash' the project has attempted 'to create a procedure in which children could actively experiment with as many media as possible in order to express, propose, question and build alternative futures with minimal interference/domination from adults'.[17] In practice this has meant making available to children art materials, sound and visual equipment, and facilities for copying, photographing and printing in an 'open' school/community context. Children are held to be 'experts' in their own right, their concerns, feelings and intuitions accorded equal weight with those of adults. Clearly, the utopian element is strong: 'children, with adults of all ages, . . . can enjoy working in harmony toward creating a better world'.[18] Hence, during the process of carrying the project through in several widely scattered sites, a number of conflicts arose with both school and civil authorities. These show that the liberal, optimistic ethos of the project stands in opposition to structural constraints acting upon schools, but is unable to resolve them satisfactorily other than by looking toward the passing away of the school as we know it. The greatest value of the project may be its convincing demonstration that children are indeed natural innovators. What is less clear is whether these promising experiments can bear the weight of interpretation placed upon them.[19] While they are certainly suggestive of what may be attempted in this field they indicate a need for a clearer theoretical base and sober evaluation.

A contrasting approach is evident in the Cities in Space project initiated by teachers at Barstable School, Essex, and timed to coincide with the launch of the first space shuttle in 1981. It represented part of a week-long enrichment course (since repeated) for gifted pupils drawn from a variety of schools. The central task involved assessing the practicability of an orbiting space colony of the type proposed by O'Neil and others in *The High Frontier* (1976). Students were supplied with basic data, proven theory and speculative assumptions. They were asked to demonstrate that a 10,000-person colony was not, in fact, possible and to give detailed reasons.

The exercise required students to handle large amounts of data, to think systematically and to distinguish clearly between claims and evidence. To consider the ecology and sociology of an enclosed system also involved looking at existing settlements in new ways. It was quickly realized that colonies of the kind proposed were not merely bio-technical constructs but socio-cultural ones involving 'the whole realm of civics'. Owing to the complexity of the task pupils found it necessary to break problems down to manageable components and later reintegrate them in their conclusions. They found defects in the system of mirrors designed to create 'day' and 'night' and a need for certain structural modifications. The communal nature of life on the colony was discussed as were issues related to the production of soil-free crops and the varied uses of a central power plant. Other questions were left unresolved and the teachers felt that future exercises would benefit from being more closely structured. Nonetheless, the course was considered a success: 'the students talked and calculated and argued, read the material and used what they could. We . . . were more than happy to see the way [they] worked and learned to work.'[20]

The value of such an exercise lies partly in its transdisciplinary perspective and in the way it presents futures issues for students to study and discuss. The idea of linking it with a key event in the development of space exploration is clearly a good one which deserves emulation. Projects of this kind provide a means for students to explore and interpret aspects of the present and future world which are often overlooked in school curricula. As with our previous examples, they can draw on widely available materials and need not involve expensive training or equipment. They also give weight to the view that final, conclusive, answers are rare, indicating that systematic monitoring of the cultural environment in a continuous search for higher-order understandings may be a more appropriate curriculum goal than many which are currently pursued.

Finally, The World Tomorrow is one of four themes in the Schools Council World Studies 8–13 Project. The latter has attracted interest in some forty LEAs and numerous schools associated with them. A section of the World Studies interim guide briefly presents some general propositions and concepts related to teaching futures.[21] In addition, about thirty practical activities are suggested. These include 'time lines', future histories, 'lifestyles' and the use of science fiction. Many have been tried in schools and the early results provide evidence of stimulating and thought-provoking work.

Intending innovators can draw on these, and other, examples to create future-focused curriculum offerings appropriate to their own situations. Some will wish to add modules or courses to existing curricula, some will emphasize prospective elements and themes in established subjects, while more ambitious souls will want to follow the example of the Montclair Futures School, New Jersey, and rethink the entire curriculum in the light of futures concepts and methodologies.[22] In most cases it will be useful to bear in mind the following five steps. They are not offered as a blueprint but may help teachers and others to clarify what is involved in introducing futures study into existing modes of practice. First, it is useful to review the relevant literature to gain an overall view of the field. Several key texts are included in the references.[23] Second, one may develop a set of guidelines. These will depend on a range of intraschool factors and may need to be negotiated with heads of departments, curriculum committees and the like. Third, decisions must be made about the types of activities that are feasible in a given situation. Teachers with sufficient autonomy and generous resource levels may wish to be fairly ambitious, but those without these benefits will still be able to locate many useful options.[24] Fourth, teaching materials and sources of information can be accumulated. Much can be gleaned from newspapers, magazines and journals and there are a growing number of futures-related publications to which schools may subscribe.[25] Finally there remains the task of evaluating the work carried out and communicating this with others. At the time of writing, several developments are in progress and it is likely that some form of association, network or institutional base will be established for such purposes. In the meantime, small-scale innovations can proceed in the knowledge that they contribute to wider changes in the climate of education in Britain.

Conclusion

There is value in regarding all curricula as being rooted in the past, enacted in the present and oriented toward futures. In this view futures study is an obscured dimension of education which requires serious and sustained attention. In contrast to the 'back to basics' movement or to de facto core curricula which hark back to the preoccupations of an earlier period of history, future-focused curricula have much in common with those drawing on analyses of contemporary culture.[26] A prospective culture map approach allows us to view students as mediators of culture and as makers of meaning. Sensitive to the transformations taking place around them, they can learn to take part in exploring, defining and negotiating humanly desirable futures. Hence, school-based innovations in the field of futures study represent a major category of responses to structural change, a way of countering technological determinism and political manipulation. They provide support for a much more active and alert notion of citizenship. But of equal importance is the way that developments in this area provide opportunities for the educational system to abandon its long-standing obsession with the past and to engage more fully with the realities of life in the late twentieth and twenty-first centuries.

Notes and references

1. Taylor, C. (1976) Hermeneutics and politics, *in* Connerton, P. (ed.) *Critical Sociology*, London: Penguin, p. 189.
2. Woods, P. (1978) Negotiating the demands of schoolwork, *JCS* 10, 4, pp. 309–327.
3. Schon, D. (1971) *Beyond the Stable State*, London: Temple Smith, p. 51.
4. See Jouvnal, B. (1967) *The Art of Conjecture*, London: Weidenfeld and Nicholson.

304 Readings in School-Based Curriculum Development

5 See Nicholson, S. (1980) Choice, Chance and Utopia. Malmo School of Education, *Educational and Psychological Interactions* 79, December.
6 The classic work on images of futures remains that by Polak, F. (1973) *The Image of the Future*, translated and abridged by Elise Boulding, London: Elsevier.
7 See Briggs, A. (1978) The historian and the future, *Futures* 10, 6, December, pp. 445–451.
8 Boulding, E. (1978) The dynamics of imaging futures, Washington DC, *World Future Society Bulletin* 12, 5, Sep/Oct, pp. 7–8.
9 The potential of computers as learning tools is explored by Papert, S. (1980) *Mindstorms: Children, Computers and Powerful Ideas*, Brighton: Harvester Press.
10 For a practical American view, see Fitch, R. and Svengalis, C. (1979) *Futures Unlimited: Teaching About Worlds to Come*, Washington DC, National Council for the Social Studies Bulletin 59. For an in-depth British approach to the theory of teaching critical futures study, see Slaughter, R. (1982) *Critical Futurism and Curriculum Renewal*, Ph.D. Dissertation, University of Lancaster.
11 This is explored in Slaughter, R. (1983) *Futures Education: Why We Need to Teach For Tomorrow*. Lancaster, S. Martin's College, Centre for Peace Studies, Occasional Paper 5.
12 See Hicks, D. (1982) *Education for Peace: What Does it Mean?* Lancaster, Centre for Peace Studies, Occasional Paper 1, p. 3.
13 Jeffery, J. et al. (1977) *Possible Futures*, London: Community Service Volunteers folder.
14 ibid.
15 ibid.
16 Nicholson, S. (1982) *The Future of Politics*, Oxford: Open University.
17 Nicholson, S. and Lorenzo, R. (1981) *The Political Implications of Child Participation: Steps Toward a Participatory Society*, Switzerland, IFDA Dossier 22, March/April, p.66.
18 ibid. p. 67.
19 i.e. whether they should be elevated to a theory of cultural evolution and/or social change. See ibid.
20 Williams, M. (1981) *Report on the Science Section of the Enrichment Course held at the Brooklands Centre*, Chelmsford, April.
21 Fisher, S. and Hicks, D. (1981) *Planning and Teaching World Studies: An Interim Guide*, London: Schools Council, pp. 35–44.
22 Prospectus, Montclair Futures School, Grove Street, New Jersey, USA, 1980.
23 See notes 10 and 11. Also Kauffman, D. (1976) *Teaching the Future*, Palm Springs: ETC Publications; and Toffler, A. (ed.) (1979) *Learning For Tomorrow: The Role of the Future in Education*, New York: Vintage.
24 See notes 11 and 21.
25 Of particular value are *Futures*, IPC, Guildford, England, and the *Future Studies Centre Newsletter*, Birmingham Settlement, 318 Summer Lane, Birmingham, England, B19 3RL. Also, from the World Future Society, *The Futurist*, *The WFS Bulletin* and *Future Survey*, 4916 St. Elmo Avenue, Bethesda, Maryland, 20814, USA.
26 See Skilbeck, M. (1982) *A Core Curriculum for the Common School*, an inaugural lecture, University of London Institute of Education.

CHAPTER 27

CURRICULUM FOR WHAT?
James Hemming

The context for change

Many ideas come together in the concept of a curriculum. The behaviourists see the role of the curriculum as that of shaping and conditioning the young so that they respond appropriately to the stimuli of life. For the cognitive psychologists, the role of the curriculum is to promote a formative reaction between the questing mind of the growing child and an ever-expanding awareness of the environment. The depth-psychologists made their contribution by concentrating on emotional development. Psychologists apart, traditional educators, as a group, are mainly concerned to hand on the culture pattern of their society; the pragmatists to prepare the young for their functional roles as husbands, wives, parents, and workers; the romantics to promote the flowering of individual personality; the moralists to assure the transmission of right values; and so forth. The problem for curriculum designers is that all these protagonists are right – and all wrong. Right because each puts stress on an essential element of the whole; wrong because what we mostly need in a modern curriculum are comprehensiveness and balance rather than the dominating influence of any particular theory or attitude.

We must also, when looking anew at the curriculum, dismiss the illusion that we can bring schooling up to date by adding subject to subject until we have put together a complete education. This additive approach has bedevilled the curriculum for many years. The classical curriculum of the nineteenth century, however inadequate in itself, was a manageable proposition for both teachers and taught. Then science achieved an entry and expanded rapidly. More recently, the schools have had to cope with demands for aesthetic education, emotional education, contemporary languages, education in practical skills, health education, social education, moral education, craft, design and technology, economics, politics, computer studies and the rest. Obviously, no student can do it all on the basis of adding subject to subject, so options and specialisms have increasingly taken over advanced schooling.

This has imposed on the young an unbalanced and fragmented educational experience, so that a movement has grown up to relate subject to subject and to fill in the lacunae between the specialist areas. Integrated Studies and General Studies appeared on the curriculum. But these developed not as principles of coherence and mutual reinforcement to bind subjects together, but as subjects, or subject groups, in their own right, demanding their own time slots and increasing the congestion of the curriculum still further.

We are now nearing the end of that road, harassed by its pressures, frustrated by its imperfections, looking for some new synthesis. So 'education for what?' becomes the search for a new approach to curriculum content and method which is appropriate to the needs and powers of the modern young and is within the competence of the schools to operate with reasonable harmony, tranquillity, and personal satisfaction for both teachers and taught. This chapter seeks to contribute to that search. It will be mainly concerned with secondary education since it is the secondary curriculum which is, at present, in urgent need of renovation, but the ideas and strategies proposed are equally relevant to primary education.

The motivation dimension

The starting point for a new curriculum is a single-minded determination to offer the young at school a highly motivating environment for learning and growth. To take full account of the students' personal interests and capabilities is not pandering but good education. Bored minds do not function well. On the other hand, the young love achievement. Equally, they – like all of us – loathe failure.

The dynamics of curriculum success can be stated in the simple formula:

$$M \sim \frac{S}{F}$$

where M stands for motivation and S and F for satisfaction and frustration.

If, over time, any task or experience we offer to the child provides more success than frustration, then motivation to continue with the activity will be generated. But, if success is small and frustration high, then motivation will constantly diminish until it is replaced by boredom.

However, success should not be too easily attainable or it becomes meaningless. Many years ago, the American educator, Carleton Washburne (1940) suggested that the essential principle was to assure 'success in proportion to effort' for every pupil. The young show in their own behaviour the validity of this principle. They willingly take on demanding challenges – like mastering skate-boards or the rubik cube – and then work hard at self-improvement, building success on success. The sticking power of young people, when provided with opportunities for self-improvement, was shown, over forty years ago, in the community research project, the Peckham Health Experiment, (Crocker and Pearse 1943). More recently the same principle has been observed in some of the special units set up to take over the education of school rejects. The energy for self-improvement is waiting to be tapped in all children.

The plague of orthodox secondary education around the developed world today is that it leaves hosts of big, healthy, vigorous adolescents profoundly demotivated by the curriculum on offer to them. At the same time, the traditional curriculum irritates many of the young people who *can* cope with its 'subjects', by the narrowness of the studies they are engaged in and the irrelevance of these studies to life.

The missing factor from the curriculum in both instances is lack of concern for personal motivation. Every young person is a unique syndrome of interests, aptitudes and abilities. Although an enthusiastic teacher can awaken interests, and build on what he, or she, awakens, the teacher has to work through *actual* interests, whether already present in the student's awareness or existing as potentialities. The curriculum for its part must be designed as a magnet to draw out interests and potentialities. A well-designed curriculum, then, sustains a cycle of learning. It will encourage the learner to engage with the opportunities on offer. If this encounter produces more satisfaction than frustration, the result will be positive reinforcement for the activity and the cycle of learning will be sustained. Sustaining cycles of learning in the service of personal growth is, then, the main role of the curriculum. When this is achieved, the problem of the schools is not to persuade adolescents to come to them but to get them off the premises at the end of the day.

The first principle, then, of the new synthesis must be: *the curriculum is for maximizing the students' motivation in the service of their own education.* This principle is absolutely crucial. We can put children in school but we cannot make them learn – without skilfully devised motivation. When motivation is lacking within the curriculum, schooling is a misery for both teachers and taught. To maintain discipline becomes a continuous struggle because schooling is a battle-ground between boredom and authority. Willing cooperation, without which no curriculum can achieve anything, is the consequence of high motivation. It has no other source. Hence, whatever our educational aims may be, arousing motivation must be the top priority.

The rest of this chapter will suggest approaches to the curriculum which combine motivation with learning. But first we must take a look at that thorny issue of education today – early specialization.

A comment on specialization

During the course of this century, specialization, based on traditional subjects, has been regarded as the acme of adolescent learning. This is now coming to be seen as misguided (Hargreaves 1982; DES 1979). The accumulation of unrelated packages of learning does not constitute an education. Nor can a few periods of general education, patched onto a subject-bound curriculum, provide coherence. Indeed, any attempt to offset the disjointed character of a subject-bound curriculum in this way may be self-defeating, because students easily come to regard the specialist subjects as the important part of the curriculum and may dismiss attempts at broadening and integration as expendable extras, if not as soft options for the less able. It is, in fact, very hard to motivate either for breadth or through breadth in a subject-bound curriculum. Yet breadth is a vital and motivating factor in education today. Without breadth of understanding – including international understanding – young people are left unrelated to the world as it is and are diminished as individuals by that separation.

On the other hand, we need specialist skills in society. Indeed, fresh specialisms are constantly emerging. The question is how best to produce the specialists society needs. In the past, the educational system has been structured as if all children were potential specialists so that they should be urged on to specialist tracks as soon as possible. The consequence has been a narrow education for those capable of intense specialization and rejection for the rest. This is clearly the wrong way to go about giving able students their chance, sustaining the self-confidence of nonacademic students, and giving society the specialists it requires.

The alternative is to stop forced feeding and to let the specialists select themselves. A broad, lively curriculum, related to what is going on in the local community and the world, cannot fail to motivate special abilities latent in students. The young, as we have noted, love to develop their powers. A curriculum that opens windows upon the world shows what the opportunities are. The rest can be left to the young people themselves so long as the teachers are prepared to act as facilitators and guides, and so long as abundant resources for learning are made available to young people both within the school and in the community.

The schools did not train the first scientists nor did they train the first computer operators. Young people with appropriate general backgrounds seized on these specialisms for themselves. The point is that schools should exist to encourage and promote any special interests among their pupils, as individual studies, but should not start by imposing specialisms. Such an approach would result in those students with a genuine specialist interest having the opportunity to get further in the time available than if tied down to a standardized programme of specialist study. It would build specialisms on genuine personal motivation. It would also permit those with individual interests, skills and abilities, not recognized as specialisms, to pursue them to the limit of their capacities. In considering what the curriculum is for, then, specialist study will not be dealt with first but last – as the logical outcome of a broad, highly motivating general education.

Basic competence

The curriculum has to be dedicated to ensuring children acquire the basic skills that permit them to live their present and future lives effectively as individuals and as members of the community. The necessity of this has always been recognized, but, often, what has been assessed as basic has been limited to 'the three Rs' while the methods used have been dull, repetitive and demotivating. Consequently, many able young people have left school lacking basic competences – social and practical skills for example – while the less able have given up their struggle with the three Rs before they have become either literate or numerate.

We now need to look beyond basic skills to basic competences. These include not only reading, writing, and calculation but also oracy – the ability to communicate information, ideas, and feelings in speech. Also to be considered as basic are practical ability, that is know-how and facility with the ubiquitous mechanical and electronic artefacts of our technological society, and the abilities needed to relate, person to person and group to group, in the conduct of social and societal life in a democratic community.

Reading, writing and calculation – including mathematical expression as in simple statistics – call for a dual approach in the curriculum. Each essential skill has to be broken down into readily assimilable units which will provide for every student the experience of gradually growing success (Becker et al. 1981). Secondly, the curriculum has to be designed so that the skills which are mastered are immediately put into practice in significant ways. The best reinforcement is effective use. Continuous assessment of ability is also necessary so that errors can be spotted and eliminated. All of which is thoroughly acceptable to the young so long as the outcome is a feeling of success instead of a sense of defeat.

This approach involves sorting out two confusions still present in educational thinking. Just because the earlier methods of teaching the three Rs were so dreadfully monotonous, mindless and discouraging, there has been a tendency to regard efforts specifically directed to teaching them as at odds with the concept of educating the child as a unique individual. This anxiety is erroneous. Competence in basic skills is the foundation for self-confident, individual development. Appropriately taught, they can be a source of high satisfaction. When they are organized as a ladder of success, the able students romp from stage to stage, while the less able achieve their own level in their own time, and both groups draw self-esteem from their sense of growth (Banks 1981).

The other common confusion is that learning by doing is the only valid method. Actually, precision teaching is an element in the learning of any skill. Precise teaching and learning by doing are both needed in the development of the three Rs.

Practical competence grows from the knowledge of how things work, partly gained from explanation and partly from active manipulation of components. A curious anomaly of education as it exists at present is that, whereas putting things together and making them work is a common experience of children at the infant stage, such practices may drop right out of later education. This omission should be remedied.

An individualized approach to the three Rs – letting each student go at his or her own pace – means that the quicker students will attain fully adequate competence well ahead of the rest. This is probably the group which should be encouraged to explore their potentialities in learning a foreign language, or languages. There is no point in loading students with the task of learning a foreign language while they are still labouring with their own.

Developing social skills warrants a section on its own.

Socialization through the curriculum

Everywhere throughout society today the cry is heard for attention within education to the development of social skills. It comes, for example, from industry, the social services, psychiatrists, the prison services, the armed forces, and the young people themselves.

Necessary skills range from social deportment – how to meet and greet people, how to maintain eye-contact without embarrassment, how to carry on a conversation – to the ability to participate confidently in communal and political life. Oral communication skills are essential to all this, including involvement at work. In a recent study (Townsend and Bevan 1983), the highest ranked of essential skills in fifty percent or more of jobs was 'Listening and Talking'. We live in the communication age, when the exchange of accurate information is the life-blood of industry and commerce. Exchanges by word of mouth continue to be the most vivid and immediate of all communication. Communication of ideas and feelings is also central in private life. Counsellors find themselves constantly engaged in helping marriage partners to express their feelings to one another.

The participant character of modern life also requires facility in a number of other social capabilities. Young people used to be taught passivity at school – to have their lives run for them. They now need to learn how to participate in identifying and fulfilling common purposes. This involves flexibility of mind, the ability to weigh issues, make plans, arrive at decisions and evaluate results. Teamwork is the name of the game in society today. Competition may provide a useful stimulus but it is cooperation that gets things done. Schools that generate intense individual competitiveness as the main motivational force are out of tune with their times.

Schools today, then, should be friendly, purposeful, democratic communities in which the range of social skills necessary in modern life – whether in or out of employment – should be specifically taught by appropriate activities, in the classroom, and should also be put to use in the day-to-day life of the school and its relationships with the wider community (Watts 1980).

Such school experience is itself a powerful influence in developing oral communication, a vital modern skill, as noted earlier. Sharing and reporting on experiences, discussing projects, answering questions from peers, preparing check-lists to use on factory, or other, visits, describing people and scenes, and the like, induce young people to search for the right words and the most effective mode of expression. Sufficient practice in oral skills requires an active style of teaching within an active school community. There is then plenty to discuss, comment on, and evaluate.

This brings us to our second principle for a new synthesis: *the curriculum and conduct of school life should ensure competence in basic skills for all children, including practical skills and the skills of participant social life.*

Orientation to life

In our era, human knowledge is moving from reductionist to holistic perceptions. This should be reflected in the curriculum. Early curriculum designers, in their efforts to provide young people with a reliable package of facts, broke up the corpus of knowledge into encapsulated subjects – history, geography, biology, physics, and the rest. Each subject was then split into age-related syllabuses, and each syllabus into chapters of a textbook. These subject divisions are now out of date (Hargreaves 1982). The contemporary alternative is the development of a broad perspective on the overall human situation. This includes awareness of mankind's evolution and place in Nature; orientation to the human past, to science, to society, to different habitats and cultures, and to mankind's worldwide involvement in, and responsibilities to, people and the environment; orientation to the universe as the physical context of all that exists; and orientation to mankind's possible futures. Orientation falls naturally into two main areas: orientation through the humanities and orientation to science. From either area specialist individual studies may develop – the hills rising from the plain.

What prevents a proper background of orientation is partly the academic illusion that the only valid knowledge is factual knowledge, and partly lack of confidence on the part of teachers about entering all the areas of human experience to which their pupils should be introduced. The answer to both these problems is the use of modern technologies to give orientation to essential fields of awareness, backed up by open discussions in which teachers and pupils learn together. Some schools are already operating along these lines (Watts 1977) but such programmes need to be universal, not exceptional.

The aim of orientation is to develop the open rather than the closed mind.

Human beings are born curious (Hodgkin 1976) so that interests, once fully aroused, tend to be self-sustaining. What education has to strive to avoid is producing young people who leave school with a 'not for me' sticker attached to areas of essential human awareness. The curriculum is for developing growing points in the mind.

Principle three of the new synthesis must, then, be: *the curriculum is for developing a broad understanding of the human situation.*

Creative and aesthetic experience

Through from the 1920s, or even earlier, there have been educators who have stressed that creative outlets and the arts have a very valuable contribution to make to education. However, the absorption of secondary education with academic attainment always ran counter to this conviction so that creative and aesthetic experiences were often forced to the fringes of education instead of being given a significant place (Read 1943).

We now face a quite new situation. Research into the bi-modality of the human brain (Sperry 1973) has made it clear that an education which neglects synthesis, intuition and creativity is denying formative experience to a mode of consciousness needed to balance the analytical–logical mode, which is so much to the fore in the traditional curriculum. Thus, the typical secondary curriculum overdevelops one mode of interacting with the environment and neglects the other, whereas optimum human functioning requires the two modes to be developed equally (Bogen 1977).

The inclusion of a generous component of aesthetic and creative experience in the curriculum goes further, however, than maintaining a proper balance in mental development. People in the future, with work often demanding less of their time, will be left at the mercy of received entertainment if they lack the inner resources to develop and share creative interests. Furthermore, this formerly neglected aspect of education is now in demand within the field of work itself. Imagination, design skills, the ability to synthesize as well as to analyse, are of vital importance in modern industry.

The arts in the curriculum – literature, creative writing, music, painting, drama, movement, pottery, craft, design – as well as being essential to a complete education, are also a source of cohesion and enrichment for the whole school community. In addition, they can provide links with the wider community. They, consequently, offer a field for the development of social skills and relationships as well as personal sensitivity.

This brings us to the fourth principle for a contemporary education: *the curriculum is for developing the creative and aesthetic potentialities of young people.*

Health education

One might have supposed that no case would need making out for time and attention within the curriculum for health education. On the contrary it – like creative and aesthetic education – often gets short shrift owing to the pressures of the academic curriculum. Health, of course, means 'whole', and health education is now coming to be seen as directed towards the attainment of personal wholeness: physically, socially, and morally, in being and relationships. Aspects of health education can be taken up in various areas of the curriculum, but a satisfactory health education programme involves also its own particular allotment of time in which developmental problems (sex, relationships), possible dangers (smoking, alcohol, drugs), and the acquisition of a dependable set of social/moral values are dealt with against the background of the students' own lives. Every year, within the adolescent population, a thorough health education programme becomes more urgent. This need is being recognized around the world as, for example, in the suggested core curriculum for Australian schools (Skilbeck 1982).

Accordingly, our fifth principle for the new synthesis must be: *the curriculum is for providing all students with a comprehensive health education which should include the development of personal qualities and values.*

Individualized study

A curriculum comprising a thorough development of the basic skills, orientation studies, aesthetic/creative opportunities and a comprehensive health education may completely absorb the time and energies of some students. Others will find the incentive in one or other of these areas, or in their experience of life, to select aspects or themes for concentrated individual study. The curriculum should set aside time for this whenever individual students reveal flair or interest.

When such specific interests exist, it is likely to be more efficacious to help individuals to work at their own pace than to bed them down in class situations, although the overlap of interests can lead to stimulating group work. Individualized study has the great advantage that students of high capacity are free to progress fast (Perry 1982) while slower learners can follow their own courses without being shown up by their swifter peers. In individualized study, competition is with oneself, not with others.

Independent study courses, based on individual interests, have now proved themselves at diploma and degree level (Adams and Burgess 1980). In earlier periods in Britain, when the academically less able adolescents were educated in secondary modern schools, the same principle was found to work well in that context. It now seems that the time is ripe for a similar principle to take over specialist study, within the context of individualized study, from, say, age 13.

Some have suggested that society will be left short of the specialists it needs if students are not dragooned into following prescribed subject courses, leading to prescribed levels of attainment in tests or examinations. This is supposition, not certainty. It is equally valid to suppose that, if we provide a stimulating learning environment, which is also related to the world beyond the school, we do not have to worry about where the craftsmen and specialists are going to come from. We have only to spot the potentialities latent in young people, and to provide the time, and resources, for their development, including work experience (Eggleston 1982). This is the way to generate application and dedication and, therefore, high standards.

Our sixth, and last, principle, then, becomes: *the curriculum is for providing opportunities for individualized study so that young people may be motivated to develop their personal interests, aptitudes and skills to the ceiling of their potentialities.*

To sum up: a contemporary curriculum should aim to provide:

1. Highly motivating learning experiences for students of all abilities.
2. A thorough grounding in, and practice of, basic skills, including practical ability, and social skills.
3. Broad orientation courses which relate students to all aspects of the human situation and develop a sense of involvement in the affairs of mankind, past, present, local and global, as well as providing opportunities for cooperation, planning and decision making.
4. Opportunities for a wide range of creative and aesthetic experiences and pursuits.
5. Courses directed to the attainment of total health: physical, personal, social and moral.
6. Opportunities for individualized study designed to foster the growth of personal interests and aptitudes, as well as the experience of dedication and application.

Curricula – and school communities – designed on those principles would tap and stimulate the competence, humanity, integrity, creativity and inventiveness of the coming generation so that the young people would be equipped to deal both with their personal and working lives and with the social and global problems that will confront them. That is what schooling is for.

References

Adams, E. and Burgess, T. (eds.) (1980) *Outcomes of Education*, London, Macmillan.
Banks, B. (1981) The Kent Mathematics Project, *The Institute of Mathematics and its Applications*, Feb/March.
Becker, W.C., Engelmann, S., Carmine, D. and Rhine, W.R. (1981) *in* Rhine, W.R. (eds) *Making Schools more Effective*, New York: Academic Press.
Bogen, J.E. (1977) Some educational implications of hemispheric specialization, *in* Wittrock, M.C. (ed.) *The Human Brain*, New Jersey: Prentice-Hall.
Crocker, L.H. and Pearse, T.H. (1943) *The Peckham Experiment*, London: Allen and Unwin.
DES (1979) *Aspects of Secondary Education in England*, a survey by H.M. Inspectors of Schools, London: HMSO.
Eggleston, J. (ed.) (1982) *Work Experience in Secondary Schools*, London: Routledge and Kegan Paul.
Hargreaves, D.H. (1982) *The Challenge of the Comprehensive School*, London: Routledge and Kegan Paul.
Hodgkin, R.A. (1976) *Born Curious*, London: John Wiley.
Perry, Lord (1982) Changing patterns of education, *in* Costello and Richardson (eds) *Continuing Education for the Post-Industrial Society*, Milton Keynes: Open University Press.
Read, H. (1943) *Education Through Art*, London: Faber and Faber.
Skilbeck, M. (1982) *A Core Curriculum for the Common School*, University of London Institute of Education.
Sperry, R.W. (1973) Lateral specialization of cerebral function in the surgically separated hemispheres, *in* McGurgan, F.J. (ed.) *The Psycho-Physiology of Thinking*, New York: Academic Press.
Townsend, C. and Bevan, S. (1983) Skills needed for young people's jobs, *BACIE Journal*, March/April.
Washburne, C. (1940) *A Living Philosophy of Education*, New York: John Day.
Watts, J.F. (1977) *The Countesthorpe Experience*, London: Allen and Unwin.
Watts, J.F. (1980) *Towards the Open School*, London: Longman.

INDEX OF NAMES

Abbott, M.G., 176, 177
Abraham, H.J., 91
Adams, E. et al, 222, 224
Adelman, C. et al, 60, 145
All Faiths for One Race (AFFOR), 61
Anderson, C.A., 82, 91
Antaki, C. and Brewin, C., 26
Arlin, M., 19, 26
Aronwitz, S., 240, 242
Atherton, B., 204
Aucott, J. et al, 90, 91
Avon Local Education Authority, 145

Baker, K. and Sikora, J., 189
Balogh, J., 214, 215
Banks, B., 310, 316
Bardell, G., 158
Barnes, D., 102, 111, 114
Baron, G., 101, 114
Bartlett, L. and Ogilvie, D., 262, 268
Bassett, G.W., 263, 268
Batten, M., 250, 269, 263, 268
Becher, T. and Maclure, J.S., 102, 114, 189
Becker, J.M., 86, 89, 91
Becker, W.C. et al, 310, 316
Benn, C. and Simon, B., 154, 158
Bennett, N., 20, 26
Bereday, G.Z. and Lauwerys, J.A., 84, 91
Bernstein, B., 23, 26, 174, 177
Beswick, N.W., 204
Bidwell, C.E., 167, 169
Biggs, J.B. and Collis, K.F., 22, 26
Black, H. and Broadfoot, P., 215

Blatchford, K., 79
Blenkin, G.M. and Kelly, A.V., 19, 26
Bogen, J.E., 313, 316
Bolam, R., 117, 123, 263, 268
Bolam, R. et al., 263, 268
Boud, D., 222, 224
Boulding, E., 297, 304
Bowmen, B., 43, 46
Brady, P. and Pope, B., 257, 268
Briggs, A., 304
Broadbent, J. et al, 60
Brophy, J.E., 19, 20, 26
Bruner, J.S., 14, 26, 107, 114
Bruyn, S.T., 134, 138
Buergenthal, T. and Torney, J.V., 83, 86, 91
Bunday, J., 79
Burgess, R.G., 241, 242
Burgess, T. and Adams, E., 215, 221, 224, 315, 316
Buswell, C., 65, 66, 71
Byrne, E., 70

Campbell, W.J. and Robinson, N.M., 257, 268
Campbell, W.J. et al, 263, 268
Carews, J. and Lightfoot, S.L., 22, 26
Central Advisory Council (Crowther Committee), 39, 41, 46, 164, 169, 178
Central Advisory Council (Newsom Committee), 39, 41, 46, 74, 80
Centre for the Study of Comprehensive Education, 216
Chalkley, B., 90, 91

Clarricoates, K., 71
Clift, P., 189
Cmd 5174: Education a Framework for Expansion, 219, 224
Cohen, D., 79
Cohen, D. and Harrison, M., 258, 261, 262, 268
Coleman, J.S. et al, 14, 20, 26
Collins, C.W. and Hughes, P.W., 257, 268
Connell, W.F., 84, 91
Consultative Committee on the Curriculum, Scotland. (Munn Report), 107, 115
Coslett, J., 153
Council for Education in World Citizenship, 88, 91
Craft, A. and Bardell, G., 61
Crittenden, B., 79
Crocker, L.H. and Pearse, T.H., 307, 316
Crone, R. and Malone, J., 124, 133

Dale, R.R., 70
Davies, E., 117, 123, 223, 224
Davies, W.J.K., 204
Davis, B., 167, 169
Davis, E., 244, 255
De Charms, R., 18, 26
Delamont, S., 65, 71
Department of Education and Science, 30, 31, 32, 33, 34, 38, 39, 42, 43, 46, 63, 70, 79, 83, 91, 102, 106, 155, 158, 204, 209, 215, 309, 316
Downing, L.L. and Bothwell, K.H., 19, 26
Dunlop, J., 87, 91
Dweck, C., 65, 71

Eastgate, C.A., 155, 158
Eddowes, M., 64, 70
Education Department of South Australia, 80
Eggleston, J., 161, 163, 315, 316
Eisner, E.W., 45, 46
Elliott, G., 32, 38, 89, 91, 189, 245, 252, 255
Elliott, J. and Adelman, C., 235, 242
Ellis, W., 153
Entwhistle, D.R. and Hayduk, L.A., 20, 21, 22, 26
Equal Opportunities in Education Project, 69, 71
Esland, G., 120, 123

Evans, G.T., 80, 245, 255, 257, 258, 260, 262, 263, 269
Evans, G.T. and Cotterell, J.L., 262, 269

Fennema, E., 64, 70
Ferguson, C., 177, 178
Fisher, S. and Hicks, D., 88, 91, 304
Fitch, R. and Svengalis, C., 304
Ford, T.J., 247, 255
Fox, G.T., 256, 269
Fraser, B.J., 244, 245, 255
Freire, P., 260, 269
Further Education Curriculum Review and Development Unit (FEU), 173, 175, 176, 178, 215
Future Studies Centre, 304

Gahagan, J., 16, 26
Galton, M. et al, 20, 27
Gammage, P., 19, 27
Geertz, C., 275, 289
Girls and Mathematics Association, 69, 71
Girls and Technological Education Project, 69, 71
Girls into Science and Technology Project, 69, 71
Giroux, H., 240, 242
Goacher, B., 214, 215
Goodlad, J.L. et al, 84, 91
Grassie, M., 262, 269
Gray, H.L., 111, 114
Gray, H. and Coulson, A.A., 119, 123
Greene, M., 238, 242
Grundy, S. and Kemmis, S., 253, 255

Halpin, A.W., 101, 114
Hamblin, D., 158
Hamilton, D., 22, 27, 173, 178
Hamilton, D. et al, 145
Harding, J., 64, 70
Hargreaves, D.H., 80, 114, 308, 312, 316
Harlen, W., 245, 252, 255
Harris, N.D.C. et al, 204
Harrison, A., 215
Heater, D., 83, 86, 91
Hemming, J., 217, 225
Herbert, J., 247, 255
Hicks, D., 304
Hicks, D. and Townley, C., 86, 89, 91
Hodgkin, R.A., 313, 316
Holland, G., 44, 46

Index of Names 319

Holt, M. (*see also* Subject entry), 114, 234, 242
Hopkins, D., 189
Hopson, B. and Scally, M., 15, 27
Houlton, E. and Willey, R., 60
House of Commons Select Committee on Higher Education, 218, 225
Howe, A., 204
Hoyle, E., 114, 167, 169, 175, 178
Hughes, P.W. et al, 244, 248, 253, 254, 255, 266, 269
Hull, C. et al, 238, 242
Hurman, A., 154, 155, 158

Ingvarson, L., 261, 263, 269
Inner London Education Authority (ILEA) (*see also* Subject entry) 60, 68, 71, 145
International Understanding at School-Unesco, 91
Irving, A. and Snape, W.A., 202

James, W., 14, 27
Jeffery, J. et al., 304
Jones, E. et al, 16, 27
Jouvenal, B., 303

Kaneti, Barry, S.M., 176, 178
Kauffman, D., 304
Kelly, A., 70, 71
Kemmis, S. et al, 255, 265, 269
Kirby, N., 19, 25, 27
Klein, G., 60
Kohlberg, L., 282, 289

Law, B. and Watts, A.G., 155, 158
Lawton, D., 114, 146, 289
Lewis, R., 204
Lloyd-Trump, J., 108, 114
Logan, L.D. and Dore, C.K., 259, 269
Lord James of Rusholme (James Committee), 219, 225
Lynch, J., 61

Marland, M., 43, 46
May, N. and Rudduck, J., 242
Meade, P., 257, 269
Middleton, M., 77, 80
Millman, V., 66, 71
Milne, A.A., 94, 102, 114
Minister of Education in Western Australia (Priest Committee), 74, 80

Minister of Labour, 45, 46
Montclair Futures School, 304
Morris, B., 16, 27
Mullard, C., 61
Murray, L., 217, 225
Musgrove, F., 101, 114
McConaghy, D., 253, 255
McCormick, R., 189
MacDonald, B., 147
MacDonald, B. and Walker, R., 145
McPherson, A., 234, 242

National Advisory Council on Education for Industry and Commerce (Haslegrave Committee), 172, 178
National Inquiry into Teacher Education (Australia), 263, 269
National Union of Teachers (NUT), 61, 70
Newson, E., 13, 27
Nicholls, A. and H., 159, 163
Nicholson, S., 300, 304
Nicholson, S. and Lorenzo, R., 304
Nisbet, J., 122, 123
Nixon, J., 242
Nottingham University School of Education, 61
Nowicki, S. and Duke, M.P., 19, 27
Nowicki, S. and Strickland, B.A., 19, 27
Nuttall, D., 189, 215

O'Neil et al, 301
Open University, 189
Organization for Economic Co-operation and Development: Centre for Educational Research and Innovation (OECD/CERI), 125, 126, 133
Owen, J.G., 162, 163
Oxfordshire Local Education Authority, 145

Papert, S., 304
Parker, J.C. and Rubin, L.J., 232, 242
Parliament of New South Wales (McGowan Committee), 75, 80
Pedersen, E. et al, 21, 27
Perrott, C., 258, 261, 262, 269
Perry, Lord, 314, 316
Pettigrew, A.M., 176, 178
Phares, E.J., 19, 27
Pike, L.W. and Barrows, T.S., 86, 91
Plaskow, M., 80
Polak, F., 304

Postman, N., 13, 27
Power, C.N., 75, 80
Prescott, D., 84, 91
Pring, R., 173, 178

Raddon, R., 204
Raven, J., 80
Read, H., 313, 316
Reid, E., 60
Reid, M.L. et al, 155, 158
Richardson, R., 85, 90, 91
Richardson, R. et al, 88, 92
Rotter, J.B., 19, 27
Rowlandson, S., 242
Royal Commission, 1861, 153
Royal Society of Arts, 218, 225
Rudduck, J., 235, 237, 243
Russell, N., 247, 255
Rutter, M. et al, 20, 27
Ryrie, A.G., et al, 158

Sanders, S.G. and Wren, J.P., 19, 27
Scanlon, D.G., 83, 92
Schon, D., 292, 303
School and Community Project, Canberra, 264, 269
Schools Commission, Australia, 80, 259, 263, 270
Schools Council for Curriculum and Examinations for England and Wales, 45, 46, 47, 61, 69, 71, 103, 114
Schools Council Sex Differentiation in Schools Project, 69, 71
Scriven, M., 22, 27
Secretary of State for Education and Science, 41, 47
Secretary of State for Scotland (Pack Committee), 74, 80
Sharpe, S., 66, 71
Shaw, K., 168, 169
Sheperd, G.D. and Ragan, W.B., 13, 27
Shipman, M.D., 118, 123, 126, 133
Simons, H., 147
Skilbeck, M., 80, 125, 133, 161, 163, 178, 229, 253, 255, 304, 314, 316
Skilbeck, M. and Connell, H., 84, 92
Skilbeck, M., et al, 260, 270
Slaughter, R., 304
Smyth, J., 260, 270
Solihull Local Education Authority, 145
Solomon, D. and Kendall, A.J., 20, 27
Spender, D., 71

Spender, D. and Sarah, E., 70
Sperry, R.W., 313, 316
Stanton, G., 212, 216
Starkey, H., 90, 92
Stenhouse, L., 44, 45, 47, 162, 163, 232, 233, 234, 241, 243
Stenhouse, L. and Torrance, H., 233, 243
Stephenson, J., 219, 225
Stipek, D.J. and Weisz, J.R., 19, 27
Stone, M., 60
Stones, R., 64, 71
Strachey, R., 70
Sussex European Research Centre (SERC), 86, 92
Swann Committee (Education of Children from Ethnic Minority Groups), 61

Tanner, J.M., 13, 27
Taylor, C., 291, 303
Taylor, L.C., 204
Tenbrink, T., 246, 255
Thelen, H.A., 23, 25, 27
Thomas, J.B., 204
Thornbury, R. et al, 204
Tipton, B., 174, 178
Toffler, A., 304
Tomlinson, J. et al, 218, 225
Tomlinson, S., 60
Torney, J.V. and Buergenthal, T., 87, 92
Torrance, P., 64, 70
Townsend, C. and Beven, S., 311, 316
Turnbull, C., 282, 289
Tyler, W., 170

Walford, C., 64, 70
Walsh, P.D., 80
Walton, J., 102, 114
Warwick, D., 103, 114
Washburne, C., 307, 316
Waterhouse, P.S., 205
Watts, J.F., 311, 312, 316
Watts, T., 35, 38
Weiner, B., 27
Weinstein, G. and Fantini, M.D., 16, 28
Wells, G., 23, 28
Whitehead, A.N., 207
Whitfield, R.C., 102, 114
Williams, M., 304
Williams, R., 275, 289
Wolpe, A.M., 71
Woods, P., 158, 292, 303
World Future Society, 304

Young, F.A., 88, 92

INDEX OF SUBJECTS

Access to Information on Multicultural Education (AIMER), 56, 60
accountability, 7, 30–31, 42–43, 93, 180, 210, 245, 246–247
action research (*see also* evaluation; research and development: teachers as researchers), 86–87, 93, 125–126, 131, 159–162, 228–229, 232, 252–253, 265, 267
adult education, 171
advisers, inspectors (*see also* curriculum – field officers; H.M.I.; LEA's), 32–33, 34, 37, 68, 101, 122, 134, 137, 187, 245, 247, 254–255, 258, 262
All London Teachers Against Racism and Facism (ALTARF), 58, 61
assessment, of students (*see also* examinations; learning; tests, testing), 20, 22, 72–74, 75, 79, 155, 190–191, 207–208, 210–216, 217–218, 220–224, 238–239
attributes, attribution theory (*see also* curriculum – psychological perspectives), 8, 15–18, 21, 22–23, 25–26, 150, 151, 307–308
Avon Resources for Learning Centre, 99

Barstable School, 301
Black Papers, 41
Boyle, Sir Edward, 38, 39
Business and Technician Education Council (BTEC), 36, 172, 211
Business Education Council, 172, 176

Callaghan, J. (Ruskin College speech), 41
careers teacher (*see also* curriculum – guidance), 157
case study, 93, 95–96, 101–114, 124, 125–133, 134–138, 139–145, 146, 155–158, 159–162, 164–169, 234–239.
Certificate of Pre-Vocational Education (CPVE), 36–37, 211
Certificate of Secondary Education (CSE), 29, 36, 37, 70, 74, 86, 104, 209, 210, 211, 217
checklists, 23, 36, 68, 107, 121–122
childhood concepts, theories of (*see also* curriculum – psychological perspectives of), 13, 25
City and Guilds of London Institute (CGLI), 36, 76, 211
class, class group (*see also* mixed ability grouping; streaming), 23, 25, 131, 201–203
Community Participation by Children in Futures Project, 300
comprehensive education, schools (*see also* secondary education), 39, 44, 97–98, 101–114, 155–158, 159–162, 210–211
computers (micro), 13, 34, 172, 298, 304
Confederation of British Industries (CBI), 43
consensus (*see also* national curriculum framework; participation; partnership), 11
Council for National Academic Awards (CNAA), 219–220, 222

Crosland, A., 39
culture (see also multicultural education),
  analysis of (cultural analysis), 272–273, 285
  concepts and definitions, 275–277
  context (cultural context), 13, 41–42, 45–46, 53–54, 81–82, 285–288, 291–292
  maps of (cultural mapping), 4–5, 25, 85, 272, 277–278, 285–288, 297, 303
  systems of, 272, 278–285
curriculum
  adaptation (see also curriculum – development, development projects; teacher roles), 232–233
  adoption, 232–233
  aims (see also education, aims of), 19–20, 50–52, 55–56, 58–59, 67–68, 103, 106–107, 109, 160, 219, 270, 286–288, 297, 306–316
  areas of knowledge and experience (see also culture – maps), 309–315
  basic skills and competences, 41, 42, 105, 138, 303, 309–312
  change (see also curriculum – development strategies; innovation), 5, 32–37, 39–46, 118–119, 159–162, 164–169, 176–177, 227, 276–277
  coherence (see also curriculum – core), 31, 103, 111, 305, 308, 315
  common (see also curriculum – core), 42, 45–46, 105, 108–109, 111, 132, 133, 155, 286
  concepts and definitions, 3, 11, 14, 25, 49, 102–103, 127, 159–161, 227, 229, 232, 233, 276, 297–298, 304, 305–306
  consultant, field officer (see also advisers), 95, 101, 106, 125–126, 131, 133, 180, 187–188, 235–241, 254
  control (see also curriculum – school roles, teacher roles; partnership), 11, 19, 29–30, 37, 42–43, 166–168, 173–177, 239–240
  co-ordinators, 182–187
  core (see also curriculum – common), 57, 67–68, 90, 95, 166, 308–314
  cultural map (see culture)
  decisions, decision-making, 99, 102–105, 106–114, 117, 154–155, 160–162, 174–176, 245
  design, 55–59, 67–68, 83–86, 103–113, 130–131, 132, 149–152, 156–157, 160–161, 193–196, 277–288, 300–303
  development, development strategies
  (see also curriculum – change; innovation), 2, 4–5, 30–33, 40, 55–59, 67–69, 75–79, 83–88, 93–96, 98–99, 117, 118–120, 124–133, 161–162, 233–240, 272–273, 297–299
  development projects, 44–45, 134–137, 231–232, 245, 270
  guidance, 67, 96, 126, 148–162, 193–196
  guidelines (see also guidelines for review and internal development), 32, 33, 59, 60, 67, 68, 180, 183, 253, 302
  hidden, 103
  matching, 11, 16–17, 20, 167, 277, 285–289, 291–292
  materials, resources, publications, 64–65, 78, 88–89, 99, 136–138, 152–153, 190–204, 265
  objectives
    in course planning (see also curriculum – aims), 173, 195
    criticisms, 173–174
  options, option system, 62–63, 67, 96–97, 104, 109–110, 112–113, 127, 128–129, 154–158, 160, 308–309
  parent roles (see also participation), 29, 33–34, 103, 117, 157
  plans, planning (see also curriculum – review, evaluation and development), 16, 108–114, 158, 165–169, 275, 277, 288, 298
  principal's roles (see also curriculum – school roles, teacher roles), 94–95, 101–114, 116–123, 140, 167, 169, 180, 185, 254, 261–262
  psychological perspectives, 12, 14–26, 73, 79, 305–308
  review, evaluation and development, process of (see also evaluation), 2, 3, 31–32, 42–43, 57, 67, 89, 93–99, 101–114, 121–122, 126, 133, 180–181, 182–186, 188
  school, college committees, 108, 140–145, 159–162, 166, 175–176
  school roles (see also primary education; secondary education), 5, 8–9, 14, 20, 42, 45, 55–59, 67, 69, 75–78, 83–87, 89–90, 102–103, 105–111, 116, 131, 133, 154–155, 168, 179, 181, 272, 291–293, 298–299
  situational analysis, 84, 90, 102, 111, 141, 142, 144
  sociological perspectives (see also social

Index of Subjects 323

change), 12–13, 23–25
studies, 4, 275
subjects, subject departments, 32, 46, 57–58, 60, 62–63, 64–65, 66, 67, 74–75, 77, 86, 87, 103, 104–106, 107, 110, 118–119, 132, 135–138, 150–151, 174, 176–177, 235–239, 257, 262, 305–306, 308, 312
syllabuses, 29, 86
teacher roles, teaching (*see also* teachers – roles), 7–8, 14–15, 23, 32–33, 40, 56, 66, 75–76, 88–90, 116, 123, 126, 157, 171, 175–176, 191–199, 201–204, 233–234, 239–240, 257–261, 266–268
units of study, 202–203
whole (*see also* curriculum – common, core), 32, 49, 67–68, 77, 98, 166, 270–272, 304–305
Curriculum Development Centre, Australia (*see also* author entry), 245

Department of Education and Science (DES) (*see also* author entry), 3, 9, 30–33, 35, 271–272

education
aims of (*see also* curriculum – aims; values), 5, 42, 43, 45–46, 53–55, 75–76, 83–84, 167, 180, 277, 292–293, 298
concepts and definitions (*see also* curriculum – aims; education, aims of), 14, 15, 42, 43, 45–46, 290–294, 297–299, 309–314
expenditure, 31, 41–43
for international life,
concepts and definitions, 51–52, 81–83, 85, 297–298, 300–302
curriculum for, 84–87
evaluation of, 89
professional development for, 88–89
resources, 88–89
school responsibilities and roles, 83–90
teacher roles, 89–90
girls and women
affirmative action, 67–69
curriculum strategies, 50–51
pioneers, 70
sex differentiation, 62–66, 69, 127, 131
Education Act, 1944, 31, 39, 42
Education Act, 1980, 33, 42

educational covenant, 103
education for capability, 218, 225
educational standards (*see also* Black Papers; Great Debate), 41, 207, 210–211, 218–219, 246
Equal Opportunities Commission, 50, 68, 69, 71
evaluation (*see also* curriculum – review, evaluation and development),
concepts and definition, 22, 246
of students (*see* Assessment)
models, 246
planner (*see also* checklist), 249–252
school self-evaluation, 96, 139–147, 159–169, 179, 228–229, 246–255, 266
examinations (*see also* CPVE; CSE; GCE), 4, 12, 29, 33, 36–37, 40, 44, 60, 63, 96, 104, 108, 116, 172, 174, 207–208, 208–211, 217–219, 222, 224, 266, 291
Eleven plus, 29, 207
Sixteen Plus, 36, 69, 71, 207

falling rolls, 30, 31, 35, 46, 111, 159, 292
first school (*see also* primary school), 12–26 139
further education, 35, 98, 171–177
futures study in the curriculum
examples, 300–302
meaning of, 273, 293–297
planning for, 302–303
rationale, 43, 291–294

General Certificates of Education (GCE), 29, 36, 37, 63, 70, 74, 86, 104, 165, 167, 209–210, 211, 217
general education (*see also* liberal education), 45–46, 127, 276–289, 291–292, 308–314
governors, governors' roles, 29, 103, 224
Great Debate, 30
guidelines (*see* curriculum – guidelines)
Guidelines for Review and Internal Development (GRIDS), 98–99, 179–188

Henbury School, 101–114
Heider, F. (*see* Attributes)
Her Majesty's Inspectorate (HMI), 9, 31, 32, 62, 101, 135
Holt, M. (*see also* author entry), 101, 106, 109, 126

Humanities Curriculum Project (*see also* Stenhouse), 44–45, 228

Industrial Training Act (1964), 172
Industrial Training Boards, 172–173
information technology, 190
Inner London Education Authority (ILEA) (*see also* Author entry), 68–69
innovation (*see also* curriculum – change, development strategies), 44, 67–69, 72, 77–78, 97, 117–123, 174–177, 291–294, 297–299
inservice education (*see also* professionalism; teachers – education of), 2, 32–33, 34, 37, 101, 106, 107, 253–254, 260–261, 263
Integrated Studies Project, 126
International Baccalaureate, 86
international education (*see* education for international life),

Joseph, Sir Keith (*see also* author entry), 43

learning
  activities, experiences and processes, 7–8, 13–14, 21–22, 25, 56–57, 74, 86–87, 99, 150–152, 159–160, 193–196, 235–237, 273–274, 306–308
  assignments, study guides, 196, 202–203
  individualization (*see also* learning-activities), 190–191, 201, 314–315
  resources (*see* curriculum – materials),
liberal education (*see also* general education), 8–9, 36, 43
Local Education Authorities (LEAs), 8, 29, 30–32, 35, 37, 42, 68–69, 101, 104, 121–122, 140, 143, 171, 179, 181–182, 187, 215
low achievers
  concept and definition, 51, 72–74
  responsibilities of schools, 75–76, 78
  school organization for, 76–78
  teacher education for, 78–79

Man: a course of study (MACOS), 231, 232–233
Manifesto for Change, 218, 225
Manpower Services Commission (MSC), 35–36, 43–44, 171
mixed ability grouping, 104, 106
multicultural education (*see also* culture)
  concepts and definitions, 50, 53–55

curriculum strategies, 55–60
National Association for Multiracial Education (NAME), 58, 61
national curriculum framework, 3, 8–9, 30–37, 39–46, 172–173
negotiation (*see also* participation; partnership), 77, 139–140, 141, 142, 145

parent roles (*see also* Education Act, 1980; participation; partnership), 33, 103, 157
participation (*see also* negotiation; partnership), 33, 35–36, 103, 167–169, 180, 224
partnership (*see also* negotiation; participation), 29–30, 32, 37, 40, 45, 120–121, 240
Pocklington School, 300
preparation for work, vocational training, 35–36, 41, 42, 43, 67, 156–157, 217–218, 219
primary education, schools, teachers (*see also* curriculum – school roles; first school), 32, 33, 72–73, 87, 117–121, 134–138, 139–147, 184–185
professional associations, 264–265
professionalism, professional development (*see also* inservice education; teacher education), 5–6, 88–89, 103, 120–121, 145, 169, 214–215, 234, 237–238, 256–268
profiles, records of achievement, 76, 208, 211–215, 223–224

remedial classes (*see also* streaming, setting), 104, 105, 109
Research and Development (R&D) and Diffusion (R.D.D.) (*see also* action research; teachers as researchers), 4, 140, 188, 227–229
Resource Centres, libraries, 196–201
Royal Society of Arts, 218

school functions, roles of (*see* curriculum – school roles),
school, college organization (*see also* class), 20, 56–57, 65–66, 74–75, 77, 103–105, 107–108, 111, 118–121, 126, 127–132, 167–169, 174–177, 198–200, 261–268
School Curriculum Development Committee, 43
School of Independent Study, North East London Polytechnic, 208, 219–224

Index of Subjects   325

school self-evaluation (*see* evaluation)
Schools Council for Curriculum and Examinations for England and Wales (*see also* author entry), 8–9, 39–40, 43, 44, 50, 76, 180, 207, 245, 276
Schools Curriculum Project, Northern Ireland, 124, 126
Schools Support Service, Northern Ireland, 95, 125, 126, 131
secondary education, schools, teachers (*see also* comprehensive education; curriculum – school roles), 28, 32, 35, 39, 42, 44, 62–63, 72, 74–78, 124–133, 148–152, 164–169, 209–224, 235–240, 308–309
Secondary Examinations Council, 43, 208
Sex Discrimination Act, 1975, 50, 62, 69
sixth form curriculum, 164–169
Skilbeck, M. (*see also* author entry), 84, 161–162
social change (*see also* curriculum – sociological perspectives), 34–36, 41–43, 45–46, 49–52, 54, 63–64, 81–82, 152, 153, 159, 165, 167, 169, 272–273, 276–289, 290–292, 295–297, 311–313
Stenhouse, L. (*see also* author entry), 228, 231, 232–234
streaming, setting (*see also* class; mixed ability grouping), 74, 103–104, 106, 107
students (*see also* attributes; learning; low achievers),
  needs and interests, 55–57, 59, 62–63, 65–66, 72–74, 76–77, 86–87, 96, 120, 150, 156, 160–161, 234, 273, 298, 306–310, 314–316
  participation
    case for, 78, 152–153
    forms, procedures, 148–153

performances (*see also* examinations; tests) 75, 86, 148–149, 222–223, 234, 239
roles, tasks, 45, 148–153, 220–223, 300–301

teachers (*see also* curriculum – teacher roles)
  as researchers (*see also* action research; research and development), 155–156, 228, 235–242
  autonomy, 9, 29–30, 173, 232, 262
  education of (*see also* inservice education), 40–41, 78–79, 240–241, 245, 298–299
  roles, 16, 20, 25, 64, 149–153, 174 182–186, 197, 201–203, 210
teachers' centre, teachers' centre leader, 40, 139–145
Technical and Vocational Education Initiative (MSC), 43–44
Technician Education Council, 172
tests, testing (*see also* assessment: examinations), 15, 19, 73–74, 195
Thatcher, M., 40
transmission, education as, 12, 15, 25, 63–66, 227, 260, 276

values (*see also* curriculum – aims; education – aims of), 22, 45, 50, 57–59, 63, 64–66, 73–75, 82, 83, 86, 122, 150–151, 273–274, 277, 278, 282–284, 288, 291, 314

World Studies 8–13 Project (*see also* author entry, Hicks and Townley), 302

Youth Training Scheme (YTS), 35, 37, 44